Vectors of Memory

Vectors of Memory

Legacies of Trauma in Postwar Europe

Nancy Wood

Oxford • New York

First published in 1999 by
Berg
Editorial offices:
150 Cowley Road, Oxford, OX4 1JJ, UK
70 Washington Square South, New York, NY 10012, USA

Berg is the imprint of Oxford International Publishers Ltd.

Library of Congress Cataloging-in-Publication Data

A catalogue record for this book is available from the Library of Congress.

British Library Cataloguing-in-Publication Data

A catalogue record for this book is available from the British Library.

ISBN: 978-1-85973-294-6
ISBN: 1859732941

Typeset by JS Typesetting, Wellingborough, Northants.
Printed in the United Kingdom by WBC Book Manufacturers, Bridgend,
Mid Glamorgan.

Contents

Acknowledgements   vii

Introduction   1

1   Memory's Remains: *Les Lieux de mémoire*   15

2   Public Memory and Postconventional Identity   39

3   The Victim's Resentment   61

4   Narrating Perpetrator Testimony   79

5   Memory on Trial in Contemporary France   113

6   Colonial Nostalgia and *Le Premier Homme*   143

7   Remembering the Jews of Algeria   167

8   Memory by Analogy: *Hiroshima, mon amour*   185

Conclusion   197

Index   203

Acknowledgements

Versions of Chapters 1 and 5 have appeared in *History and Memory*, Chapter 6 in *French Cultural Studies*, and Chapter 7 in *parallax*. Chapter 3 appeared in a shorter version in B. Cheyette and L. Marcus (eds), *Modernity, Culture and the Jew* (Cambridge: Polity, 1998) and Chapter 8 in H. R. Kedward and Nancy Wood (eds), *The Liberation of France: Image and Event* (Oxford: Berg, 1995).

For their comments on individual chapters during the book's long gestation, I am grateful to Rod Kedward, Katherine Lacey, Susan Tarrow, Dominick LaCapra, Raymond Jonas, Sue Collard, Roger Silverstone, David Mellor and Anne Berger.

A year at the Society for the Humanities at Cornell University advanced research for the book considerably and I am grateful to friends and colleagues who supported me during that year, especially Dominick LaCapra, David Rodowick, Tom and Christine Lamarre, Shirley Samuels, Neil Saccamano, Susan Tarrow, Tim Murray, David Bathrick, Alain Boureau, Bob Wise, Mary Ahl, Linda Allen and Aggie Serrine.

This book would not have been completed without steadfast encouragement from Trisha Purchas, who kept the faith during the long, wet summer of 1998.

Introduction

Memory is decidedly in fashion. Whether attention is focused on the so-called return of 'repressed memories' of the abused individual, or on the 'black holes' in a nation's recollection of its past, the topic of memory has become a compelling preoccupation of academics and non-academics alike. It has also become a subject of intense contestation amongst vying social groups and an essential bulwark of the identity politics that motivates many of these debates. As the renowned historian of France's 'Vichy Syndrome', Henry Rousso, has remarked, memory has become a 'value' reflecting the spirit of our times.[1] To be against the retrieval of neglected memories or their commemoration is to be out of step with the general public's reverence towards, and willingness to engage in, a wide range of memorial activity. In contrast to the future-oriented gaze of post-war decades, any injunction to 'turn the page' of history, especially those pages from which resentments still fulminate, is greeted with suspicion or scorn. But while much is said and done in the name of 'collective memory', the concept has suffered from conceptual haziness on the one hand, and over-frequent deployment on the other.

Such imprecision is hard to avoid, and indeed this book invokes terms like 'collective memory', 'public memory' or 'national memory' without always making explicit the conceptual underpinning that justifies this usage. The difficulty arises because while it is axiomatic to acknowledge that since memory arises from lived experience only individuals can remember, the notion of 'collective memory' allows us to signal some tangible presence of the past that can be discerned beyond the level of the individual and in specific social milieux. Moreover, as the first modern theorist of collective memory, Maurice Halbwachs (1877–1945), observed, any hard and fast distinction between individual and social memory is questionable precisely because the very 'words and ideas' out of which 'autobiographical memory' emerges are appropriated from a social milieu. Thus for Halbwachs the meaning of individual memories had to be sought not only in the recesses of the unconscious, or in the familial nexus whose intimate dramas it inscribed, but with reference to the social milieux in which the child's life was always and already immersed. Halbwachs therefore proposed that collective memory be conceived as the 'social frameworks' (*cadres sociaux*) onto which such personal recollections were woven.[2]

But these frameworks also require further specification in the light of a tendency to see this process as one where amorphous residues of the past, conjured by individuals, are amassed into shared imagery until they receive social expression. Again, Halbwachs would insist on viewing memory – whether individual or collective – not as a repository of images, stored 'in some subterranean gallery of our thought', but as the selective reconstruction and appropriation of aspects of the past that respond to the needs of the present. In other words, the representations to which we give the appellation 'collective memory' do not pre-exist their expression at a specific conjuncture. This book develops Halbwachs's insight further by treating 'collective' memory – or 'national' or 'public' memory – as essentially *performative* – i.e. as only coming into existence at a given time and place through specific kinds of memorial activity.[3] As will be seen below, I mobilize the concept of 'vector' to designate the conduits of this performativity, whether these be commemorations, historical narratives, political debates, or other cultural forms.

In light of the fact that memory, now understood in its performative dimension, is engaged in the work of representing a past, it is tempting to draw an analogy between individual and collective modes of remembering. After all, both modes of memory avail themselves of mechanisms like selection, narrativization, repression, displacement or denial. But individual memories, however much they are socially mediated, do not have the same status as the representations of the past to which a larger collectivity adheres. Nor is the memory-work eliciting the words, images and symptoms that alert us to memory's presence in the individual psyche – or in the case of repression and denial, its determined absence – analogous to the forces that generate memorial activity in the public sphere. What differentiates these two modes of memory is that while the emanation of individual memory is primarily subject to the laws of the unconscious, public memory – whatever its unconscious vicissitudes – testifies to a will or desire on the part of some social group or disposition of power to select and organize representations of the past so that these will be embraced by individuals as their own. If particular representations of the past have permeated the public domain, it is because they embody an intentionality – social, political, institutional and so on – that promotes or authorizes their entry.[4] This relationship between memory and power has inspired much work on so-called 'collective memory' – from the social marginalization of 'popular memory' that oral histories sought to redress,[5] to the political will to relativize German responsibility for the Holocaust that Jürgen Habermas so forcefully unmasked. This relationship between memory and power traverses the individual chapters of this book, though before turning to the specific 'politics of memory' that each navigates, I shall persist in my attempt to theorize collective memory as not only performative and embodying a social intentionality, but as an agency that has assumed *evolving* functions in the modern – and now postmodern – era.

It is by now a commonplace to refer to memory's function as an agency of individual and collective identity and as a mechanism of social differentiation among groups. Memory performs this task by situating representations of the past within recognizable temporal and spatial structures and sensibilities. Individuals may thus be bound into a collectivity by virtue of their endorsement of these representations, regardless of whether or not they have shared the experiences upon which they are based. And as Halbwachs, again, was among the first to note, memory organizes representations of the past into a structured sequence that produces a consciousness of an identity through time. Whereas the discipline of history, 'interested primarily in differences', tends to emphasize the alterity of the past, collective memory, for which 'resemblances are paramount', looks to the past to confirm continuity with the present. Collective memory is thus a representation of time as continuous duration, and of a subjectivity inscribed within that temporality. At the same time, Halbwachs drew attention to the use of collective memory as a spatial framework that groups carved out in order '*to enclose and retrieve*' their remembrances. While Halbwachs considered the nation as the privileged locus of this circumscription within modernity, he also pointed out that between the individual and nation were more 'restricted groups' that demarcated specific places as sites to which their memories were exclusively attached and within which only their memories could be commemorated. By means of such spatial and temporal delimitation, Halbwachs contended, groups simultaneously laid claim to distinctive social identities and came into being as distinct memory communities.[6]

Since Halbwachs, attention to the socially-constitutive function of collective memory has tended to focus on the temporal dimension, and in particular on those narratives by which a given social group represents its relation to past. The emphasis has fallen primarily on the *content* of these representations and on the kinds of socio-political needs and interests they embody.

While the temporal dimension remains paramount in many of the memories this book examines, Pierre Nora's concept of *lieux de mémoire*, to which the first chapter is devoted, puts the emphasis less on memory as a narrativized representation of the past than on specific 'sites' or 'realms' that individuals and groups have invested with affective ties of longing and belonging.[7] From Nora's extended elaboration of the concept of *lieux de mémoire*, collective memory emerges as a symbolic 'topography' or 'dynamic ensemble' of diverse representational forms, both material and immaterial in nature, that articulate the heritage of a given community. In the case of his specific object of analysis, French national memory, these *lieux* assume coherence in their bid to embody the quintessential features of the Nation and the Republic. Moreover, Nora follows Halbwachs in insisting that the exigencies of the present dictate the selection and consecration of these sites by official commemorative bodies or by various memory communities. Thus his project is not only concerned with the identification of the memorial sites that are most deeply and pervasively inscribed in the French national imaginary, but with the elucidation of the *intention to remember* that distinguishes these *lieux de mémoire* from mere *lieux d'histoire*. As Nora will argue, 'what matters [. . .] is not the identification of the site, but the opening up of that of which the site is the memorial trace'.[8]

If the emphasis so far has primarily been on memory as a symbolic topography, it is worth considering how Nora treats memory's temporal dimension, especially in light of Halbwachs's claim that a key task of historical memory is to produce a consciousness of an identity through time. Of course, the spatial and temporal dimensions of memory are not easily separable: a *lieu de mémoire* takes on a revered patrimonial status – or, in the case of events like the Holocaust, represents a traumatic impasse – precisely because of the history that its attempted commemoration evokes. But it is Nora's contention that our historical sensibility has itself been transformed from one that looks to the past to affirm a causal relation between past and present to one that views the past as mere heritage. This, Nora argues, is in turn the consequence of the different role that memory has assumed in modernity, which is being recast once more by the changing spatial and temporal structures of the postmodern life-world.

Nora contends that a major shift in temporal consciousness already characterized the transition from the pre-modern to the modern era. Indeed, the very term 'sites of memory', which designates memory's presence with reference to external signs, indicates to Nora that modern societies no longer live *within* the 'environments of memory' of the pre-modern era, where memory led a spontaneous and unself-conscious existence. The corollary of this claim is that once modern societies carved out a 'past', distinct from the present, a historical consciousness of time began to prevail over a memorial one. This, not coincidentally, is the era of the rise of the modern nation-state, whose legitimacy depended on narratives of the nation that forged unchallenged continuities between a nation's past, present and future. In other words, the nation itself was the 'cause' to which these historical narratives rallied.

If these propositions are familiar enough,[9] the uncertain future that many observers predict for the nation-state suggests that historical narratives of the nation are losing their foothold as the key structures within which citizens situate their collective trajectories. On the one hand, this may be a response to an era of supranational integration on the one hand and national disaggregation on the other, where national narratives no longer perform the same legitimizing function. But it is also indicative of a postmodern scepticism towards 'compromised teleological notions of history'[10] and towards the Enlightenment confidence in the inherently progressive forces dictating relations between past, present and future. And yet if such a historical consciousness is indeed on the wane, it is significant that memory has stepped in once again to forge a 'retrospective continuity' between past and present. For Nora, as we shall see, this is not a reincarnation of pre-modern memory but a postmodern memory steeped in patrimonial reverence for the past, one that promises to tell us who we are rather than to offer insights into where we ought to be going, as modern memory purported to do. However, if other theorists of the collective memory of postmodernity also lament its nostalgic, melancholic or even regressive function,[11] a more progressive – or at least ambivalent – prognosis can also be envisaged.

Andreas Huyssen for his part has argued that this revival of memory's fortunes expresses both a crisis in the modern structure of temporality and

> our society's need for temporal anchoring when, in the wake of the information revolution, the relationship between past, present and future is being transformed. Temporal anchoring becomes even more important as the territorial and spatial coordinates of our late twentieth-century lives are blurred or even dissolved by increased mobility around the globe.[12]

One key agent of this sense of erosion of temporal and spatial boundaries and increased global mobility is, of course, the media – a realm which, critics assert, increasingly trades in simulation rather than referentiality, and whose technology has made possible a 'world of information networks that function entirely according to principles of sychronicity while providing us with multiple images and narratives of the non-synchronous'.[13] Faced with a mass-mediated world of disorienting temporalities, where a sense of 'before' and 'after' increasingly gives way to (mis)perceptions of simultaneity, memory must once again assume the task of providing the sense of identity through time that Nora maintains was previously performed by national narratives. Memory, according to Huyssen, is now intervening in an attempt to slow down the pace of information processing and 'to recover a mode of contemplation outside the universe of simulation and fast-speed information and cable networks, to claim some anchoring space in a world of puzzling and often threatening heterogeneity, non-synchronicity, and information overload'.[14]

As we shall see, Huyssen's almost lyrical defence of memory's resistance to a synchronicity run rampant, to a sense of simultaneity reinforced dramatically by new distribution technologies like the Internet, touches upon one crucial theme of this book: the relationship between the modern media and the contemporary politics of memory. However, unlike Huyssen, I do not see the two domains as sworn enemies of each other, but as entwined in a mutual embrace. At the same time, unlike those critics who would conflate the modern media with memory on the basis that its simulated images of the past have colonized our memorial consciousness, I treat the media as one 'vector' of memory – a pre-eminent one, but by no means the only cultural practice that is charged with 'anchorage' and representing and transmitting a society's relationship to its past.

The term 'vector' was first used in this context by Henry Rousso in his now classic study, *The Vichy Syndrome: History and Memory in France since 1945.*[15] Rousso analyzed a number of cultural and political practices that had organized the representation of *les années noires* in the post-war period and related these to the affective dimensions that the evolving memories of Vichy had assumed in French public life. In particular, Rousso cited the importance of political discourse, commemorative rituals, films and new histories of Vichy as 'vectors' of French memory. This book also considers a number of 'vectors' of public memory: historiography, survivor testimonials, trials, novels and films. And while France and Germany emerge as the primary national contexts within which these vectors are located – notwithstanding predictions of the nation-state's imminent demise – my concern is less to chart the trajectory of a single national memory than to reflect on the kinds of public debates these vectors have elicited.

However, the focus on France and Germany is not by chance. In recent years, most European countries have engaged in a politics of memory about episodes in their recent past. The Swiss have had to shed their self-image as a nation above reproach and acknowledge the material exploitation of Holocaust victims in which some of their key institutions were directly implicated. In the former Yugoslavia, 'ancient tribal hatreds' and ethnically-based enmities arising from the Second World War became a legitimating weapon in a genocidal war waged entirely on behalf of a contemporary nationalist agenda. After 1989, public exorcism of memories of the recent communist past preoccupied the countries of east-central Europe. What distinguishes the French and German context is not only the duration and extent of national introspection, particularly concerning the events of the Second World War, but the fact that the public debates they have generated have become a *defining* feature of political culture itself. German historian Dan Diner has described the Holocaust as an 'identity-forming foundational event' for Germany, and its memory 'basic to Germany's moral and historical self-awareness',[16] while Nora has maintained that 'France as an identity constructs a future only by deciphering its memory'.[17] Nora's comment refers not only to the French public's current obsession with its *patrimoine* and local or national *lieux de mémoire*, but to the 'singular destiny' that the memory of Vichy and French involvement in the Final Solution has taken on in national life over the past three decades. And in both Germany and France, it has been the domain of historiography, wherein the very mode of writing history is the object of critical reflection,[18] that has played a major role in animating and shaping the contours of these debates. As Nora has noted, 'when history begins to write its own history, a fundamental change takes place. Historiography begins when history sets itself the task of uncovering that in itself which is not history, of showing itself to be the victim of memory and seeking to free itself from memory's grip'.[19] This suspicion that history had become the victim of memories driven by specific political agendas mobilized, though in very different ways, historiographical initiatives within Germany and France that turned their respective critical spotlights on dominant narratives recounting their nation's responsibility for, or participation in, the Holocaust.

For the past two decades, French historians of Vichy have increasingly found themselves in the limelight as memories of Vichy and French involvement in the Final Solution were seized upon by a wider constituency dissatisfied with previous narratives that referred only to France's heroic struggle against Nazi Occupation. Summoned to rectify this one-dimensional portrait, and to detail the complicity and dereliction that had been relegated to the shadows by Gaullist glorifications of a 'nation-in-Resistance', historians of Vichy have enjoyed a media attention and public influence that must be the envy of their largely ignored European counterparts. But their status has been further magnified and problematized by the additional role they have been expected to play not only as historical experts, but as judicial witnesses and as arbiters of public memory. The trial of Maurice Papon, a former Vichy functionary accused of crimes against humanity, put historians in the position of negotiating all three roles simultaneously. This was not the first time the courts had summoned historians to the witness stand – historians had also testified at the trials of Klaus Barbie and Paul Touvier; but the tensions generated by this juridical 'instrumentalization' of historiographical expertise were made more explicit. Not only does the Papon case raise important questions about whether belated legal proceedings for crimes against humanity can serve the needs of justice and memory simultaneously; it has also served to highlight the contradictory aims of the judicial system and historiography as distinct 'vectors' of the memory of Vichy and the Final Solution.

Over roughly the same period, Germany has witnessed two major furores that have focused upon how historians have written about the Nazi past. The first of these, called the *Historikerstreit* or 'historians' debate' of the mid-1980s, though ostensibly about new interpretations of the Nazi past by neo-conservative historians, was, as Jürgen Habermas indicated, a vehicle for a wider debate about the relationship between Holocaust memory and contemporary German identity. And while Pierre Nora was trying to wrest the concept of *lieux de mémoire* from the nostalgic and celebratory overtones with which it was being endowed in France, Habermas was elaborating a concept of memory as the assumption of collective 'liability' for Germany's Nazi past in order immediately to foreground its critical and self-reflexive nature. Indeed, Habermas has promoted his concept of collective liability as a vigorous defence against a neo-conservative politics of national identity that increasingly made its presence felt in Germany from the mid-1980s onwards and whose orchestration Habermas considered symptomatic of a will to forget Nazi crimes – or at least to relativize the liability that flows from them. I look at why Habermas has repeatedly insisted, even more emphatically following the unification process, that 'Auschwitz' must remain the primordial *lieu de mémoire* in contemporary Germany, and why 'postconventional' identity is the only identity-formation consistent with an awareness of what this memorial site represents.

A decade after the *Historikerstreit* was launched, German historians were once again up in arms, though this time unified in their condemnation of an account of German perpetrators of the Holocaust written by a young American scholar, Daniel Goldhagen. A larger German public, by contrast, rushed to purchase Goldhagen's text, and thronged to venues where he debated publicly with his critics. Unlike the *Historikerstreit*, the response to Goldhagen could no longer be characterized in terms of a left–right political division between those who opposed the continual invocation of Auschwitz and those who considered this reference point basic to German self-understanding. Instead, a 'paradigm shift'[20] seemed to have taken place, where the stakes of historical memory were no longer whether Germany was entitled to become a 'veritable continental nation' – this had been achieved by unification – but why the generation raised in this atmosphere of rehabilitated nationhood approved the portrait of their forebears that Goldhagen's accusatory treatise drew.

The accusatory voice is also dominant in the writings of the Auschwitz survivor Jean Améry. Améry readily acknowledged that his memories were steeped in 'resentment'; but I argue that, far from being an expression of Nietzschean *ressentiment*, as some critics maintain, Améry's resentments, as well as those of Primo Levi, function as an agency for the kind of critical moral reflection that Habermas would advocate several decades later. In the manner in which they are wielded by Améry and Levi, memories of resentment should be seen not as the 'festering wound' for which the victim refuses treatment, as Nietzsche would have it, but as a trenchant rebuke of the moral dereliction of societies in whom victims placed their trust. Moreover, I contend that these reflections on memory-as-resentment still speak to us today, not because the genocides to which we are witness are analogous to the Holocaust, but because, like Améry, victims have experienced their fate as one of abandonment by the outside world.

The public debates about memory in Germany and France have another distinguishing feature: both have engaged a wider public thanks to the resources of the modern media. Several of the debates that are examined in this book – notably, the *Historikerstreit*, the Goldhagen 'phenomenon' and the trial of Maurice Papon – were conducted in the full glare of publicity, and their meaning and significance cannot be extricated from the mass-media forms by means of which specialists and a larger public alike consumed or participated in them. For someone like Habermas, it was precisely because neo-conservative historians had taken to the German print media to disseminate 'revisionist' accounts of the Nazi past that he regarded his own mass-mediated interventions as a necessary contribution to the struggle over the 'public use of history'. In response to media and public acclaim for Daniel Goldhagen's thesis of a specifically German version of 'eliminationist anti-Semitism', German historians were forced to temper their own initially hostile reactions and to take the measure of the new memorial climate to which Goldhagen's text seemingly responded.[21] Thanks to the saturated media attention devoted to

Maurice Papon's trial for crimes against humanity, conflicting interpretations of France's collaborationist past were not confined to the courtroom or to restricted historiographical circles, but spilled onto the pages of national newspapers, into national television space and on to the World Wide Web. However, in these instances, the question of the media's role is primarily one of public access to contested fields of historical knowledge and their ensuing terms of debate. While the issue of access is of fundamental importance to the nurturing of a democratic public sphere, an argument that Habermas in particular has developed at length elsewhere,[22] it does not exhaust a consideration of how the modern media impinge on our historical and memorial consciousness.

As Huyssen reminds us, 'memory, even and especially in its belatedness, is itself based on representation'.[23] Conversely, the media, as Huyssen goes on to note, are 'central to the way we live structures of temporality in our culture'.[24] But it is by no means a simple step to move from this recognition of the entanglement of media and memory to an incisive account of how media influence or determine 'the ways we think and live cultural memory'.[25] I have already referred to the widespread acknowledgement that the media now function as the key vectors of cultural memory, and the most proliferating source of images and narratives of the past. Some critics look upon this development only with despair, ascribing to the media responsibility for the waning of historical consciousness because of their subordination of all historical meaning and significance to the 'live event', to the genre of hyper-realism or the public's appetite for sensationalism and the 'scoop'. At the same time, the media are credited by others not only with stimulating many of the public debates about memory discussed in this book, but with giving representational form to cultural memories that official vectors have largely ignored or treated only within the confines of conventional historical narration. Films in particular have been at the centre of debates concerning the 'limits of representation' of historical events like the Holocaust[26] or, in the case of the film that is treated as a 'mnemonic symptom' in this book, of the atomic conflagration that engulfed Hiroshima. In short, the media's role in the production and distribution of memories is ambivalent and differentiated, and can be neither condemned nor condoned in sweeping generalizations.

And as the discussion of the *Historikerstreit* made evident, the problematic of representation and its limits could not be restricted to cultural vectors like the media, but had to be extended to include historiographical discourse itself. Yet when the Goldhagen controversy erupted, it was remarkable how little attention was paid to the representational aspect of *Hitler's Willing Executioners*. In attempting to account for the appeal this book exerted on a non-specialist public, I argue that even more than his contentious claims about the ideological mind-set of 'Ordinary Germans', it is the 'limits of representation' that Goldhagen's historiography of the Holocaust broaches (and perhaps breaches) that lie at the heart of his provocation.

Finally, if we treat memory's performativity not only as the *mise-en-scène* of representations of the past, but as the organization of forgetting – in short as a mnemonic agency 'contingent upon the social formation that produces it' (Huyssen) – then it is clear that our analysis must embrace not only memories that achieve public articulation, but those that are denied expression or recognition, as well as those memories that are displaced or merely alluded to. This book turns its attention to several *lieux d'oubli*[27] – sites that public memory has expressly avoided because of the disturbing affect that their invocation is still capable of arousing. Until recently, both official memory and Vichy historiography shunned any reference to *les femmes tondues* – the shaven women of the Liberation. This long-standing and pervasive silence surrounding the memories of women accused of 'horizontal collaboration' with the German enemy makes all the more astonishing and prescient Alain Resnais's 1959 film *Hiroshima, mon amour*, whose central protagonist relates to her Japanese lover her traumatic memories of love and punishment during the Occupation and Liberation. Because the release of these memories is triggered by a visit to Hiroshima, itself a site of trauma and repressed memory, the film sets up an *analogy* between individual and collective memories of trauma that must negotiate the pitfalls of comparison and the insights of juxtaposition.

Until the 1970s, Jewish memories of wartime persecution and deportation were the primary *lieux d'oubli* in the French memorial landscape.[28] Franco-Jewish memory is now in the vanguard of commemorative politics and in the demand for *lieux de mémoire* that designate the nation's responsibility for the fate of its deported Jewish citizens or those who sought refuge on French soil. In the decades following France's infamous *guerre sans nom* or 'undeclared war', France's decolonization *débâcle* in Algeria came increasingly to occupy that non-site of memory. That memories of France's 'last stand' in Algeria have in their turn gradually assumed a more tangible – and recognized – form in the national imaginary is the consequence of a combination of cultural and political forces that it is beyond the scope of this book to appraise.[29] However, I do try to broach the reasons for this earlier memorial lacuna in a more tangential way. Albert Camus's most autobiographical – and belatedly published – novel, *Le Premier Homme* (*The First Man*), has been widely celebrated as a poignant *Bildungsroman* by Algeria's famous native son. However reviewers, with notable exceptions, have largely ignored the extent to which Camus's childhood memories are 'framed', in Halbwachs's sense, by memories of a colonial Algeria whose profound ambivalence betrays the crisis into which Camus's *pied-noir* identity has been precipitated by the struggle for Algerian independence.

One subset of that *pied-noir* community – the Jews of Algeria – invoke memories of the colonial period and decolonization that warrant their demarcation as a separate 'memory community' – also in the Halbwachsian sense. I try to show how the memories of writers whose 'judeo-franco-maghrebian' identity has been reasserted of late interweave with the narratives of Jewish existence in colonial

Algeria that have come to the fore in recent historiography, and I suggest that both are a complex response to the civil war that is tearing Algeria apart even as I write. Pierre Nora has gone a step further and speculated that France's neglect of the welfare of Algerian Jews at several crucial historical junctures, and especially at the moment of their massive repatriation in 1962, fuelled resentment in this diasporic community that would later be channelled into the memorial militancy that accompanied Jewish demands that the French nation assume symbolic responsibility for the crimes of the Vichy state.[30] In other words the *lieux d'oubli* that bespoke the nation's circumvention of traumatic moments in Jewish-Algerian history, found displaced embodiment in the *lieux de mémoire* that now commemorate Jewish suffering during the Holocaust. If Nora's hunch is correct, it only strengthens my claim that 'collective memory' should be treated as a complex field of representations that requires careful theorization and analysis, since it is never quite what it purports to be.

Notes

1. Henry Rousso, *La hantise du passé: entretien avec Philippe Petit* (Paris: Les éditions Textuels, 1998), p. 14.
2. See Maurice Halbwachs, *The Collective Memory* (New York: Harper and Row, 1980).
3. See Marie-Claire Lavabre, 'Du poids et du choix de passé, Lecture critique du Syndrome de Vichy', in Denis Peschanski, Michael Pollak and Henry Rousso (eds), *Histoire politique et sciences sociales* (Brussels: Complexe, 1991). Of course the notion of 'performativity' has been most widely deployed within gender studies, and I adapt its usage for my own purposes here.
4. See Lavabre, 'Du poids et du choix du passé'.
5. The Popular Memory Group of Birmingham best represent this approach. See Richard Johnson *et al.*, (eds), *Making Histories: Studies in History-Writing and Politics* (London: Hutchinson and CCCS, 1982). Michel Foucault also made an intervention on behalf of 'popular memory' in response to the film *Lacombe Lucien* by Louis Malle, whose message Foucault situated in the context of a 'healing of the breach between the national right and collaborating right'. See his interview in *Cahiers du Cinéma*, nos. 251–2.
6. Halbwachs, *The Collective Memory*.
7. *Les Lieux de mémoire* (sous la direction de Pierre Nora), *Vol. 1, La République; Vol. 2, La Nation; Vol. 3, Les France* (Paris: Gallimard, 1984; 1986; 1992).

8. Pierre Nora, 'Comment écrire l'histoire de la France?' *Les Lieux de mémoire, Vol. 1, La République*, p. 20. My translation.

9. The proliferating literature on national identity has increasingly foregrounded the role of memory in nation-building. Anthony D. Smith, for example, dismisses global culture as a fallacy and 'memory-less construct' and makes 'common myths and historical memories' a constitutive feature of national identity. See Anthony D. Smith, *National Identity* (London: Penguin Books, 1991). For a discussion of modern temporality, see especially Reinhart Koselleck, *Futures Past* (Cambridge, MA: MIT Press, 1990).

10. Andreas Huyssen's term in 'Introduction: Time and Cultural Memory at Our Fin de Siècle' in *Twilight Memories: Marking Time in a Culture of Amnesia* (London: Routledge, 1995), p. 6.

11. See Frederic Jameson, 'Postmodernism, or the Cultural Logic of Late Capitalism', *New Left Review*, no. 146, July–August 1984, for the programmatic statement of the relationship between postmodernism and a nostalgic view of history. See also Eric L. Santner, *Stranded Objects: Mourning, Memory and Film in Postwar Germany* (Ithaca: Cornell University Press, 1990), for an incisive discussion of postmodernism's 'discourses of bereavement' that tend to celebrate melancholia rather than engage in a labour of mourning.

12. Huyssen, 'Introduction: Time and Cultural Memory at our Fin de Siècle', p. 7.

13. Ibid., p. 9.

14. Ibid., p. 7.

15. Henry Rousso, *The Vichy Syndrome: History and Memory in France since 1945* (London: Harvard University Press, 1991).

16. Dan Diner, 'On Guilt Discourse and Other Narratives: Epistemological Observations regarding the Holocaust', *History and Memory*, vol. 9, nos. 1–2, Fall 1997, p. 301. By contrast Michael Geyer claimed – at least before the eruption of the Goldhagen debate – that disputes over history and memory in Germany have faded in recent years, as a result of the absence of an intellectual public able to mobilize opinion. See his 'Why Cultural History? What Future? Which Germany?', *New German Critique*, no. 65, Summer 1995.

17. Pierre Nora, 'L'Ère de la commémoration', in *Les Lieux de mémoire, Vol. 3, Les France* (Paris: Gallimard, 1993), p. 1009. My translation.

18. For reflections on the rise of historiography see Nora, 'General Introduction: Between Memory and History', in the selected English translation *Realms of Memory: The Construction of the French Past, Vol. 1: Conflicts and Divisions*, edited by Lawrence D. Kritzman and translated by Arthur Goldhammer (New York: Columbia University Press,1997); originally published as 'Entre Mémoire et Histoire: La problématique des lieux' in *Les Lieux de mémoire, Vol. 1, La République*, and first translated as 'Between Memory and History: *Les Lieux de Mémoire*' in *Representations*, no. 26, Spring 1989.

19. Pierre Nora, 'Between Memory and History', p. 4.
20. The term is Dan Diner's in 'On Guilt Discourse and Other Narratives', p. 306.
21. This is discussed fully in Chapter 4; but see Josef Joffe, 'Goldhagen in Germany', *New York Review of Books*, 28 November 1996 for a discussion of the critical retreat of a number of prominent historians of Nazism faced with massive public acclaim for *Hitler's Willing Executioners*.
22. This is the theme of Habermas's *The Structural Transformation of the Public Sphere: An Inquiry into a Category of Bourgeois Society* (Cambridge: Polity Press, 1989); first published in Germany in 1962 as *Strukturwandel der Öffentlichkeit: Untersuchungen zu einer Kategorie der bürgerlichen Gesellschaft*.
23. Andreas Huyssen, 'Introduction: Time and Cultural Memory at Our Fin de Siècle', p. 3.
24. Ibid., p. 4.
25. Ibid., pp. 4–5.
26. See especially Saul Friedlander (ed.), *Probing the Limits of Representation: Nazism and the 'Final Solution'* (Cambridge, MA: Harvard University Press, 1992). Films like Claude Lanzmann's *Shoah* and Steven Spielberg's *Schindler's List* have been most frequently discussed in these terms.
27. I use the term *lieux d'oubli* to emphasize the intentionality of their avoidance – even if the 'will to forget' may be embedded in the vicissitudes of a cultural unconscious. In his contribution to *Les Lieux de mémoire*, for example, Pierre Birnbaum observes that those groups 'who cannot claim a privileged relation to a specific area, to memories rooted in a particular region, are more or less excluded from the national scene: no public *lieu de mémoire* gives them substance'. See 'Grégoire, Dreyfus, Drancy, and the Rue Copernic: Jews at the Heart of French History' in *Realms of Memory*, pp. 380–1. While the term *non-lieux de mémoire* is also in use, it carries different connotations. The anthropologist Marc Augé, in his *Non-lieux: Introduction à une anthropologie de la surmodernité* (Paris: Seuil, 1992), (translated as *Non-places: Introduction to an Anthropology of Supermodernity*, London: Verso, 1995), refers to these as the characterless and anonymous spaces – airports, shopping malls – that individuals increasingly frequent as part of their postmodern lives.
28. Pierre Birnbaum notes the absence of physical sites commemorating Jewish memory of the Holocaust in France in the essay cited above.
29. The literature is now enormous, but an essential point of departure is Benjamin Stora's *La Gangrène et l'oubli: la mémoire de la guerre d'Algérie* (Paris: La Découverte, 1992).
30. Nora makes this suggestion in an interview 'Tout concourt aujourd'hui au souvenir obsédant de Vichy', *Le Monde*, 1 October 1997.

–1–

Memory's Remains: *Les Lieux de mémoire*

Introduction

Virtually all writing on national memory in France now pays tribute to the influence of *Les Lieux de mémoire*, a monumental study of the key symbolic matrices that have figured French nationhood. This seven-volume work, compiled under the direction of the French historian Pierre Nora between 1984 and 1992, has not only garnered an impressive number of intellectual accolades, but has enjoyed consider-able media attention as well. It would be tempting to credit the project's success to a passing vogue for the topic of memory that has gripped intellectuals and the wider public alike. As the editors of the journal *Esprit* remarked, public discussion in France has become so 'saturated' by the theme of memory that it has virtually relegated to the shadows any discourses oriented to the future.[1] Certainly the rapid demise of ideologies promising 'radiant tomorrows' has played a part in rendering suspect any preoccupation with futurity. However the repeated invocation of memory in the French public sphere preceded 'really existing socialism's' fall from grace, and looks set to endure for some time. The compelling interest of Pierre Nora's project lies in its attempt to explain and analyze memory's ascent to such an elevated social status.

Nora's aim, expressed in the introduction to the first volume of *Les Lieux de mémoire*, *La République*, published in 1984, was to give memory a history and, in particular, to offer a history of France from the perspective of its most salient memories – in Nora's own words, 'une histoire de France par la mémoire'.[2] He approaches this task, with his team of eminent historical researchers, by identifying, classifying and analyzing an array of *lieux de mémoire* – 'sites' or 'realms' of memory that have been invested with enduring and emotive symbolic significance. The definition of a *lieu de mémoire* that comes to inform this enquiry over a decade of research (and indeed gains official endorsement by its entry in the 1993 edition of the *Grand Robert* dictionary) consists of 'any significant entity, whether material or non-material in nature, which by dint of human will or the work of time has become a symbolic element of the memorial heritage of any community'.[3] Thus we can say provisionally that *lieux de mémoire* are quintessentially symbolic (whatever form they assume), a product of human or temporal agency, and constitute the bedrock of a community's symbolic repertoire. In this first volume, these *lieux de mémoire* range from symbols (the *tricolor* of the French flag) and monuments (the Pantheon) to pedagogic manuals (*Le Tour de la France par deux enfants*), institutions (La bibliothèque des Amis de l'instruction), and personages (Lavisse), to commemorative events (14 July), honorific dates (the centenaries of Voltaire and Rousseau) and exhibitions ('L'Exposition coloniale' of 1931). Across their material and ideational diversity, Nora and his researchers identify in these *lieux de mémoire* a common memorial function: all manage to evoke powerfully a set of civic values that together figure the nation through the idea of *La République* and that draw their adherents into a social collectivity – 'a veritable civil religion' – united in the sanctification and defence of these values.[4]

In the second instalment, *La Nation* (comprising three volumes), published in 1986, Nora attempts to chart across an even vaster symbolic terrain the role played by memory in the construction of 'the Nation', and to identify the key *lieux de mémoire* that produced the 'memory-nation' as the main principle of social identity and cohesion. Here again we find a plethora of material and conceptual elements – institutions (Le Collège de France), texts (*L'Histoire de France* by Lavisse), historiographical schools of thought (the *Annales* School), mottoes ('Mourir pour la patrie') and national heritage sites (Rheims). These in turn are categorized not on the basis of common forms or substances but because of their convergence on a delimited set of symbolic matrices that are seen to be constitutive of France as a memory-nation. Some of these matrices – 'L'État', 'Héritage', 'Le Térritoire' – might be anticipated, since they resonate with other studies of national identity that have also found these elements to be constituent features of the nation-building process. However, Nora's inclusion of other nodal points like 'Le Patrimoine', 'Paysages', 'La Gloire' and 'Historiographie' begins to suggest the novel dimensions of his approach to national identity, in so far as all of these categories also contain – and rely upon – a substantial complement of historical memories.

Finally, with the third and final tome (also comprising three volumes), published in 1992, *Les France* (as will be seen, the use of the plural article is both intentional and meaningful), Nora takes as his starting-point the historical eclipse of France as a 'memory-nation'. Over the last twenty years, France has witnessed the demise of national memories, a proliferation of 'patrimonial' sites of memory and a corresponding multiplication of conflictual social identities that have riven the French national landscape. The symbolic matrices of this culminating work ('Minorités Religieuses', 'Enracinements', 'Partage de l'Espace-Temps', etc.) thus evoke this more fragmented and partisanal sense of belonging, founded on division among groups within the national polity as much as on adherence to more local claims of allegiance. Moreover, according to Nora, in this passage from the reign of the 'memory-nation' to the 'era of commemoration' in which France is now immersed, sectoral memories have restructured the way the relationship between past, present and future is experienced, and reshaped the forms of collectivity that now cohabit in the national space.

This thumbnail sketch suggests the broad trajectory of Nora's enquiry, but its achievements as 'une histoire de France par la mémoire' should not obscure its more general significance beyond the national framework within which it is primarily located. *Les Lieux de mémoire* represents nothing less than a radical upheaval in the way the phenomenon of 'collective memory' can henceforth be conceived. Certainly Maurice Halbwachs's theory of collective memory forms an essential backdrop to Nora's project. In the introduction to the first volume of *Les Lieux de mémoire*, Nora pays tribute to Halbwachs's insights on the multiplicity of collective memories and, in the final essay of the final volume, Nora notes that a 'rediscovery' of the writings of Halbwachs in the 1970s was one of the effects of the new interest that French historians were showing in the question of memory. But the theory of collective memory that emerges across Nora's work represents such a radical reworking of this early conceptualization that it will no doubt become a historiographical landmark in its own right.

Nora follows Halbwachs in treating memory not as a monolithic mental image of the past internalized in the same way by all members of a given society, but as the diverse representational modes by means of which communities imagine, represent and enact their specific relationship to the past. 'Sites of memory' are in turn conceived as 'symbolic fixations'[5] of these heterogeneous forms that crystallize some key attributes of that relationship. The project of identifying such sites, according to Nora, must be less concerned with accumulating an exhaustive inventory than with demonstrating how these memorial sites articulate with each other and function as a category of 'contemporary historical intelligibility'. For, as Nora remarks, 'without an intention to remember, *lieux de mémoire* would be *lieux d'histoire*'.[6] He thus places the semantic emphasis not on memory as remembrance (*souvenir*), but as 'rememoration' – a concept he defines in Halbwachsian terms as 'the general economy of the administration of the past in the present'.[7] And despite his recourse to the metaphor of collective memory as a 'symbolic topography', Nora's *lieux de mémoire* are emphatically performative – 'dynamic ensembles' rather than static places on a memory landscape. However, in order to understand how it is that memory has acquired this performative dimension – a dimension that Nora believes to be qualitatively different from a memory that is merely lived and experienced – he proposes to chart the broad sweep of memory's history. It is in the course of treating memory not as an immutable 'given' of either individuals or communities, but as a historically-evolving entity, that Nora helps us to grasp the crucial transmutation of the phenomenon of memory itself.

The History of Memory

Nora in fact starts his history in the present, citing the pervasiveness of the subject of memory in contemporary discourse that I evoked at the outset of this chapter. However, he interprets this discursive omnipresence as a symptom of the *diminution* of memory as an integral component of everyday life: 'Memory is constantly on our lips because it no longer exists.'[8] The more talk of memory, the less it is unselfconsciously experienced. Modern societies have separated memory off from the customs, rituals and traditions that it quietly inhabited in the pre-modern world, and by insisting memory declare its presence through external signs, they have weakened memory's endogenous grip on collective life. Nora's *lieux de mémoire* are themselves impoverished substitutes for the *milieux de mémoire*, 'environments of memory', which have all but disappeared. By treating memory primarily as an arena of cultural display, modern societies have ensured its compartmentalization as an experience:

> If we still dwelled among our memories, there would be no need to consecrate sites embodying them. *Lieux de mémoire* would not exist, because memory would not have been swept away by history. Every one of our acts, down to the most quotidian, would be experienced in an intimate identification of act and meaning, as a religious repetition of sempiternal practice.[9]

Modern societies, however, are based on the mediation of experience, on its strict temporal demarcation, and on the interpretation of act as signification. Pre-modern societies live within memory, Nora observes, whereas modern societies put memory at a distance and in so doing become 'historical' societies.

This profound transformation in the way memory is experienced inaugurates a new form of historical perception. Societies living within memory made no sharp distinctions between the past and present. Temporal continuity was assured by the repetition of rituals, by the transmission of collectively-held values, and by the stamina of tradition confronted with the forces of change. These were societies whose memories were 'without a past' in the sense that they lived a present infused with the past; the past was apprehended by memory only as a 'perpetually actual phenomenon'. However, according to Nora, the perception of time in modern societies, aided and abetted by the media (about which more later), has undergone a 'tremendous dilation'. The past is now apprehended as a ransacked storehouse of historical traces, while the present appears as a 'thin film of current events'. As a consequence of this ephemerality, the present seems caught in the wheels of the 'acceleration of history'; it appears to slip all too rapidly 'into a historical past that is gone for good'; and with its precipitate decampment from consciousness, our recollection of it becomes that much harder to conjure. This leads Nora to characterize modern consciousness of the past as 'historical' rather than memorial; it is a consciousness whose only recourse is to represent and invent what it is no longer able deeply and spontaneously to experience.

But if this depiction so far seems to teeter on the precipice of a nostalgia for what he portrays as the 'integrated', 'unselfconscious', and 'all-powerful' memory of the pre-modern world, Nora – the historian – is compelled to acknowledge that it is also only in historical societies that memory itself can become an object of history and in particular of a critical history such as the one he has embarked upon:

> Places, *lieux de mémoire*, become important even as the vast fund of memories among which we used to live on terms of intimacy has been depleted, only to be replaced by a reconstructed history [. . .] if history did not seize upon memories in order to distort and transform them, to mold them or turn them to stone, they would not turn into *lieux de mémoire* which emerge in two stages: moments of history are plucked out of the flow of history, then returned to it – no longer quite alive but not yet entirely dead, like shells left on the shore when the sea of living memory has receded.[10]

So, in keeping with this elegiac metaphor, we might describe the historical forays of Nora and his team of researchers as the sifting of these beached remains for whatever traces of a memorial consciousness they might yield.

Yet this historiographical enterprise is not undertaken for mere intellectual diversion. The critical history envisaged by Nora has a more urgent agenda. He believes that although memory has been dissipated by the incursions of the modern world, its residues have nonetheless coalesced around particular social loci. Of these, the nation-state has been particularly privileged as a site for the regroupment of memory's forces. Hence Nora wishes to trace the role that memory has played in constructing the idea of 'the Nation' in modern nation-states, and in France in particular.

Again, at this point Nora's work rejoins that of a number of contemporary historians and political sociologists who foreground the central place accorded to historical memories (or the 'invention of tradition') in the forging of a modern national consciousness and 'imagined communities'.[11] As I shall show below, his delineation of the memorial figures that have coalesced into the dominant representations of 'the Nation' in France yields a particularly rich profile of this constituting dimension of collective memories.[12] However, Nora makes a radical and controversial departure from analogous accounts in two related respects. On the one hand, he asserts that the nation-state as a unifying *framework* of collective identity is in rapid decline. Contrary to the claim that the nation-state has so far held at bay the various forces of attrition seeking to dismantle it, Nora believes that it has definitively succumbed to these forces. On the other hand, he maintains that, despite this demise, the *memory* of 'the Nation' has continued to play an integrating role in the larger polity. One of the central analytic tasks of *Les Lieux de mémoire* is to explain this apparent paradox and to identify the binding mechanisms of national memories in the face of the historical eclipse of their erstwhile framework of cohesion, the nation-state itself.

This explanation is first broached by considering the manner in which memory has traditionally performed its integrating function on behalf of the nation-state. In the era of the nation-state's unassailable supremacy as the key organizing principle of modern societies, memory relied primarily on narratives of a national past to provide the thread of continuity between past, present and future. Moreover, these reassuring narratives generated a historical consciousness of the nation that was embraced by the state in order to legitimize its hegemony in the present and its indispensability to the national future. But Nora's proposition is that a new coupling has gained ascendancy – that of state and society. Symptomatic of this new social alliance is a collective memory that no longer takes the nation – and in the case of France, the nation-as-Republic – as a 'cause' legitimized by recourse to a historical chronology that secures its present and orients it to the future. Instead, this memory takes the nation as a 'given'; its narratives only serve to verify what is (not endorse what was and therefore what should be), since it is now *society* alone that dictates the cast of the future: 'Once society had supplanted the nation, legitimation by the past, hence by history, gave way to legitimation by the future . . .'.[13]

Here, perhaps, lies Nora's most contentious claim: that for all intents and purposes, 'society' rather than the nation-state has increasingly become the linchpin of social organization, at least in France and, by implication, in the rest of Europe, even if in the prevailing consciousness, 'the Nation' remains the nostalgic and enduring figure of the larger social collectivity. (The newly-independent states of Eastern and Central Europe would require a more nuanced adaptation of this argument, but it is by no means irrelevant to their present troubled realities.) Moreover, under the sway of this prevailing framework of social organization, memory is detaching itself from narrative history and from the task of forging that 'retrospective continuity' between the national past and present that historical memories of the nation-state had hitherto established. Now memory can attest only to the 'discontinuity of history' and thus to its own rarefied relation to the past. Meanwhile, severed both from the tradition of memory and from its identification with the nation, history has 'lost its subjective force as well as its pedagogical mission, the transmission of values'.[14] Bereft of its legitimizing function, history can only act at the behest of the 'self-knowledge of society'. For Nora, this functional separation of history and memory is a defining feature of contemporary societies and provides the key to investigating the fate of the idea of the nation in modern times. His (preliminary) conclusion in the first tome is that the 'memory-nation was thus the last incarnation of memory-history'.[15] 'Society', like its predecessor the nation-state, relies no less heavily on national memory; but it is a memory that has shed its own intimate reliance on a historical sensibility.

Finally, if, despite its detachment from the narratives of national destiny that underpinned the political logic of the nation-state, this memory of 'the Nation' might nonetheless appear as the durable basis of collective identity, Nora sees its synoptic function also giving way under our century's wholesale preoccupation with the individual psychology of remembering. Because we no longer enact memory in the social rituals of everyday life, it is both compartmentalized as an experience and appropriated as an internal agency of the self: 'This transformation of memory marks a decisive shift from the historical to the psychological, from the social to the individual, from the concrete message to its subjective representation, from repetition to remembrance.'[16]

From this perspective, the memory of 'the Nation' that anchors the new alliance of state and society is best conceived not as an overarching, consensual representation of a common national past, but as an affective investment in a specific set of *lieux de mémoire* that resonate with social and individual needs for collective belonging. For it is the *emotive* force of national memories that has given them their magnetic, contagious and volatile character in the life of modern nation-states (and aspiring nation-states). Nora's emphasis on the 'psychologization of contemporary memory' suggests that this affective investment in national memories is due not only to the conjunctural 'fit' of social and individual memories, but to the changing psychic economy of memory itself. Under the impact of the waning fortunes of 'environments of memory' in the modern world, individual memories acquire ever-greater significance as the guarantors of social continuity, instilling a 'duty to remember' that assumes 'great coercive force'. But if these pressures turn their bearers into 'memory-individuals', compelled to remember for their own and society's sake, they also generate a counterforce in the form of a need for expressive outlets that would articulate the burden of memory that modern individuals now shoulder. Nora points out that psychoanalysis, literature and philosophy have primarily attended to this expressive need over this last century. But the atomized and highly-cathected agency of individual memory has increasingly sought a wider social arena of expression, and the 'idea of the nation', for reasons that Nora will explore in subsequent volumes, has proved an extremely fertile and receptive terrain.

La Mémoire républicaine

I shall return in due course to Nora's ongoing theorization of collective memory, but it is first necessary to take a detour via his overview of the main transformations in the character of French national memory. These abbreviated but suggestive overviews conclude every tome of *Les Lieux de mémoire* and attempt to tease out the main contours of French national memory (what Nora calls '*un dispositif de mémoire*' – a 'memory apparatus') by drawing together the constellation of meanings that the diverse sites of memory elected for scrutiny have elicited. Yet inasmuch as these constellations have been selected because they have managed to consolidate their hold on individual and collective memory resources, and to provide the foundations and reference points of French national identity, they have also been subject to the forces of change – 'the ponderous realities of our twentieth century'.[17] Nora's laconic remarks on how French national memory has negotiated these periods of instability and change must thus be read against the backdrop of his more general propositions on memory's indispensable vocation in the halcyon days of the nation-state.

As has already been mentioned, the first volume of *Les Lieux de mémoire* takes as its core representation the image of the nation-as-Republic. This representation is sustained by a set of 'founding principles', values that have been so powerfully inscribed in the national polity as to become more than a mere description of French civic consciousness – '*La France républicaine*' – but the signifier of the French nation-state – '*La République*' – itself. Nora maintains that this has been achieved over the nineteenth and twentieth centuries by 'the systematic construction of a memory that is at the same time authoritarian, unitary, exclusivist, universalist and intensely *passéiste*'.[18]

The authoritarian character of this memory derives from an appropriation of the French revolutionary tradition in the guise of a 'centralizing Jacobinism'. In political terms, this entailed a permanent mobilization of this revolutionary memory against potentially destabilizing forces, and on behalf of certain efficacious social alliances. In cultural terms, it required a collective memory that rallied to the cause of national unity and to the defence of the revolutionary tradition, diverse social constituencies that had until the nineteenth century remained outside any common national rubric. Nora observes that a host of national institutions – schools, military service, electoral rituals, political parties – not only congregated individuals and groups into a common public sphere, but were able to exact 'the absolute obligation to enroll local memories in the common fund of a national culture'. And, according to Nora, the extent of this republican 'conquest' of the state – and ultimately of society – can be measured by the fact that *La République* came to signify not only the political regime and its philosophy and policies, but 'a system, a culture and virtually a moral civilisation'.[19]

By definition, a memory that sought to dictate and unify also consolidated itself by that which it excluded: 'It defined itself through opposition, it thrived on enemies [. . .] The Republic needed adversaries in order to develop its genetic aptitude to embody the social totality. . .'.[20] To adapt a familiar adage, had the fledgling French Republic not had enemies, it would have been obliged to invent them as the condition of its own sense of indivisibility. As the true offspring of the revolutionary tradition it had selectively assimilated, *La République* demanded social solidarity in the face of the alleged adversaries that permanently assailed it. Though here Nora conjures a dramatic image of a republican identity shored up by the very social cleavages its state has deliberately incited, the point is well worth registering. For Nora does wish to emphasize that France has only known democratic politics in its republican guise, that is, wherein the social contract is interpreted as the exclusivist expression of the general will – 'the general will which requires the excluded'.[21] The 'republican consensus' forged by national memory thus has an inherently 'combative' rather than conciliatory dimension, and in this respect can be seen as a distinctive figuration of the French nation-state. In seeming opposition to this particularism, the memory of *La République* was also intent on yoking its revolutionary heritage to the universalist claims of the Declaration of the Rights of Man. Yet Nora observes that even the goal of universal emancipation was envisaged as a project in which the French Republic would play a leading and exemplary role.

Finally, Nora characterizes the memory of *La République* as one that was fundamentally *passéiste*. Acknowledging that this seems a tautological observation in so far as memory necessarily refers to, and relies upon the past, he nonetheless insists on this description in the specific sense that memory's trenchant efforts on behalf of forging a republican consensus immediately became the object of national commemoration. To put it another way, if republican identity was founded on memory, it was to a great extent the reverent memory of its own founding activities. *La République*, solemnly venerated, quickly commemorated the very 'traditions' that were bringing it into existence. This leads Nora to propose that the *tradition républicaine* be seen as the true *lieu de mémoire* of *La République*, and grasped not as the historic evolution of time-honoured republican traditions, but in *ses foyers d'expression* – political, cultural, pedagogic and so on – by which *La République* invented and celebrated its immediate claims to posterity.[22]

To recapitulate: French national memory must first be apprehended in its republican incarnation and with the key attributes that Nora summarily recounts. But more than the content of this republican memory, Nora is concerned to emphasize the task it triumphantly carried out: namely, the articulation of 'the State, society and the nation in a patriotic synthesis'.[23]

The decline of the republican memory occurs under the pressure of a series of factors. The first, in Nora's view, is the very success of its bid to generalize this memory throughout French society. The challenges this century that have been mounted to the republican order – whether real or imagined – (Nora's examples include the Vichy government, fear of a communist coup at the time of the Liberation, and the French generals' putsch during the Algerian war) were initially met with a defensive reflex that testified to the infusion of the republican spirit throughout the body politic, its 'durable entrenchment in the memorial capital of the nation'.[24] However, its ability to fend off external threats successfully did not protect republican memory from erosion from within. Under the impact of its own internal weaknesses (ministerial instability, parliamentary impotence, institutional paralysis) and the betrayal of its principles (non-intervention in the Spanish civil war, Munich, torture in Algeria) the social cement of the republican memory began to crumble and to expose itself to the corrosive forces of competing memories. In particular, Nora highlights the Gaullist and communist attempts of the post-war period to refashion republicanism in their own image – the former claiming to offer an alternative to its weaknesses and prevarications; the latter to embody its logical fulfilment. For Nora the significance of these bids is twofold: however different their political philosophies, Gaullism and communism were able to mount for a time a plausible challenge to the monopoly of a single republican representation of the national polity, but to do so only by affirming their own loyalty to *La République* in the alternative versions of national identity they sought to impose. In other words, *La République* remained the central figure of a republican memory that was increasingly on the defensive.

But more than any other factor, Nora highlights the fact that republican memory was irrevocably undermined by the exceptional economic development that France enjoyed over a period of thirty years, roughly from the 1950s to 1980s. In the throes of this rapid development, the aims of 'growth' increasingly functioned as the central mechanism of national cohesion, not only displacing the binding civic values of republicanism, but installing a whole new social ethos incommensurable with its predecessor: '. . . growth moved the national consensus that was the achievement of republican memory toward values that had been alien to it: the economy, the present, prediction, consumption, peace, the social, modernity; and in this way it powerfully contributed to the neutralization of republican values and rendered them somewhat obsolete'.[25] Not only does republican memory lose its dynamic powers of moulding, shaping and enforcing a national consensus, but the 'patriotic synthesis' of State, nation and society that had been its culminating achievement is now progressively dismantled, and each instance regains a more autonomous social status.

Nora's final ruminations on the fate of the republican memory take the form of a diagnostic of the present (that is, the early 1980s, when this essay, 'De la République à la Nation', was written). He admits the acute difficulty of measuring the impact on memory of developments that are still taking place. But at the same time, he is convinced that these changes are of such a scale and happening in such a concentrated period of time that they must be indicators of a 'new configuration' of the national memorial landscape. They include a cluster of key elements: accelerated growth followed by protracted economic stagnation; a left in power that has become identified with the very institutional instruments it once saw as irredeemably anti-republican; and new political trajectories along which Gaullism and communism have been propelled. The final discrediting of Soviet-style socialism has virtually put French communism beyond the pale of a national republican consensus. Gaullism, meanwhile, has been busy reconsolidating its identity around a version of national history in which it enshrines its own unique place.

From these disparate trends, Nora discerns a new memorial consciousness awakening in the French political landscape: 'The return of the national and the withdrawal into the minimal values of the Republic.'[26] Each political constituency, shaken by different forces (the left by its unholy alliance, the right by lingering suspicions about its Pétainist precursors), knows its political fortunes now hinge on its ability to be seen as the true standard-bearer of an enduring republican 'vigilance'. However, in so far as the strength of republican values has been dissipated by the more pragmatic values that accompanied the intervening period of growth, Nora perceives a far greater investment in a *national* memorial coinage. Popular memory and conventional historiography, supported by the revamped political agenda of all parties, have trained their sights on national history as the most promising foundations of a new national identity. Moreover, as France attempts to forge this new identity in the face of its declining economic fortunes and diminished status as a *puissance moyenne* in international affairs, the temptation to bask in the glories of national history is proving irresistible. *La République* may still be ritually invoked as the nation's revered memorial figure, but for Nora it has been superseded by a considerably greater preoccupation with the national; hence *La République* has become a mere *lieu de mémoire*.

La 'Nation-mémoire'

It would be misleading to give the impression that national memory came into existence only as the republican memory caved in to the political and economic pressures of the post-war period. Nora's comments on *la nation-mémoire* that conclude the three-volume study of specific national *lieux de mémoire* attest to the presence of a national memory dating back to France's monarchical period, a *mémoire-royale* draping itself in royal robes and enacting itself in timeless rituals.[27] He also identifies a national memory that embedded itself in the institution of the early modern state, a *mémoire-État*, basking in 'monumental and spectacular' representations of itself (the key *lieu de mémoire* here is Versailles) and seeking to affirm by these ostentatious displays of power its unitary and affirmative vocation. He also sees as one of the spin-offs of the national-republican adventure, the creation of a *mémoire-citoyen*, a citizenry self-conscious of itself as a mass and as the ultimate arbiter of democratic politics. All these are moments when collective identification takes on a specifically national character. However, the national memory that forms the crux of this tome, and of Nora's reflections, is the moment when the nation becomes conscious of itself as 'a Nation'.[28] By 'moment' Nora does not mean a temporally discrete apprehension of national self-consciousness, but an ongoing memorial process. It is when 'the Nation' serves as the primary point of collective identification and, aware of its unrivalled unifying function, undertakes the work of self-consecration.

The individual chapters of 'La Nation' map this process over several centuries of French national life, though, in the spirit of the *œuvre*'s general theoretical enterprise, the ensuing demarcations act not as chronological signposts but as conceptual clusters whose constitutive *lieux de mémoire* articulate a particular aspect of national self-consciousness ('Héritage', 'Le Térritoire', 'Paysages', etc.). However, as compelling as these are in their own right, I would like to continue to follow Nora's own analytic trajectory, since it seems to me essential to understanding the 'return of the national' in French collective memory that he signals in his diagnostic of republican memory.

Rather than ponder the permutations of French national memory over the centuries, Nora concentrates on its present incarnation (a reminder: 'the present' is 1986, when this tome was published, and, as will be seen, this periodization is itself of tremendous significance). To grasp the national self-consciousness of France in the mid-1980s, Nora introduces the notion of a *mémoire-patrimoine*. This concept will become of vital importance to his final study, *Les France*, but at this stage the concept serves to highlight what Nora sees to be the distinctive feature of contemporary French memorial consciousness: the apprehension of the national past through the very memorial objects that have hitherto served to signify its existence. *La mémoire-patrimoine* is a society's appropriation of its national-memorial past as a shared and (largely) edifying collective heritage – 'the transformation of the traditional stakes of memory itself into common property and a collective heritage'.[29] When these include not only the edifying but the more painful and shameful episodes of the national past (the wars in the Vendée, Vichy, the Algerian war, to cite only the best-known), patrimonial memory is still compelled to embrace (even if it is unable to 'master') their troublesome memorial legacy.[30]

Nora believes that this *mémoire-patrimoine* is primarily responsible for activating the renewed feeling of national belonging that is manifesting itself in French public life, though he is concerned to distinguish this manifestation from the traditional nationalism that has characterized previous outbursts of nationalist sentiment. He specifies that this assertion of national belonging is expressing itself in the form of a 'renewed sensibility of national singularity'.[31] But in light of the forces he has earlier highlighted that have eroded France's more grandiose self-image and demoted its standing to that of a *puissance moyenne*, and referring to a Europe that, as Nora writes, is compelling all nation-states to waive their rights to supreme political and economic authority, this sensibility is building its sense of singularity on a new configuration. In Nora's mind, its most prominent elements include, apart from the thrust of Europeanization, 'the generalization of modern modes of life, the aspiration toward decentralization, contemporary forms of state intervention, the strong presence of an immigrant population not easily adaptable to the traditional norms of "Frenchness", the waning of the francophone world.'[32]

At this stage, Nora offers no judgement on, or prognosis of the type of national collective consciousness that this combination of elements is in the process of generating (this diagnosis must await his final essay in *Les France*). But he does attempt to reflect upon how *la nation-mémoire* in its larger sense is figuring *La France* in the mid-1980s.

First of all, Nora is adamant that *La France* has no reality *but* a memorial one. As the expression of the general will, as the binding force of diverse social groups, and as the instance of supreme political legitimacy, *La France* exists only to the extent that collective memory validates such claims. In substance, this representation has lost its putative integrating powers: 'France is no longer a convincing and viable object of analysis. Whether one examines economic factors, cultural practices or the evolution of attitudes, membership of such a unit is no longer self-evident and the existence of a single "France" has become entirely problematic.'[33]

In large part Nora attributes this loss of confidence to the very feature that made the French nation-state distinctive amongst others – its 'stato-centric' character. Invoking a theme that was central to his study of the 'authoritarian' character of *la mémoire républicaine*, he recalls the historic identification of the French nation with the State, an identification that inscribed itself in the collective consciousness and that seemed immutable. However, if the ubiquity of this statist historical memory at one time confirmed France in its grandeur, and endorsed the French state's role as 'director, protector, unifier and educator' in many spheres of life, in Nora's view this very omnipotence is at the root of its endemic failure to triumph in the face of contemporary developments. For the State's insinuation into collective consciousness as a major benchmark of French national identity depended upon an exclusively *political* self-consciousness (though Nora doesn't specify here, presumably he means this rather than, say, a moral, ethical or wider social self-consciousness). He points out that the paradox of this seemingly unshakeable foundation of the French Nation in an authoritarian State is the fact that it relies on the solidity of a domain – the political – that is by nature transitory. French national memory therefore evolved not only in an especially 'conflictual mode' thanks to the turbulence of French political life, but also in a restricted domain that was blind to other forces that were making their social impact above or below the level of the nation-state.

Nora's insistence on the politically partisanal nature of French national memory (in this specific sense of being constituted by the political sphere) leads him to describe this memory's claims to historical continuity as the results of its own intensive labours: 'It is entirely the effect of the exhumation of a *continuity*, the valorization of a *singularity*, and the apparition of a *chronology*.'[34] While he acknowledges that this work of memory construction is undertaken by all nation-states, the French version of *la nation-mémoire* can be distinguished by its exceptional degree of dependence on the political vicissitudes of the modern French state.

It is therefore no wonder that the French state has shown such an intense interest in Nora's own historiographical enterprise – a fact that Nora himself makes the basis of his final ruminations.

L'Ère de la commémoration

The concluding essay of the last tome, *Les France*, contains Nora's final reflections on the fate of national memory in France; but the extraordinary feature of this analysis is that it is obliged to consider the effects that *Les Lieux de mémoire* as a historiographical project has had on the very transformations Nora is trying critically to apprehend. Whatever its academic and intellectual accomplishments (and the highly favourable reviews throughout its gestation show these to be considerable), *Les Lieux de mémoire* has been a resounding *popular* success. The entry of the term *lieu de mémoire* into *Le Grand Robert* has already been mentioned. But this endorsement followed on the heels of other accolades in the late 1980s and early 1990s – perhaps most notably, a commission from the then French Minister of Culture Jack Lang, asking Nora and his team to lend their assistance to an official campaign designed to protect specified *lieux de mémoire*. More widely, the term *lieu de mémoire* entered into common cultural currency: it could be found in lifestyle magazines intent on drawing readers' attentions to the tastefulness of rural architecture or in the campaigns of local heritage associations concerned to claim a rightful place for their own locality's cherished monuments. And it is precisely in this increasing enthusiasm of diverse social constituencies to consecrate their own *lieux de mémoire* that Nora identifies both the conservative recuperation of his own critical project and the distinctive symptoms of a new memorial era – the 'era of commemoration'. On a rather plaintive note, Nora records that '. . . the tool forged for the purposes of critical distance [the notion of *lieux de mémoire*] has become the instrument *par excellence* of commemoration'.[35] This appropriation is driven, however, by a strong social impetus to commemorate – virtually a 'commemorative obsession' – a force with which Nora's project clearly resonates and perhaps that it even fuels, but that has its own specific conditions of existence.

In his previous essay, Nora highlighted several of these formative conditions – in particular, the fact that as France sees its status as a great world power ebbing away, it makes a compensatory grab at those features that seem to affirm its lingering grandeur – its cultural *richesse*, revolutionary heritage, and exalted sense of historical mission. But in this volume, Nora pinpoints a decisive shift in France's commemorative sensibility: '. . . the subversion and violation of the classical model of national commemoration [. . .] and its replacement by a splintered system, composed of disparate commemorative languages, which presupposes a different relation to the past – more elective than imperative [. . .] There is no longer a commemorative superego, the canon has disappeared.'[36]

Nora traces this shift to the erosion of the 'unitary framework' of the nation-state and an ensuing decentralization of social power. The order and hierarchy of authority implied by its erstwhile key figures – 'La France', 'La République', 'La Nation' – is now suffused throughout the social body. The alliance of state and society that Nora maintains in his first essay has supplanted the cohesive structure of the nation-state is now fully revealed. And the traditional instruments of the state's commemorative activity – schools, official memorial rituals and the like – find their tasks usurped by new mechanisms and forms of representation: on the one hand by the spectacularization of collective memory effected by the mass media and especially film and television; on the other hand, by the 'deluge' of particularistic commemorative events housed in museums, folkloric displays, local monuments and a proliferating multitude of heritage associations. The state's presence in memorial activity, once overbearing and directing, is now 'discrete' and 'enabling' – a clear indication of its own demotion to the sidelines of contemporary memory-politics. Nora interprets Mitterrand's involvement in this politics – his controversial laying of the wreath at Pétain's tomb and his declaration, after protracted resistance, that a national day of commemoration, 'Vél d'Hiv' Day, would recall the round-up of French Jews in Paris in July 1942 – as a sign that official attempts at national commemoration have exhausted all but their political meaning and import.

In this new order of things, the significance of certain national commemorative events is better measured by their purely memorial status than by any predicted impact on current social or political behaviour. Thus in Nora's account, the controversies accompanying the 1789 Bicentenary commemorations were waged not over the contemporary political ramifications of certain interpretations of the revolutionary heritage as against others, but over the memorial status of the competing celebrations themselves. Far from being divisive, however, these very rivalries had a unifying effect and offered a rare opportunity for a truly national identification. From sporting events to town fêtes, the Bicentenary elicited a common sense of purpose in the sense that the populace was united in a shared activity of commemoration – if not in shared understandings of the Revolution that was its ostensible object. Nora therefore proposes that the contemporary era of commemoration be distinguished by an *inverse* relationship between the popular success of national commemorations and a critical apprehension of the event that is their inspiration: '. . . commemorations without an object have been the most successful; the emptiest from a historical and political point of view have been the most replete from a memorial point of view'.[37] Reinvigorated but pacified, national sentiment no longer functions as the agent of *un nationalisme agressif*, but instead fosters *un nationalisme amoureux*.[38]

Local commemorative activism, by contrast, is in the ascendancy, very often relying heavily on the support of state agencies (the Ministry of Culture, the new *Direction du patrimoine*) and state policies (decentralization, tourism, conservation). But Nora notes that this situation is not to be construed as one of local dependency on the official, but a dynamic reversal of the former state of affairs: now memorial militancy comes from below rather than above, and its own particular interests (regional, corporative, institutional) dictate the values to be venerated in relation to which the once sacrosanct values of the national and patriotic must find their assigned place. In this sense, he suggests that such widespread memorial activism might also have a certain 'democratizing' potential in so far as it reclaims from a 'stato-centric' tradition of commemoration the power to determine and regulate commemorative activity.[39] It is a localized, sentimental reinvestment in the past that also manages to subvert traditional political divisions: even if motivated by different forces – the Left's growing ecological sensibility, the Right's conservative revalorization of regional tradition – both sides of the political spectrum find themselves united 'in the defence of old stones and menaced landscapes'.[40]

Notwithstanding the challenge to national memorial orthodoxies that this description seems to imply, this characterization of a shift of social power from national to local memorial activities also highlights a more ambivalent side. Nora believes that the withdrawal into the 'refuge' of patrimonial memory may be one means of negotiating the painful transformation in national self-consciousness that France is undergoing, and that the accompanying 'cult of commemoration' might even play a role in regulating the accompanying tensions.[41] But even this functional interpretation is tempered by Nora's awareness of the conflicts that can be produced when memory is recruited on behalf of a particularistic cultural ethos and the corresponding demands for recognition of what he calls 'sectoral identities'. If local groups and interests each vociferously claim the right to determine their own commemorative activity and its significance, they are also susceptible to the 'internal conflicts' and 'inevitable contestations' which such assertions necessarily bring in their wake. On the one hand, Nora seems to suggest that the more benign result may be a reconstituted national polity, wherein the national functions not as 'the militant expression of the unity of a group' but as 'the conflictual unity of all groups within a democracy'.[42] On the other hand, there is a more sinister prognosis that surfaces repeatedly in his analysis, deriving from the growing strength of 'sectoral identities' and the corresponding inability of the national imaginary to represent an inclusive *political* identity of any kind – including the founding collective identity of republicanism itself. As Nora points out, with the exploration of patrimonial forms of identification comes the discovery of *la patrie*, with all the emotional ambivalences towards 'strangers' – within and without – that such an emotionally-laden term implies. Moreover, an identity politics that promotes the accumulation of patrimonial capital as the key asset of national belonging necessarily excludes

from its embrace those diasporic groups who do not have the same emotional investment in *les lieux de mémoire* of *la patrie*.[43] It is perhaps not surprising, then, that in
contrast to his earlier thoughts on the matter, Nora now has little faith in the ability
of the 'European idea' to forge a new inclusive identity on the ruins of the crumbling
national edifice. It would seem that even as Nora entertained that hope, the new
stakes of collective identity were being firmly driven into the soil of *la patrie*.

Precisely because these reflections have wider political import, this may be the
appropriate place to leave Nora's *histoire de France par la mémoire* and to conclude
with a more general summary and appraisal of the fate of collective memory in our
times.

Identity/Memory/Patrimony

It has been commonly assumed that collective memory provides communities with
historical narratives by which they apprehend their identity over time. If this
assumption has been able to account for the importance of representations of
temporality to collective identity formation, it is a formulation that now requires
considerable revision in the light of Nora's reworking of the transformations
undergone by collective memory in the modern world. On the one hand, he has
highlighted the fact that modern societies live within a 'historical' rather than
'memorial' consciousness of time. With the demise of the 'environments of memory'
of the pre-modern world in which time is perceived as continuous (for Nora, their
last vestiges disappear with the peasantry), a modern historical consciousness
emerges that *represents* temporal order according to the instances of past, present
and future. Modern memory assumes the function of an agency that orders these
discrete temporalities into specific configurations of consciousness.

To simplify: in the era of the modern nation-state, memory has primarily worked
on behalf of narratives that have linked the national past and future in a causal
relation. National destiny has been derived from myths of the national past, in
which the cause of the nation itself has been the unifying and driving force. With
the decline of the nation-state as the main institution of social cohesion, and its
replacement by a social consciousness of the nation, past and future are no longer
interdependent. The 'dissolution of the national myth', according to Nora, has the
effect of making past and future into virtually autonomous instances. The future
can no longer be predicted on the basis of an assumed historical trajectory, and
therefore in its very capriciousness becomes all the more menacing and pre-
occupying. The past, 'detached from the organizing coherence of a history', is
rendered wholly patrimonial.

Here Nora is clearly referring to a more widespread phenomenon that is now
considered a defining feature of postmodern societies – the transformation of
national pasts into 'heritage' cultures. Faced with the disappointed promises of

late modern history, it is alleged, memory has returned in force as the cult of heritage. The consciousness of being a subject-in-history has ceded place to a voracious appetite to possess one.[44] Nora is well aware that the 'patrimonialization of history' has transformed most Western political cultures over the past twenty years. But he is convinced that France has experienced in a particularly distinctive manner a 'decisive passage from a historical consciousness of itself to a patrimonial one, a transformation from one model of the nation into another . . .'.[45]

In the throes of such a decisive transformation, memory also comes into a new alliance with the present. In an era of obsessive patrimonial commemoration, the present can perhaps be best characterized as a 'memorial culture'. It is a present that operates under the compulsive injunction to remember, yet also generates a consciousness acutely aware of the horizon of uncertainty that the future now represents, or, in the more emphatic words of Nora, 'a present that the anticipatory gaze to which we are condemned nails to the necessity of remembering'.[46] A present that, under a historical consciousness of the nation, was a transitory and 'translucent' temporal order, has become 'the burdened category which the oppressive weight of the future obliges to take charge of a totalized past'.[47] It is under the sway of contemporary society's effective dissociation of past and future that Nora identifies memory's promotion to such an elevated social stature – 'as dynamic agent and sole promise of continuity'.[48]

Nora does not elaborate upon the main cultural instruments that orchestrate this new disposition of temporality; but his remarks in the first essay, which see the present projected onto consciousness as an ephemeral 'film of current events', hint at the main culprits. Indeed, following Nora's lead, *Esprit* editor Olivier Mongin observed that the essential task of the 'society of communication' is to construct a present 'in the form of successive moments (*coups*) without historical relation to one another'.[49] The contemporary media are thus held primarily responsible for the 'ideologization' of the present – an ahistorical present that, on the one hand, is deemed 'self-sufficient', yet whose elements, on the other, are rapidly relegated to historical obscurity. At the same time, the media are posited as a central institution of the memorial culture that saturates the present, offering up for mass consumption recycled memorial images and sounds that are emptied of any historical plenitude. The media are therefore also charged with complicity in the 'ideologization' of memory that contemporary culture as a whole has effected.[50]

This accusation is certainly persuasive, and must strike a resonant chord with, for example, the ordinary viewer of television news, who senses the manipulation of present events by the hierarchy and duration of reportage, and by the immediate relegation of today's eminently newsworthy item into tomorrow's televisual archive. That same viewer will also 'remember' history and commemorate particular events by conjuring a repertory of images whose origins are primarily filmic or televisual.[51] Yet, convincing as this characterization of the contemporary media might be in general terms, it is nonetheless too sweeping in scope and too hasty in its outright condemnation of the media's ideologizing role. After all, as we shall see in subsequent chapters, the very historical events that Nora suggests continually return to haunt the 'era of commemoration' in France, and to trouble its placid memorial surface – Vichy and the Algerian war, for example – have made their entry into public consciousness courtesy of the resources of the modern media.[52] Nora's account has put its finger on the crucial role that the contemporary media play in constructing and shaping the distinct temporality of modern consciousness and the form and substance of collective memories (hence the vital relevance of Nora's work to media and cultural analysis); but we will not find in *Lieux de mémoire* the precise mechanisms by which they do so.

Finally, this realignment of temporality, whose corresponding consciousness Nora designates as a 'historicized present', gives rise to another correlative – that of 'identity'. He cites 'identity', 'memory' and 'patrimony' as the sovereign troika that now rules contemporary consciousness – each in symbiotic union with the other two. In 'identity', the singularity and permanence of the self (or group) is asserted and repeatedly rehearsed; in 'memory', the repertoire of representations of an individual or collective past is embraced as the distinctive repository and resource of a present consciousness; in the patrimonial, a specific heritage is claimed as a precious possession that constitutes the founding proof of one's singular identity. '*Le patrimoine*', Nora states, 'is no longer the inventory of totemic masterpieces of national grandeur. It has become the collective possession of a specific group which, through its recuperation, validates an essential and constitutive part of its identity.'[53] The circularity, overlapping and virtual interchangeability of these terms and their meanings is for Nora the sign of a 'new internal configuration', a new economy of memory-politics centred on 'identity' that now dominates so much cultural and political discourse. While Nora is clearly sceptical of this new constellation and the politics it supports – he makes a mocking reference to these terms as 'the three new faces of the new continent Culture'[54] – it does provide him with the grounds for asserting that memory is once again pervasive in the social landscape. This memorial omnipresence should not be confused with the 'environments of memory' evoked above – our contemporary society is too self-conscious of the temporal hierarchy that now determines its distinct sensibility; but it nonetheless signals in Nora's view a transition from a more 'restrained' memorial presence to a 'generalized' one. Indeed, Nora suggests that our era may be succumbing to memory's tyranny once more.[55]

Whether Nora's prognosis is correct is a question that will be addressed frequently within the remaining chapters of this book. And while *Les Lieux de mémoire* may stop short of condemning the obsession that it purports only to have exposed, I would contend that it provides a compelling – and indeed essential – analytic framework for the construction of this more critical agenda.

Notes

Unless otherwise stated, translations from the French are my own.

1. *Esprit*, no.193, July 1993, p. 5.
2. *Le Monde*, 5 February 1993.
3. *Les Lieux de mémoire* (sous la direction de Pierre Nora), *Vol. 3, Les France*, tome III (Paris: Gallimard, 1992), p. 1004. I am drawing upon the definition that appears in Nora's 'Preface' *Realms of Memory: The Construction of the French Past, Vol. I: Conflicts and Divisions,* trans. Arthur Goldhammer (New York: Columbia University Press,1997), p. xvii. As this book goes to press, two other volumes have been published: *Volume II: Traditions* and *Volume III: Symbols*. These contain selections from the corresponding French volumes. In his review of the project, Tony Judt comments on the difficulty of finding a suitable English translation of *lieux*: "'sites' or 'places' may be too 'misleadingly spatial', whereas 'realms' dilutes 'some of the emphasis on soil and territory that is so important in French memory'. See Tony Judt, 'A La Recherche du Temps Perdu', *New York Review of Books*, 3 December 1998, p. 55.
4. Nora, 'De la République à la Nation', in *Les Lieux de mémoire, Vol. 1, La République* (Paris: Gallimard, 1984), p. 651.
5. Nora's term in 'From *Lieux de mémoire* to *Realms* of Memory',' in *Realms of Memory*, p. xvii.
6. Nora, 'General Introduction: Between Memory and History', in *Realms of Memory*, p. 15.
7. Nora, 'Comment écrire l'histoire de la France?', in *Les Lieux de mémoire, Vol. 1, La République*, p. 25.
8. Nora, 'General Introduction: Between Memory and History', in *Realms of Memory*, p. 1.
9. Ibid., p. 2.
10. Ibid., pp. 6–7.
11. See Eric Hobsbawm and Terence Ranger (eds), *The Invention of Tradition* (Cambridge: Cambridge University Press, 1983); Anthony D. Smith, *National Identity* (London: Penguin, 1991); Benedict Anderson, *Imagined Communities: Reflections on the Origin and Spread of Nationalism* (London: Verso, 1991); and David Lowenthal, *The Past Is a Foreign Country* (Cambridge: Cambridge University Press, 1985).
12. For appraisals of Nora's assemblage of memory-sites see Steven Englund, 'History in a Late Age', *French Politics and Society*, vol. 14, no. 1, Winter 1996, and Tony Judt, 'A la Recherche du Temps Perdu'. Judt also comments on noteworthy exclusions, such as Napoleon Bonaparte, Louis Napoleon and the political tradition of *bonapartisme*, as well as the massacre of Protestants

on St Bartholomew's Day, 1542. The absence of colonial *lieux de mémoire* has also been remarked upon by critics, though the reader is referred to Chapters 7 and 8 for Nora's distinctive contribution to the understanding of France's colonial past in Algeria.

13. 'Between Memory and History', p. 6.
14. Ibid.
15. Ibid.
16. Ibid., p. 11.
17. Nora, 'De la République à la Nation', p. 651.
18. Ibid., p. 652.
19. Ibid.
20. Ibid.
21. Ibid., p. 653.
22. This is a case where, to use the formulation of Slavoj Žižek, 'the "external" ritual performatively generates its own ideological foundation'. See 'Superego by Default' in *The Metastases of Enjoyment* (London: Verso, 1994) p. 59.
23. Nora, 'De la République à la Nation', p. 654.
24. Ibid., p. 655.
25. Ibid., p. 657.
26. Ibid., p. 658.
27. Nora, 'La nation-mémoire', in *Les Lieux de mémoire, Vol. 2, tome III, La Nation* (Paris: Gallimard, 1986), pp. 648–9.
28. Ibid., p. 648.
29. Ibid., p. 650.
30. Tony Judt argues that '. . . the French have no narrative to which they can attach "Vichy" that would give to it an agreed, communicable meaning. Without such a narrative, without a history, "Vichy" has no place in French memory.' See 'A la Recherche du Temps Perdu', p. 58. However, I would suggest that Vichy is part of the national 'patrimoine' *precisely because* of the 'negative identification' with crimes committed in the name of the nation that it solicits – an identification that can also serve a collective, binding function. As Žižek again alleges: '. . . identification with community is ultimately always based upon some shared guilt or, more precisely, upon the fetishistic disavowal of this guilt'. See 'Superego by Default', p. 57.
31. Ibid., p. 651.
32. Ibid.
33. Ibid., p. 653.
34. Ibid., p. 655 (emphasis in the original).
35. Nora, 'L'Ère de la commémoration', in *Les Lieux de mémoire, Vol. 3, tome III, Les France* (Paris: Gallimard, 1992), p. 977.
36. Ibid., pp. 983–4. In 'A la Recherche du Temps Perdu', Judt observes that

France, 'like other modern nations, is living off the pedagogical capital invested in its citizens in earlier decades', p. 58. Judt believes that owing to the 'virtual disappearance of narrative history from the school curriculum in many school systems', citizens are being plunged into 'realms of forgetting' about their common past. Judt perhaps underestimates the extent to which these narratives are being disseminated in popular culture – for better or worse.

37. Ibid., p. 988.
38. Pierre Nora, 'La Loi de la mémoire', *Le Débat* no. 78, Jan.–Feb. 1994, p. 189.
39. Nora describes this (tongue-in-cheek?) as its 'toquevillian' moment. See 'Un entretien avec Pierre Nora', *Le Monde*, 29 November 1994.
40. Pierre Nora, 'La ruée vers le passé', *Magazine littéraire', Hors série, 1966-1996, La passion des idées*, p. 69.
41. 'Un entretien avec Pierre Nora', p. 2.
42. 'L'Ère de la commémoration', p. 986.
43. As we shall see in later chapters, this is the explanation offered for France's periodic anti-Semitic outbursts and for the sense of exclusion encountered by certain categories of the citizenry, however long-standing their presence in France.
44. For the analysis of heritage in the British context, see Patrick Wright, *On Living in an Old Country* (London: Verso, 1985); Robert Hewison, *The Heritage Industry* (London: Methuen, 1987), and more recently, Raphael Samuels, *Theatres of Memory, Vol. I, Past and present in contemporary culture* (London: Verso, 1995). Samuels's book defended the popular passion for heritage against intellectual sceptics, notably Wright, Hewison and the journalist Neil Ascherson, and thereby ignited yet another round of debate. The critique has been renewed most recently by David Lowenthal, *The Heritage Crusade and the Spoils of History* (Cambridge: Cambridge University Press, 1998)
45. Nora, 'La Loi de la mémoire', p. 189.
46. 'L'Ère de la commémoration', p. 1009.
47. Ibid.
48. Ibid.
49. Olivier Mongin, 'Une mémoire sans histoire? Vers une autre relation à l'histoire', *Esprit* no. 190, Mar.–Apr.1993, p. 102.
50. Ibid., p. 108.
51. See Anton Kaes, *From 'Hitler' to 'Heimat': The Return of History as Film* (London: Harvard University Press, 1991).
52. See Henry Rousso, *The Vichy Syndrome: History and Memory in France since 1944* (London: Harvard University Press, 1991) for an account of the role played by the French media in mobilizing debates about Vichy, particularly key films like Marcel Ophuls *Le Chagrin et la pitié* (1971). In a later text that Rousso co-authored with Éric Conan, *Vichy, un passé qui ne passe pas* (Paris:

Fayard, 1994), which charts how the concept of the Vichy syndrome has been instrumentalized by '*le devoir de mémoire*' or the 'obligation to remember' imposed by memorial 'militants', the authors display a profound scepticism about the capacity of the media to encourage a critical, historical memory. Their example of the media's surrender to the value of the 'scoop' is the treatment of the allegation, made by journalist Thierry Wolton in 1993, that Resistance hero Jean Moulin was a Soviet agent. I discuss this text more fully in Chapter 5.

53. 'Un Entretien avec Pierre Nora', p. 2.
54. Nora, 'L'Ère de la commémoration', p. 1010.
55. Ibid. If, in Nora's view, this 'commemorative obsession' has 'overdetermined' social consciousness in France, he nonetheless remains circumspect about whether this is a largely positive or negative phenomenon when it concerns, for example, Jewish memory of Vichy. See his comments prior to the trial of Maurice Papon on the 'obsessive memory' of Vichy, 'a wound which continues to fester rather than heal'. 'Tout concourt aujourd'hui au souvenir obsédant de Vichy', *Le Monde*, 1 October 1997.

Public Memory and Postconventional Identity

Introduction

In an era that is allegedly rife with the 'return' of memories stemming from childhood that have entirely escaped the subject's conscious apprehension, Jürgen Habermas's model of memory may seem on first encounter naïvely voluntaristic, or at the very least, over-reliant on a belief that memory can be decisively shaped by the forces of rationality and consciousness. Indeed, in an article summarizing post-war Germany's modalities of 'coming to terms' with its Nazi past, Habermas summons the analogy of the individual who critically examines and selectively appropriates aspects of a personal past by proceeding 'in an almost counterfactual way'. The individual, says Habermas, must first of all 'take full responsibility for the outcome of the processes that shaped one's identity and then discriminate those strands that one affirms and wants to continue from those to be rejected'. However, if this depiction might conjure for the reader the image of an individual rummaging through the clothes closet, separating threadbare and outmoded garments from those still serviceable for another season, the simplicity is deceptive. For Habermas acknowledges that even for the individual, accepting or rejecting elements of one's past is not sufficient. Especially when what is recalled entails 'painful episodes of failure and the appalling aspects of one's life that ought no longer to determine one's identity', the outright repudiation or denial of such negative moments is more likely to ensure their unconscious persistence and ongoing psychic effectivity rather than their successful exorcism. In order to avoid a compulsion to repeat – or what Habermas calls the past's 'compulsory reign over the present' – he argues that a process of consciously 'working through' such memories must be attempted.[1] And while aware that individual and collective memory must not be conflated, Habermas goes on to stipulate that like individuals, the wider German polity must also find a corresponding mode of working-through painful memories in the nation's recent past.

Again, this emphasis on a conscious working-through of painful memories contrasts markedly with the more recent emphasis on the unconscious dimensions that memory engages and that escape the volitional capacity of individuals and collectivities: affective structures like mourning, melancholia and trauma or mechanisms of repression, displacement and denial. Moreover, Habermas's approach must appear all the more incongruous coming as it does from a former member of the Frankfurt School. After all, Habermas's Frankfurt School predecessors Theodor Adorno and Max Horkheimer were among the first to turn to psychoanalysis in order to address the failure of social theory to explain Nazism's deep-seated appeal to the 'ordinary German'. In their analysis, it was the unconscious personality structures shaped and nurtured within the intimate confines of the German family that were drawn to Nazism's authoritarian strictures and ideology.[2] Habermas appears to upend these insights by suggesting that only a working-through of the Nazi legacy that takes place in the *public* sphere and assumes *collective* responsibility for Nazi crimes can foster individuals capable of coming to terms with this past at the deepest subjective levels. As Dominick LaCapra has pointed out, rather than making an individual labour of mourning in the private sphere the precondition for a collective coming to terms with Nazism and the Holocaust, Habermas invokes public memory as 'a prerequisite for any process of mourning and working through collective traumas'.[3] Or, to put it another way, Habermas believes that only memory's constant performativity in the public sphere can generate in individuals a subjective foundation receptive to the kind of critical memory-work in which he believes the German national polity must constantly engage. This is not a rejection of the psychoanalytic precepts of memory so much as an awareness that subjective identities in Germany take form partly in relation to the prevailing terms of public discussion and debate about the nation's Nazi past. The issue Habermas has been tackling for well over a decade now is how to work-through such memories in the German public sphere in a manner that can foster and consolidate a 'postnational' or 'postconventional' identity – in his view the only viable identity-formation now available to Germany's citizenry. This chapter will seek to trace Habermas's elaboration of the link between public memory and postconventional identity, in the context of the political events that inspired and shaped his reflections.

Habermas, one of Germany's leading political philosophers, is not a figure one would at first associate with the rough-and-tumble world of newspaper journalism and the invectives of 'mediatized' political polemic. It is therefore all the more interesting that Habermas's first sustained interventions on German memory appeared in *Die Zeit*, the German weekly newspaper, between 1985 and 1990. In these articles, Habermas is trying to intervene actively in the politics of the moment – in his first riposte, in a controversy about official 'commemorative politics' (to use Nora's term); subsequently, in a debate that became known as the *Historikerstreit* or 'German historians' debate' of the mid-to-late 1980s; and in 1990, in the immediate aftermath of the breach of the Berlin Wall, in debates about how to conceive of German national identity in the light of unification.

But the significance of using the media in this interventionist way is not confined to the fact that a political philosopher had temporarily assumed the role of political journalist. Proponents of Habermas's theory of the 'public sphere' will find this intervention consistent with his (now famous) elaboration of this concept and the importance that he attributes to the media as the key site in modernity of an actual or potential 'democratic public sphere'. As one commentator has observed, these writings

> raise the broader question of the status of the intellectual and his or her role in the public sphere. Quite consciously, Habermas has claimed the role of the intellectual for himself and deliberately transcended the boundaries of his academic appointment [. . .] [this role] is based on free and immediate access to the media of mass communication. It presupposes the existence of a general public sphere as a forum for intellectual exchange, an exchange of opinions and arguments that ought to be accessible to the general public.[4]

If Habermas's recourse to print media can therefore be interpreted as a conscious putting into practice of his public sphere philosophy, Habermas himself points out that his own contributions were prompted by more immediate political circumstances – namely, the prolific appearance of articles in the German print media by renowned conservative historians disputing widely-accepted interpretations of the Nazi past. In other words, the use of the media to disseminate 'revisionist' accounts of recent German history was itself an 'unequivocally political question'. The need to expose why this very 'public use of history' (the title of one article) represents an important shift in the political culture of the (then) Federal Republic provides the strongest grounds for the mass-mediated nature of Habermas's own interventions.

The Politics of *Aufarbeitung*

Since the 1960s, the politics of *Aufarbeitung* ('coming to terms with the past'), more commonly – but misleadingly – referred to as *Vergangenheitsbewaltigung* ('mastering' or 'overcoming' the past), have been a constant feature in the German political and cultural landscape. The first formulations of the need for such a politics can be traced to several influential sources. I've already referred to Adorno and Horkheimer's early work on the 'authoritarian personality'; however, in 1959, Adorno wrote an essay 'What Does Coming to Terms with the Past Mean?', wherein he attempts to answer the question posed in his title by formulating the interplay of subjective and objective forces behind a specifically German response to the recent past.[5] The features typical of this response ranged, according to Adorno, from a wish to hastily 'turn the page' of history to a resentful 'guilt complex', from 'massive affect' in situations that didn't warrant it to 'lack of affect' in contexts that did, from claims of not having known about Nazi crimes to postures of indifference in the face of such knowledge. What these diverse responses had in common, in Adorno's view, was not so much the overwhelming power of the unconscious processes allegedly producing them, as the effacement of memory achieved by an 'all-too-wakeful consciousness'. While not denying that the collapse of Hitler's regime had triggered a host of psychopathological responses – a damaged collective narcissism being the most evident – Adorno insisted that the 'forgetting of National Socialism should be understood far more in terms of a general social situation than in terms of psychopathology'.[6] Such responses served 'highly realistic ends', and anyone displaying such emotions and modes of behaviour could in fact feel 'at one with his time', was indeed conforming to a mood only 'held in check by the official taboos'. The 'general social situation' to which Adorno referred was a political culture in which democracy, though more deeply rooted than during the Weimar period, was still not subjectively anchored. Democracy in Germany, Adorno observed, was introduced belatedly and by the victors, leaving the German citizenry's relation to it 'without strong emotional connections'. Consequently, Germans had adopted a passive view of democracy as something which had happened *to* them rather than a political process of which they were the agents. Thus, according to Adorno, democracy had

> not domesticated itself to the point that people really experience it as their cause, and so consider themselves agents [*Subjecte*] of the political process. It is felt to be one system among others, as if one could choose from a menu between communism, democracy, fascism, monarchy – yet not as something identical with people themselves, as the expression of their own maturity.[7]

Faced with the question of how 'public enlightenment' about the past could be broached in such a political context, and more urgently how 'to work subjectively against the objective potential for disaster', Adorno conceded the limitations of an approach that merely insisted on recounting the historical facts. Instead, he proposed that one 'should rather turn the argument toward the people whom one is addressing'. In a typically suggestive but elliptical comment, Adorno defined coming to terms with the past as 'essentially that sort of *turn toward the subject*: reinforcement of a person's self-consciousness and, with that, of a sense of self'.[8] However, he concluded his article by warning that individual enlightenment was not sufficient – that if 'the potential for fascism is linked to human interests', then Germans must be reminded that any revival of fascism, whether 'open or disguised', would lead to a 'politics of catastrophe' that would bring about their own downfall as well.

The 1960s saw the publication in Germany of *The Inability to Mourn*, a psychoanalytic treatise by Alexander and Margarete Mitscherlich, which also attempted to elucidate the subjective and objective factors structuring Germany memory of the recent past. While acknowledging at the outset the individual nature of the 'unconscious constellations that underlie psychic processes', the Mitcherlichs insisted on the applicability of certain psychoanalytic conceptualizations 'to the behaviour of individuals subjected to the very severe group pressure of political passions'.[9] German behaviour under Nazism clearly invited such clinical interest, and the Mitscherlichs' study included several case histories of former Nazi functionaries whose symptoms of neurotic and psychosomatic illness the Mitscherlichs linked to experiences during the Nazi period. But what was more remarkable in the Mitscherlichs' view was the fact that post-war clinics saw so *few* cases of such illnesses – what they observed was the 'meagerness of any outward signs of an inner burden'. This they explained by reference to, on the one hand, the powerful psychic defences of the culpable individual and, on the other, the larger social environment within which such defensive reactions would be registered. With respect to the individual, the Mitscherlichs suggested that a 'new phase of the neurotic process' had set in, 'the chief feature of which is no longer the acting out of destructive fantasies with the permission of an "upside down" conscience [Nazi criminality] – rather, there is a denial of these drive impulses and a detached indifference to the crimes committed'.[10] However, if this move from acting out destructive fantasies to their denial was a stage in the individual's neurotic disorder, it could only be perceived as a pathological reaction by the individual concerned if this was reinforced by the weight of social reproval for such culpable behaviour. Notwithstanding Germany's war crimes trials of the early 1960s (in any event resented by the majority of the population as a repetition of Nuremberg and 'victors' justice'), the social climate of post-war Germany not only lacked a morally judgemental climate against culpable individuals, but such individuals themselves formed a substantial community whose 'degree of guilt [was] determined by universal consensus'. Thus an exculpatory consensus operated on behalf of both the individual and the community, since, as the Mitscherlichs put it, 'a guilt-laden individual is isolated from society; but in a group he does not endure this fate, being merely a sinner among sinners'.[11]

However, the main diagnostic concern of the Mitscherlichs was not with those individuals who had not come to terms with actual crimes committed, but with German society more generally and its way of collectively dealing with its recent Nazi past. And here the Mitscherlichs also perceived a fundamental link between individual response and the character of the social environment, and more precisely, 'a determining connection between the political and social immobilism and provincialism prevailing in West Germany and the stubbornly maintained rejection of memories, in particular the blocking of any sense of involvement in the events of the Nazi past that are now being so strenuously denied'.[12] According to the Mitscherlichs, the social symptoms of this disorder were twofold: on the one hand, a general apathy toward issues like political rights, usually of vital concern to an engaged citizenry, and on the other, an intense – indeed for the Mitscherlichs 'manic'

– investment of energy in the process of Germany's economic reconstruction. Here they followed Adorno in explaining lack of interest in the political process by the fact that Germany's post-war democratic state had been established by an edict of the victors and hence was not normatively grounded. However, if this 'autistic attitude' toward the political process was contrasted not only with the 'political passions' that had so recently mobilized virtually an entire nation, but with the general zeal with which post-war economic reconstruction had been tackled, then a more psychoanalytically-oriented explanation was called for. The so-called 'German Economic Miracle', or *Wirtschaftswunder*, the Mitscherlichs maintained, should be seen essentially as a collective displacement activity, a defence mechanism that recapitulated at a social level the individual's resistance to remembering and working though 'a traumatic devaluation of the ego ideal [i.e. Hitler] with which identification had been so extensive'. Had the Germans responded to this loss of a narcissistically-invested love object in the 'typical' manner, they would have 'succumbed to melancholia', whose main symptom Freud had identified as a severe 'disturbance in self-regard'. Instead, this melancholic reaction was warded off through the activation of new defence mechanisms that took the form of socially-sanctioned displacement activities – the ardour of economic reconstruction foremost among these, though the Mitscherlichs also noted a 'de-realization' of the past, and a ready identification with the position of the victim.

I have dwelt in some detail on Adorno and the Mitscherlichs' study not only because these form the essential historical backdrop to, and inspiration for, many subsequent interventions in Germany's politics of memory, but because both establish a link between modalities of remembering the recent past – whether individual or collective – and the character of German political culture. As we shall see, Habermas, too, insists that the evolution of democratic convictions in Germany is intimately related to the extent to which the German public sphere has nurtured a collective capacity for self-reflexive memory.[13]

Handshakes at Bitburg

It should first be noted, however, that Habermas has consistently refused to pose the issues at hand in terms of a collective German *guilt* for crimes committed under Nazism. He repeatedly refers to Karl Jaspers's famous speech of 1946, *Die Schuldfrage*, in which Jaspers distinguished between individual guilt and collective *liability*.[14] Not only is collective guilt a notion incompatible with what Habermas calls a 'postconventionalist understanding of justice', it also, he warns, 'serves particularly the purpose of those who wish to escape collective liability by rejecting the pretension of a wrongly imputed collective guilt'.[15] This notion of 'collective liability' is at the core of Habermas's various interventions in Germany's debate about coming to terms with the Nazi past.

It first makes an appearance in an article by Habermas in *Die Zeit* occasioned by President Ronald Reagan's visit to the military cemetery at Bitburg, a small Eifel town, in May 1985. Chancellor Kohl had issued the Bitburg invitation to President Reagan as part of a spate of fortieth anniversary VE Day commemorations. The presence of Reagan, representative of the world's most powerful democracy, was to signal that the stigma attached to Germany because of her Nazi past had finally been removed and that her status as a 'normal nation' was now generally sanctioned by her former enemies.[16] The blemish on this designated commemorative landscape, however, were the Waffen SS graves in the Bitburg cemetery that were revealed in a storm of prior publicity. Despite all the subsequent official manoeuvres that tried to extricate the two leaders from this massive public relations blunder, the ceremony went ahead (and after last-minute damage-limitation measures, also included a visit to Bergen-Belsen).[17]

In his article published several weeks after this fiasco, Habermas accused Kohl of attempting to defuse the German past 'by means of the *veteran strategy*', a strategy in which 'chivalrous war enemies were to demonstrate their mutual respect [. . .] in order to bestow on the present the aura of a past that [has] a settled look'. For Habermas, this enactment of a 'forced reconciliation' was symptomatic of Kohl's neo-conservative attitude to the German past. If at one level the 'Bitburg handshake' between former enemies was a gesture governed by the 'purposive political rationality' of the present – 'a symbolic reaffirmation of the loyalty of the alliance' – at a deeper level it was expressive of a more profound official desire for Germany's rehabilitation from the burden of a criminal past so that the case for 'German continuities' could once again be pleaded.[18]

The widespread derision that greeted this symbolic strategy, both in Germany and abroad, was, for Habermas, evidence that 'the population of a modern society is less and less able to recognise itself as a whole in the "show business" of its official representatives'.[19] At the same time, however, Habermas acknowledged that if Bitburg proved that 'collective regression cannot be staged by administrative fiat alone', this did not mean that Kohl's neo-conservative bid to normalize German history had not struck a popular chord. Public scorn in Germany was directed at the clumsy manner in which this 'extorted reconciliation' was enacted, rather than at Kohl's intentions, for which Habermas sensed wider public sympathy. In opposition to what he perceived as a widespread desire to circumvent a specifically *German* responsibility for the recent past, Habermas issued the emphatic reminder: '*We are not living in just any country.*'[20] The question Germans needed to be asking themselves was not whether the nation had finally earned forgiveness by a protracted period of atoning for 'collective guilt', a formulation that Habermas claimed was in any case anachronistic, but what it would mean for Germans to finally assume 'communal liability for crimes that could not have been committed without collective silence'.[21] This is turn leads him to pose a broader question concerning the relation between collective liability and the traditions and values 'with which our own identity as well as that of our children and grandchildren is inextricably entangled'.[22] In official circles, Habermas discerned a pattern of response to these questions that typically took the form of 'laundering' or 'disburdening' the Nazi past. Rather than assuming liability for those traditions that had condoned collective silence in the face of crime, a 'defensive displacement' reaction prevailed wherein 'one touches one's own past with one's fingertips and makes it into the past of the others'.[23]

In concluding this (albeit short) article, Habermas did derive some measure of hope from the fact that it was public debate that exposed the political opportunism of Bitburg, since it suggested to him that the German public was not inclined to leave fundamental issues like identity and self-understanding to politicians acting as 'functionaries of a managerial idea that keeps them in power'. How prescient this remark would turn out to be would be revealed only several years later with the breach of the Berlin Wall; but in the meantime, and again in the public forum of the German press, Habermas found himself addressing to powerful neo-conservative historians the same charge he had addressed to Chancellor Kohl – namely, that of normalizing the Nazi past in order to reassert the case for a rehabilitated national identity.

Habermas and the Historians

The *Historikerstreit* is launched with an article by the historian Ernst Nolte, published in the *Frankfurter Allgemeine Zeitung* in June 1986 and entitled – significantly – 'The Past That Will Not Pass'. This article has been subjected to innumerable appraisals from political, historical, moral, rhetorical, psychoanalytic and textual standpoints.[24] These will not be rehearsed here, except in so far as they bear on the key points of Habermas's response. As the title suggests, the article concerns the enduring legacy of the National Socialist past, which, Nolte says, is 'suspended above the present like an executioner's sword'.[25] Nolte does not claim that this Damoclean spell is unwarranted. Instead, he asks whether there is not 'a core of truth in many of these questions and arguments that [. . .] erect a wall against the desire to ceaselessly deal with Nationalism Socialism?'[26] Nolte does not elaborate either on what these questions and arguments might be, but instead makes a further claim that if one does engage in historical enquiry about National Socialism, such scholarship runs up against the inhibitive effects of this 'non-passing of the past' in an intellectual attitude that refuses complexity in favour of self-interested polemic. In order to highlight this struggle between 'objective' enquiry and the tyranny of 'collectivist thinking' about the Nazi past, Nolte proposes to put forward his own perspective, 'using a few questions and key words'.

The clutch of questions he poses are as follows:

Did the National Socialists or Hitler perhaps commit an 'Asiatic' deed merely because they and their ilk considered themselves to be potential victims of an 'Asiatic' deed? Was the Gulag Archipelago not primary to Auschwitz? Was the Bolshevik murder of an entire class not the logical and factual *prius* of the 'racial murder' of National Socialism?[27]

If the answers to these questions are 'yes' – and this rhetorical style clearly invites affirmatives rather than negatives – Nolte's central thesis boils down to the following proposition: with the benefit of historical hindsight, we can identify the Bolsheviks as the main originators and perpetrators of crimes against whole populations in this century, and therefore Nazi crimes are neither singular nor original but can be seen to derive in a causal and mimetic way from their Bolshevik predecessors. In fact, Nolte states that all the monstrous deeds attributed to National Socialism had been described in the literature of the Soviet Union of the 1920s, 'with the sole exception of the technical process of gassing'.[28]

Having put forward such provocative questions,[29] Nolte then beats a hasty retreat by saying that although such a 'causal nexus is probable', the 'greater context' in which these questions might be asked suggests that in fact 'despite all similarities the acts of biological annihilation carried out by the National Socialists were qualitatively different than the social annihilation that Bolshevism undertook'.[30] In other words, the singularity of Nazi crimes in denied in Nolte's snowballing, interrogative strategy, only to be affirmed in this rhetorically weaker, qualifying statement.

Habermas's first intervention in this debate, 'A Kind of Settling of Damages: Apologetic Tendencies', published in *Die Zeit* one month later, cites at the outset Nolte's interrogative propositions on the Bolshevist origins of Nazi atrocity. It is evident from all the writings on the *Historikerstreit* that these remarks of Nolte's constitute the debate's inflammatory core. But Habermas is less concerned to engage in a debate about the historical status of Nolte's claims, than to situate them within a larger political agenda. This he describes as the activation of particular explanatory mechanisms whose main function is, as with Kohl's 'veteran strategy', to relativize the twelve years of National Socialism in order to restore to German history a renewed sense of historical continuity. Diminishing the singularity of Nazi crimes – reducing the uniqueness of Auschwitz to the 'format of technical innovation' – is one means by which this normalization of history is set in motion.[31]

It is important to emphasize here, since many have misunderstood Habermas on this point, that it not an opposition to historical comparison of totalitarian crimes as such that he was registering; rather, it was Nolte's summoning of other genocides and forms of mass terror in order to lessen the burden of a specifically German liability that Habermas opposed – what he would later qualify as 'the political attempt to use historical comparisons for the purpose of setting off one crime against another, thereby relativizing, even minimizing, the ethical implications of crimes emerging from and embedded in one's own history.'[32] Moreover, Nolte's suggestion that Nazi crimes were a pre-emptive response to a perceived Bolshevist threat of annihilation may not have been intended to justify the former, but nonetheless bestowed on them a logic that gained credibility not from any historically convincing evidence,[33] but primarily from the heightened anti-communist consensus of the 1980s to which such an explanation was appealing.

If relativization was one means by which Germany's specific liability for its Nazi past was being circumvented, Habermas also identified another defensive strategy in the new function that was being assigned to the writing of national history, and indeed in the very manner in which this past was being recounted. The public sphere was increasingly witness to a 'seizure of national history for purposes of promoting identification'.[34] Historical narratives had been recruited to provide, in the words of one neo-conservative historian cited by Habermas, the 'higher meaning' of which individuals had been progressively deprived by the processes of secularization and modernization. If it is an axiom that one of history's tasks is to demythologize and interpret a nation's past, according to this neo-conservative view, this should not be its exclusive function. Rather, historical scholarship should be required to balance this imperative with the needs of a national polity for 'positive' images and narratives that promote self-confidence and 'elementary patriotism' (to invoke the term of one conservative minister). History's capacity to foster a national consciousness, to instil an awareness of a community's existence through time, was a socially-integrating mechanism especially needed in a divided Germany, neo-conservatives maintained, where national identity could not be grounded in the unbroken continuity of the nation-state experience.

For Habermas, this 'identificatory grab at national history' not only served the needs of political legitimation rather than critical reflection; it also sanctioned a form of historical narration that, *in its very telling,* obscured crucial moral distinctions. This is the effect which he ascribed to the work of Andreas Hillgruber. In the first part of his study entitled *Two Sorts of Destruction* [*Zweierlei Untergang*], Hillgruber described the events of the Eastern front in 1944–5, and in particular the defensive actions of the German army – the Wehrmacht – on behalf of the population of the German East and against the Red Army's 'orgies of revenge'. Hillgruber suggested that one obstacle for the historian in rendering such accounts was the 'problem of identification' with the various actors involved and the inhibitions imposed by a stance of critical retrospection. He argued that the only plausible perspective available to a German historian concerned to elucidate the behaviour of Wehrmacht soldiers, and the experience of the inhabitants whom they were so courageously defending, was one which identified 'with the concrete fate of the

German population in the East and with the desperate and self-sacrificing efforts of the German army in the East . . .'.[35] Hillgruber acknowledged that such determined efforts on the Eastern Front permitted the extermination operations in the camps to continue. However, since admitting such facts into his account would cast a shadow over the image of suffering he wished to render, and cloud the experiential perspective he felt compelled to adopt, Hillgruber postponed the recounting of the 'End of European Jewry' to the second part of his book.[36] In Habermas's view, this separation into a 'tragic linkage' of two causally-related events conformed precisely to the neo-conservative agenda of writing history 'for the project of meaning-creating normalization'.[37] On the one hand, as with Bitburg, this strategy allowed 'veterans' memories to remain 'unframed' and thus immune from critical retrospection. On the other hand, writing the final period of the Third Reich as 'empathic narration', Habermas contended, redistributed the 'moral weight' of suffering, aligning the sufferings of Germans during the war with those German forces inflicted. A narrative that elicited identification with a beleaguered German population at the expense of Nazism's victims only fed the desire to identify retrospectively with the organic bonds of national solidarity rather than with universalist principles that, Habermas insisted, 'could only be formed after – and through – Auschwitz'.[38]

But in order not to be drawn into a narrowly historiographical quarrel, Habermas drew the political stakes of his objection to Nolte and Hillgruber (and indeed a host of other historians who had joined the fray) more sharply. He proposed that the protagonists of the dispute could be divided between those who assumed 'that the work of detached understanding liberates the power of reflective remembrance' and those who 'would like to put a revisionist history to work furnishing a conventional identity with a national history'.[39]

This very condensed and abbreviated account of the original terms of the *Historikerstreit* cannot do full justice to any of the positions engaged in it. But my aim in sketching the broad contours of the polemic is to show that central to Habermas's intervention is the relationship that he established between modes of remembering and contested forms of contemporary identity. He welcomed the debate as an opportunity for Germans to reflect on their 'identity-forming traditions in their ambivalences' in the hopes that the historical consciousness that emerged from this process would prove 'incompatible with closed images of history that have a secondary quasi-natural character and with all forms of conventional, that is, uniformly and prereflexively *shared* identity'.[40] Several months later, the *Historikerstreit* was in full and venomous stride, eliciting contributions from across the historico-political spectrum, with Habermas's critique of Nolte and Hillgruber serving as the focal point for most participants.

In his second contribution, entitled 'On the Public Use of History', Habermas was now more explicit about situating this new historiography with respect to the political agenda which he believed it implicitly promoted. This is a revisionist history, which, he claimed, had been 'impatiently urged on by the [conservative] government of the "ideological shift"'[41] – i.e. Chancellor Kohl's *Wende* or 'government of change'. Such historiographical discourse had translated into politics the neo-conservative desire to relativize the Nazi period so that it could no longer obstruct the confident reassertion of German national identity. Moreover, it did so not within the confines of academic institutions, but in the full glare of the mass media, thereby making its 'apologetic production of images of history [. . .] a directly political one'. However, for Habermas it was not only a matter of unmasking the political impulses fuelling recent historiography, but of attending to the more urgent question of what coming to terms with the Nazi past now meant for the wider public, who, Habermas maintained, whatever their generation and political leanings, still all 'have the same point of departure: the images of that unloading ramp at Auschwitz'.[42] To be sure, Habermas conceded that Jaspers's distinction between individual guilt and collective liability carries a different implication for those generations who do not have on their personal consciences either the failure to act, or the collective silence with which their parents or grandparents had been largely complicit. Yet the assumption of shared liability for that enduring image of Auschwitz remained of singular importance to Habermas. To the neo-conservative assertion that the process of coming to terms with the past had exhausted its ethical efficacy for these generations, Habermas retorted that the principle of shared liability for the past has no such statute of limitations. And to expand upon how this relates to the identity-forming processes so central to the neo-conservative agenda, Habermas emphasized that collective liability must now be conceived not only as the expression of an 'indebted memory' to the victims of Nazism, but as a process that is *constitutive* of individual and collective identities. On the one hand, 'indebted memory' continued to serve as the basic reminder of the obligation that all Germans had 'to keep alive the memory of the suffering of those murdered at the hands of Germans', so that Jewish fellow-citizens and descendants of the murdered victims could be assured that they would be able to 'breathe' in contemporary Germany. But Habermas insisted that the ongoing process of assuming collective liability for the past not only entailed an empathetic relation to the injured Other, but a critical apprehension of the *constitutive* aspects of the particular 'life-world' to which all Germans were subjectively and objectively bound, a task he described as the more 'narcissistic' one of deciding 'the attitude we are to take – for our own sakes – toward our own traditions'. In his most emphatic statement of how this collective liability should be conceived, he pointed out:

> . . . there is the simple fact that subsequent generations also grew up within a form of
> life in which *that* was possible. Our own life is linked to the life context in which
> Auschwitz was possible not by contingent circumstances but intrinsically. Our form of

life is connected with that of our parents and grandparents through a web of familial, local, political, and intellectual traditions that is difficult to disentangle – that is, through a historical milieu that made us what and who we are today. None of us can escape this milieu, because our identities, both as individuals and as Germans, are indissolubly interwoven with it.[43]

It is because German subjectivity in a deeply existential sense remains entangled in this historical milieu that Habermas believed that conventional national identities cannot be achieved and should not be sought. He interpreted the identificatory use of national history by revisionist historians as an attempt by the Right to undermine this basic premiss of social self-understanding in the Federal Republic so that German traditions might be once again available for appropriation on behalf of contemporary identities. Habermas was adamant, however, that since Auschwitz had altered for ever the conditions for the continuation of historical life-contexts, Germans must relinquish the quest for a conventional national identity once and for all. In the face of the irreparable breach with human solidarity that Auschwitz represented, Germans must settle for a collective self-understanding achieved only in the 'light of the traditions that stand up to the scrutiny of a gaze educated by moral catastrophe, a gaze that is, in a word, suspicious'.[44]

How, then, might we characterize the process that produces this 'more sober political identity' that Habermas espoused? When pressed to specify its conditions of emergence and delineate its constituent features, Habermas drew upon Kierkegaard's existentially-based and religiously-inspired conception of the manner in which the moral individual takes responsibility for his or her life history and, in so doing, reshapes individual identity. Kierkegaard described a process of transformation that, whatever its unconscious vicissitudes, favours a cognitive dimension and a strong element of choice that ultimately makes an 'ethical view of life' possible. Habermas proposed that this particular model of 'an ego-identity produced through the reconstruction of one's own life history in the light of an absolute responsibility for oneself'[45] might be pushed into a more secular direction in order to account for how an Enlightenment consciousness of the self-as-citizen emerged. And although aware of the pitfalls of conflating the process of identity-formation for individuals and for groups, Habermas proposed to retain from the Kierkegaardian model the principle that a polity too must foster a historical consciousness based on the critical examination of 'intersubjectively shared traditions'. The collective identities that are forged during this process will not necessarily reject tradition *per se*, or even sentiments and expressions of collective belonging, but these will be continually subject to critical scrutiny in the arena of a 'publicly conducted debate'.[46] This is all the more necessary, Habermas observed, faced with a widespread and deeply-rooted conviction that the act of saying "we" must necessarily remain 'untouched by reflection'.

Before this defence of 'postconventional' identities could really test its social mettle, however, the Berlin Wall was breached, and Habermas was witness to the assertion of a national sentiment that seemed to mock the 'keenly scrutinizing' attitude toward national identity that he had just been advocating.

When Germans Say 'We' . . .

Habermas was one of a handful of German intellectuals to express early and adamant opposition to the Federal Republic's hasty annexation of the German Democratic Republic via currency union and constitutional law (in particular Article 23 of the Federal Republic's Basic Law, whose original terms allowed individual German states to enter the federation). It was not the demise of the GDR regime to which he objected – on the contrary, this was an event he warmly welcomed – but the 'mode and tempo' of the unification process. On the one hand, he believed that the Federal Republic's *rapprochement* with the former GDR might have been carried out in the context of a wider *European* effort on behalf of the economic and political transformation of east-central Europe. He described this not as a missed opportunity for European philanthropism, but as an occasion when all Europeans might have demonstrated their indebtedness to the citizens of east-central Europe for shouldering the harshest burdens that resulted from the post-war division of Europe.

But his more serious objection was that the precipitate nature of the unification process had regressive consequences with respect to the forms of self-understanding it encouraged in citizens of the Federal Republic. Habermas reiterated key components of this political self-understanding as it had developed in the post-war period, particularly the extent to which a pragmatic dimension, founded on identification with the state's economic success, had progressively relegated to the 'back burner' the question of an all-German national consciousness and pride. The German Question had for all intents and purposes been settled by the acceptance of the 'liberal consensus' of 'two states – one nation'. However, precisely because the normative convictions anchoring the West German citizenry's acceptance of the constitution and democratic institutions were initially weak (as Adorno and the Mitscherlichs had observed), the ethos of a 'constitutional patriotism' based on the civic model of the nation had to be constantly reiterated and defended against a political culture inclined toward the organic bonds of community.

And yet it was not civic sentiments but the desire to rehabilitate the German nation that clearly provided the emotional momentum for the unification process. Indeed, Habermas believed that this desire had been nurtured in the years prior to unification by the neo-conservative attempt to explain loss of national self-confidence with reference to the 'loss of history' that the continual insistence on coming to terms with the Nazi past had allegedly instilled. While there was no political basis at the time upon which to spearhead a 'return to the nation', certain seeds of a traditional patriotism were nonetheless sown. With the opening of the Wall, these 'pre-political' values could now thrive under an overtly nationalist banner: on the one hand, by appealing to the nation as *Volk*, in Habermas's words, as a 'historic community of fate [. . .] as a linguistic and cultural community', and, on the other, by inviting an identification with the nation as a 'performance community' based on the 'expanded empire of the D-mark' (or in his more scathing description on 'chubby-faced DM-nationalism'.)[47]

Habermas's outrage at the path to unification that was adopted was directed not only at the mentality it promoted but at the actual *experience* of constitutional patriotism of which the German citizenry has been deprived – namely, 'a direct vote, within the framework of a non-occupied public sphere that has not already been willed away'.[48] What had been lost, according to Habermas, was the 'historic chance of carrying out the process of state unification with the clear political understanding of constituting a nation of state-citizens'.[49]

How a civic disposition was to be nurtured in an 'occupied' public sphere in the grip of national euphoria was precisely the crux of the matter. As even his most severe critics acknowledged, Habermas was well aware that constitutional patriotism – in essence, loyalty to the ideals and norms of democracy, the rule of law and open discussion – could not win hearts and minds if it was reduced to the 'anemic presence of democratic loyalty, drummed in with pedagogical rigour'.[50] And as recent history had proved, German citizens needed not only formally to *display* but progressively to *internalize* their commitment to constitutional patriotism as an essential dimension of their life-world. The difficulty was compounded by the fact that the postconventional identity elaborated by Habermas was not in fact offering an *identity* in its vernacular sense, so much as a social self-understanding of oneself as a citizen. In other words, Habermas was asking Germans to relinquish claims to a common national identity, with all its linguistic, historical and cultural resonances, and to settle for the more modest status of a nation of state-citizens.[51] And his appeal to the Kierkegaardian imperative by which state-citizens would actively forge their democratic future by taking responsibility for 'traditions in their ambivalences', was simply no match for the lure of a rehabilitated national identity that claimed to have already expurgated its negative legacy.

This is why Habermas felt compelled to foreground once again the question of Germany memory. If his criticism of the unification process seemed to stray some way from this path, Habermas retrieved the connection by pointing out that a unification that had been achieved through the logic of the nation as *Volk* would be inclined to protect its alleged integrity against a threat perceived as coming from the outside. And it was precisely National Socialism's construction of an external threat to an organic national community – the 'unassimilable' Jew – that had paved the ideological way to Auschwitz. Habermas was adamant that 'Auschwitz' must stand as an emphatic reminder – a primordial *lieu de mémoire*, to invoke Nora's terminology – of what happens when there is a confusion between 'the "demos" as bearer of political sovereignty with a specific "ethnos" . . .'. By failing to recognize that this same confusion underpinned the process of unification and therefore should have been addressed as such in a democratic public sphere, Habermas believed that Germany was once again short-circuiting the lessons of historical memory:

> Because of that horrible break in continuity, the Germans have given up the possibility of constituting their identity on something other than universalistic principles of state citizenship, in the light of which national traditions can no longer remain unexamined, but can only be critically and self-critically appropriated. Post-traditional identity loses its substantial, its unproblematic character; it *exists* only in the method of the public, discursive battle around the interpretation of a constitutional patriotism made concrete under particular historical circumstances.[52]

Germany's Memorial Prospects

Despite the temporary setback that unification represented to Habermas's vision of how a new kind of German citizenry might be cultivated, fantasies of nationhood were soon to be fractured by a host of divisive issues – not least amongst these, revelations of political crimes committed by the post-Stalinist regime of East Germany. As Habermas was to note subsequently, these revelations in their turn fostered a 'disburdening' comparison between Nazi and Stalinist terror that once again allowed the Holocaust's singularity to be buried within an antitotalitarian consensus.[53] They also allowed West Germans to point the accusing finger at their East German counterparts for being massively complicit in this repressive culture. Memories of betrayal and conformity on the part of former GDR citizens were exposed with considerable accusatory zeal by former West Germans, and there was the attendant assumption that the baton of 'coming to terms with the past' had now been passed once and for all to their Eastern counterparts.[54]

However, memory of the Holocaust was not to remain submerged for long, as the fiftieth anniversaries of the liberation of the concentration camps and of Germany's liberation from Nazism reclaimed the public spotlight. While revisionist attempts to re-interpret the meaning of the 8th of May ultimately failed, Habermas conceded that their efforts nonetheless demonstrated the reluctance on the part of many Germans to accept unequivocally the end of the war as a 'liberating transition to democracy'.[55] Their efforts also indicated that, in the domain of public memory, the Right was once again taking the offensive and equating the continual insistence on foregrounding the memory of the Holocaust with the Left's own brand of 'political correctness'. At the same time, as if echoing concerns expressed by Pierre Nora about the obsessive character that France's politics of memory was assuming, Habermas pointed to the coincidental danger of memorial work that, operating on a 'reflexive level of discussions about discussions', threatened to have the 'same neutralizing effect once brought about by an escape from discussion'.[56] This disturbing depiction of an ongoing battle over the control of public memory waged by left and right political interests sat uneasily alongside the qualified optimism that Habermas simultaneously expressed in the wider German public's acceptance of a 'particular liability for the consequences of the moral catastrophe of Auschwitz'.[57]

There has been yet another twist in Germany's contemporary politics of memory – one that, in the view of Dan Diner, has rendered the left–right distinctions of the *Historikerstreit* and its aftermath largely irrelevant.[58] These new political faultlines were created by the public controversy in Germany that accompanied the publication of Daniel Goldhagen's book, *Hitler's Willing Executioners*. As we shall see shortly, this was a text that was accused by German scholars – and indeed a wider scholarly community – of a multitude of sins, amongst them the revival of the category of collective guilt that Habermas had been at such pains to reconfigure in terms of a collective liability for the crimes of Nazism. For his part, and to the surprise and dismay of his many supporters, Habermas took the side of the wider German public who enthusiastically applauded Goldhagen's contribution.[59] Many believed that Habermas must have severely misconstrued the terms of Goldhagen's analysis and the extent to which it 'essentialized' the character of Germans rather than referring this character to features of the German 'life-world' as Habermas himself had done – features that he had insisted could and should be profoundly transformed. Others believed he had warmed to the indictment of national tradition that Goldhagen's treatise contained and delighted in the neo-conservative ire it had provoked. However, since it is Habermas's fundamental conviction that nurturing a post-conventional identity in Germany requires an ongoing *public* debate that puts German history and traditions under a permanently 'suspicious' gaze, it is easier to see why he might have considered congratulations to Goldhagen were in order on these grounds alone. Moreover, in Goldhagen's profile of the 'Ordinary German' who became a 'willing' accomplice to Nazi crimes, Habermas may well have identified issues relevant to individual and collective choice and responsibility that his own ethico-political agenda has attempted to foreground.[60] As we've seen, Habermas is convinced (and Goldhagen professes to believe) that post-war Germany has ultimately made a decisive break with the past and has firmly chosen the path of 'demos' over 'ethnos'. But it is Habermas's distinctive achievement to have shown why this choice remains *contingent* upon the conscious use of historical memory as an agency of critical self-reflection.[61]

Notes

1. Jürgen Habermas, 'On How Postwar Germany Has Faced its Recent Past', *Common Knowledge* vol. 5, no. 2, 1996, p. 1.
2. Theodor Adorno *et al.*, *The Authoritarian Personality: Studies in Prejudice* (New York: Harper, 1950).
3. Dominick LaCapra, 'Revisiting the Historians' Debate: Mourning and Genocide', *History and Memory* vol. 9, nos. 1–2, Fall 1997, p. 97. Other versions of this article appear in 'Reflections on the Historians' Debate' in *Representing the Holocaust: History, Theory, Trauma* (Ithaca: Cornell University Press, 1994), and 'Revisiting the Historians' Debate: Mourning and Genocide' in *History and Memory after Auschwitz* (Ithaca: Cornell University Press, 1998). The most sustained account of the constitutive dimension of individual mourning for the wider German polity can be found in Eric L. Santner's *Stranded Objects: Mourning, Memory and Film in Postwar Germany* (Ithaca: Cornell University Press, 1990).
4. Peter Hohendahl, 'Foreword', *The Past as Future: Jürgen Habermas Interviewed by Michael Haller* (Cambridge: Polity Press, 1994), p. viii.
5. Theodor Adorno, 'What Does Coming to Terms with the Past Mean?' in Geoffrey Hartman (ed.), *Bitburg in Moral and Political Perspective* (Bloomington: Indiana University Press, 1986). For a discussion of the important distinction between *Aufarbeitung* and *Vergangenheitsbewältigung*, see the editor's introduction to Adorno's article.
6. Ibid., p. 117.
7. Ibid., p. 118.
8. Ibid., p. 128.
9. Alexander and Margarete Mitscherlich, *The Inability to Mourn* (New York: Grove Press, 1975), p. xvi. Originally published in 1967 as *Die Unfähigkeit zu trauern*.
10. Ibid., p. 33.
11. Ibid.
12. Ibid., p. xxv.
13. For a discussion of the Mitscherlichs, Habermas, the *Historikerstreit* and other dimensions of post-war German memory to which my own thinking is heavily indebted, see Eric L. Santner, *Stranded Objects*.
14. Karl Jaspers, *Die Schuldfrage* (Heidelberg: Lambert Schneider, 1946). Translated into English in 1947 as *The Question of German Guilt*.
15. 'On How Postwar Germany Has Faced Its Recent Past', p. 2.
16. See Richard Wolin, 'Introduction', in Jürgen Habermas, *The New Conservatism: Cultural Criticism and the Historians' Debate*, trans. Shierry Weber Nicholsen (Cambridge: Polity, 1989). Wolin points out that the previous year,

Kohl had not been invited to the Allied commemoration of the Normandy landings, so that Bitburg can be seen as Kohl's deliberate attempt to redress this snub. Wolin's essay provides an insightful overview of many of the issues raised in this chapter.

17. As Habermas would later remark, '. . . the juxtaposition of the mass-graves in the concentration camp and the SS graves in the cemetery for those buried with honors, Bergen-Belsen in the morning and Bitburg in the afternoon, implicitly contested the uniqueness of Nazi crimes'. See 'On the Public Use of History', in *The New Conservatism*, p. 231.

18. 'Defusing the Past: A Politico-Cultural Tract' in Geoffrey Hartman (ed.), *Bitburg in Moral and Historical Perspective* (Bloomington: Indiana University Press, 1986). See also Habermas's comments on Bitburg in 'On How Postwar Germany Has Faced Its Recent Past'.

19. Ibid., p. 45.

20. Ibid., p. 48.

21. Ibid., p. 46.

22. Ibid.

23. Ibid.

24. See Peter Baldwin (ed.), *Reworking the Past: Hitler, the Holocaust and the Historians' Debate* (Boston: Beacon Press, 1990), for a wide-ranging collection of essays related to the *Historikerstreit*.

25. Ernest Nolte, 'The Past that Will Not Pass: A Speech That Could Be Written but Not Delivered', in James Knowlton and Truett Cates (eds), *Forever in the Shadow of Hitler? Original Documents of the Historikerstreit, The Controversy Surrounding the Singularity of the Holocaust* (New York: Humanities Press, 1993), p. 18.

26. Ibid., p. 19.

27. Ibid., p. 22.

28. Ibid.

29. Dominick LaCapra has characterized this well as Nolte's 'ploy of posing presumably daring, experimental questions that the norms of liberalism and pluralism would require one to entertain in open-ended scholarship. But the ploy is deceptive because the apparent questions are rhetorically converted into pseudo-interrogatives whose dogmatic, incantatory effect is to suggest the actuality of an implausible if not historically absurd postulation.' See his 'Revisiting the Historians' Debate: Mourning and Genocide', p. 91.

30. Ibid., p. 22.

31. See 'A Kind of Settling of Damages: Apologetic Tendencies', in *The New Conservatism*.

32. 'On How Postwar Germany Has Faced its Recent Past', p. 9. In his psycho-analytic interpretation of Nolte's tracts as a form of 'acting-out' of 'unresolved

aspects of the past', Dominick LaCapra concludes that Nolte 'forecloses the possibility of mourning precisely because [his approach] forecloses the need for it'. See 'Revisiting the Historians' Debate', p. 94.

33. One support Nolte cites for his pre-emptive thesis is Hitler's statement from 1943 speculating that captured German officers in Stalingrad would cave in to Soviet pressure because they would have in their minds the image of the 'rat cage'. The common historical view is that this reference is to Lubjanka prison, but Nolte argues instead that the 'rat cage' evokes a well-known Soviet torture method described in anti-Bolshevist literature. 'The Past That Will Not Pass', p. 21.

34. 'A Kind of Settling of Damages', p. 214.

35. Hillgruber cited by Habermas in 'A Kind of Settling of Damages', p. 216.

36. Habermas also points out that the titles for each section, 'The Smashing of the German Reich' and the 'End of European Jewry', are hardly commensurate in their interpretative connotations: '"Smashing" requires an aggressive opponent; an "end" takes place on its own.' 'Apologetic Tendencies', p. 219.

37. 'Closing Remarks' in *The New Conservatism*, p. 244.

38. 'A Kind of Settling of Damages', p. 226.

39. Ibid., p. 224.

40. Ibid., p. 227.

41. 'On the Public Use of History', p. 229.

42. Ibid.

43. Ibid., pp. 232–3.

44. Ibid., p. 234.

45. 'Historical Consciousness and Post-Traditional Identity' in *The New Conservatism,* p. 260.

46. Dominick LaCapra has noted in this regard that '. . . with respect to the tense conjunction of universalizing constitutional principles and more specific – to some extent nonreflective – bonds, there is a need for continual rethinking, and reworking rather than speculative synthesis or *Aufhebung*'. See his 'Revisiting the Historians' Debate', p. 98.

47. 'Yet Again: German Identity – a Unified Nation of Angry DM Burghers?', *New German Critique*, no. 52, Winter 1991. See also 'The Normative Deficits of Unification' in *The Past as Future*. It should be emphasized that Habermas welcomed the fall of the Wall, and especially what he described as the GDR's 'liberation from globally penetrating surveillance by a secret police that shadowed everyone with a dogged and cold-blooded perfection . . .', p. 33. His criticism was primarily directed at the Kohl government's orchestration of the process, or what became popularly known as the 'heave-ho unification of 1990'.

48. 'Yet Again: German Identity', p. 95.

49. Ibid., p. 96.
50. The phrase is Karl-Heinz Bohrer's in his response to Habermas, wherein Bohrer defends a concept of the nation that retains a 'spiritual-symbolic' dimension as a bulwark against the technocratic fiction of a European identity on the one hand, and against a moralistic and provincial German cultural identity on the other. While he believes unification is serving this end, he also expresses admiration for Habermas's 'sublime variation of the tabooization of the nation'. See 'Why We are Not a Nation – And Why We Should Become One', *New German Critique*, no. 52, Winter 1991.
51. James Donald has taken Habermas to task for attempting to give the legal status of citizenship a cultural identity. While I agree with the thrust of Donald's critique, I think Habermas's concept of liability attempts to mediate between an identity located in tradition, culture and history and a civic self-understanding derived from a modality of historical memory. See 'The Citizen and the Man About Town' in James Donald and Stephanie Donald (eds), *Identity, Authority and Democracy, Research Papers in Media and Cultural Studies* (Brighton: University of Sussex, no date).
52. Ibid., p. 98.
53. 'On How Postwar Germany Has Faced Its Recent Past', p. 11.
54. Habermas noted that the West German attitude of virtually extracting confessions of culpability ignored the fact that if 'such problems aren't faced in one's house, from one's own initiative, and under one's own power, they become unsolvable'. 'The Normative Deficits of Unification', p. 50. See Jane Kramer, *The Politics of Memory: Looking for Germany in the New Germany* (New York: Random House, 1996), for an excellent account of the more recent controversies concerning the GDR's Stasi past.
55. 'On How Postwar Germany Has Faced its Recent Past', p. 13.
56. Ibid., p. 3. In *The Politics of Memory*, Jane Kramer argues that commemorations of the Holocaust have become a veritable 'industry' in contemporary Germany and that a suspect identification with the Holocaust victim has become the dominant attitude.
57. 'On How Postwar Germany Has Faced Its Recent Past', p. 13.
58. See Dan Diner, 'On Guilt Discourse and Other Narratives: Epistemological Observations regarding the Holocaust', in *History and Memory* vol. 9, nos. 1–2, Fall 1997.
59. Habermas delivered the *Laudatio* on the occasion of the award of the 'Democracy Prize' to Daniel Goldhagen for *Hitler's Willing Executioners*. The speech was printed in *Die Zeit*, 14 March 1997. For a discussion of the *Laudatio*, see Dan Diner, 'On Guilt Discourse and Other Narratives', and José Brunner, 'Pride and Memory: Nationalism, Narcissism and the Historians' Debates in Germany and Israel', *History and Memory* vol. 9, nos. 1–2, Fall 1997.

60. I am indebted to Brunner's discussion of Habermas's *Laudatio* for this insight. Brunner notes that Habermas might also have found in Goldhagen's emphasis on choice a necessary 'counterweight to complex structural arguments that have been made in recent years by German historians such as Gotz Aly and Susanne Heim, who place their emphasis on technocratic processes of decision making which leave no space for individual moral choices and hence fail to lend themselves to the kind of public ethico-political debates that Habermas seeks.' See 'Pride and Memory', p. 279.

61. The relevance of this message has been once again demonstrated by the 'Walser Affair' – the controversy that followed the awarding of the 1998 German Peace Prize to German writer Martin Walser. On his acceptance speech of 11 October 1998, Walser castigated intellectuals and the media for preventing him, and the larger German community, from finding inner peace because of the constant reminder of Nazi crimes – "our opprobrium" in Walser's words. This affair broke as this book was going to press; suffice it to say that the terms of the controversy revive the deep qualms voiced by Habermas about the German use of the first-personal plural.

   For an account of the Walser Affair, see Lothar Baier, 'Un Romancier reconverti en oracte national', Las Temps Modernes, No. 603, March–April 1999.

–3–

The Victim's Resentment

In his introduction to Lyotard's *Heidegger and 'the jews'*, David Carroll makes the following acute observation:

> In the case of extreme injustice – of which there is certainly no shortage in recent history – it is difficult to avoid writing history (and evoking memory) in a spirit of revenge, even if the resentment of revenge will undoubtedly repeat and perpetuate in a different form the past events one is attempting to represent precisely in order that they never happen again. Memory in itself guarantees nothing; it all depends on what kind of memory and how, within memory, one goes about combating the revenge the memory of injustice often calls for.[1]

The thematic of this chapter is drawn from the essay 'Resentments' written in 1964 by the journalist, philosopher, Jew and Auschwitz survivor Jean Améry. My interest in this essay is threefold: in part it arises from Améry's attempt to elaborate a 'phenomenology' of the victim's resentment, which he wishes to distinguish from prevailing conceptions of 'revenge' and whose recognition he believes to constitute the fundamental moral basis of any memorialization of the Holocaust. Améry ultimately fails to hold fast to this distinction, but rather than surrendering to the compulsion to repeat which is allegedly fuelled by the 'resentment of revenge', I shall argue that Améry demonstrates instead how these sentiments can function as ethical agencies in a post-Holocaust world.

Secondly, Améry's defence of his resentments has been compared by some commentators to Primo Levi's allegedly more reconciliatory stance as revealed in his many accounts of his own incarceration in Auschwitz. Indeed, the two men themselves drew such a contrast with regard to their post-Holocaust attitudes – Améry describing Levi as 'the forgiver', Levi speaking of the 'positions of severity and intransigence' adopted by Améry. Yet in the later Levi one also finds an articulation of resentments, whose intended function is conceived in terms very similar to those expressed by Améry. And it is in this deployment of their resentments against what both perceived to be the growing memorial *entropy* of post-Holocaust societies that I wish to locate the contemporary and enduring value of their respective testimonials. For both Améry and Levi, the danger arose not from a failure to combat the resentments that remained active in survivor memories, but from the inability of post-Holocaust societies to accept the responsibilities and historical self-reflexivity incumbent upon the recognition of these. One might counter such concerns today by noting that contemporary societies are more disposed than ever to commemorate victims of the Holocaust. To take just two examples: the popularity of *Schindler's List* or of the Holocaust Memorial in Washington suggests that the current memorial climate is one very receptive to such commemorations – perhaps even to the point of displaying the 'commemorative obsession' evoked by Pierre Nora. However, the fact that this activity occurred at the same time as a genocidal war was taking place on European soil has led a number of observers to question whether historical memories, including memories of the Holocaust, have indeed become encased in an entropic system where, to invoke its physical analogy, the energy devoted to remembering that past has proved itself incapable of being 'converted' into relevant action in the present.

This leads directly to the third reason why critical reflection on the relation between memory and resentment remains compelling in the contemporary context. Linked inextricably to Améry's delineation of his own resentments as a victim of Nazism is a self-reflexive enquiry into his identity as a Jew. In an essay entitled 'On the Necessity and Impossibility of Being a Jew', Améry describes himself as the 'Jewish Nazi victim, which I was and am'. According to his translator Sidney Rosenfeld, Améry incurred the irritation and misunderstanding of numerous Jewish writers, intellectuals and spiritual leaders who contested his right to call himself a Jew 'because of Améry's inability to identify with Judaism in any other way except that of the Jewish Nazi victim'.[2] In a contemporary world in which there are many competing claims for victim status, Améry's embrace of this singular and exclusive identity might be interpreted as an intransigent refusal to 'overcome the past' and to extricate Jewishness from what Améry calls a 'Holocaust-determined existence'. However, Améry insists that what binds him to this identity is less the material experience of the subjugation he endured than a *memory* of the abandonment that had condemned him to this physical fate and his subsequent loss of 'trust in the world'. In other words, it was not the injuries inflicted by the perpetrator as such, but the fact that they represented society's failure actively to defend him against such persecution, that Améry believes to be constitutive of his irreducible identity as a victim. I shall suggest that this legacy of memories of abandonment remains of vital contemporary relevance in the context of the 'extreme injustices' that characterize our times.

A Phenomenology of Resentment

First of all, a brief biographical note on the author of the essay 'Resentments'. Jean Améry, whose original name was Hans Maier, was born in Vienna in 1912, son of a Jewish father and mother of mixed Jewish–Christian descent. In 1938, he fled Austria for Belgium, where, in 1940, he was arrested by the Belgians as a 'German alien', and deported to the detention camps of southern France. He escaped from one of these – Gurs – and returned to Belgium, where he joined the Belgian Resistance. He was arrested by the Gestapo under suspicion of being a German military deserter engaged in subversive activity, tortured in Brussels and then, recognized as a Jew, deported to Auschwitz. After the liberation of the camps, he returned to Belgium and adopted the name Jean Améry. He lived by freelance writing until he was asked in 1964 to deliver a radio talk in Germany on his Auschwitz experience. This talk, and the essays which followed, were published first in German in 1966 under the title *Jenseits von Schuld und Sühne (Beyond Guilt and Atonement)* and in 1980 in English with the title *At the Mind's Limits*. This is the work for which Améry is primarily known, especially among German and American readers, though he also wrote books on ageing and suicide and several novels, and a selection from his prolific journalistic contributions has been collected into a volume, *Radical Humanism*.[3]

Améry wrote his essay 'Resentments' at the time of the big Auschwitz trial that began in Frankfurt in 1964 and when a wider debate was taking place in Europe about whether further judicial proceedings relating to Nazi war crimes should henceforth be subject to a statute of limitations. While the juridical outcome of this debate in Germany was the extension of the statute of limitations for major war crimes, Améry nonetheless felt the weight of a cultural climate that attributed to victims of Nazism an enduring resentment and a vengeful desire for retribution. However, rather than entering into a political polemic about war crimes trials, Améry proposed instead to examine the nature of his resentments, to offer a 'description of the subjective state of the victim' in which, he readily acknowledged, 'resentment' figured as an 'existential dominant'.

The essay is above all a defence of the victim's resentment against its Nietzschean depiction as the 'imaginary revenge' of those 'who are denied genuine reaction, that of the deed . . .'. Améry insisted that the victim's resentment was 'a matter neither of revenge on the one side nor of a problematic atonement . . . on the other'.[4] Instead, it was to be understood primarily in two dimensions, one temporal, the other intersubjective. The victim's resentment, Améry declared, was in the first instance a 'protest against the antimoral natural process of healing that time brings about'; its 'historical function' was to protest against a consciousness of time based on this 'physiology of wound-healing', precisely because such a social conception of temporality negated the victim's experience of how time's passage mediated his or her perceptions of the injury suffered. The resentment of the victim of Nazism, noted Améry, was nailed 'onto the cross' of a 'ruined past', locked by memories of the deed into a temporal order resistant to the forces of attenuation that remoteness through time otherwise effected.[5] However, if for Améry the vivid longevity of the victim's resentment represented a revolt against a social conception of reality that had not yet apprehended the violent psychic legacy of the recent traumatic past, he maintained that his resentment was also there 'in order that the crime become a moral reality for the criminal, in order that he be swept into the truth of his atrocity' (p. 70).

Again, while this language might be reminiscent of the Nietzschean 'man of resentment' condemned to 'feel' rather than to react to the injuries undergone, Améry's demands are of an emphatically active and intersubjective nature. They certainly include the demand that war criminals be tried and punished, and Améry comments with contempt on the number of major war criminals in Germany who, as he is writing and despite the extension of the statute of limitations, have not been brought to justice and therefore 'have a good chance to attain a venerable old age and triumphantly to outlive [survivors]' (p. 64). But Améry's demand that the 'criminal be nailed to his deed' has a phenomenological as well as legal dimension, and is explained by invoking the need for a moral relation to the victim's suffering in which perpetrators are confronted with the existential fundamentals of the victim's experience. He describes his own experience of persecution as 'at the very bottom, that of an extreme *loneliness*' and goes on to explain that what is at stake for him in any demand for retribution 'is the release from the abandonment that has persisted from that time until today' (p. 70). Thus when Améry learned of the execution of one of his Nazi torturers who had beaten him with a shovel handle on numerous work details in Auschwitz, it is not a Nietzschean *ressentiment* that best grasps the nature of his reaction, but the breach he experiences in his own memory of acute abandonment: 'When SS-man Wajs stood before the firing squad' says Améry, 'he experienced the moral truth of his crimes. At that moment, he was with *me* – and I was no longer alone with the shovel handle. I would like to believe that at the instant of his execution he wanted exactly as much as I to turn back time, to undo what had been done' (p. 70). Formulated this way, Améry's demand for retribution focuses less on the nature of the act, than on the *condition* that it induce in the perpetrators the desire to nullify the deed that condemned the victim to fundamental solitude. Only through such an enactment, says Améry, would the torturers be compelled to 'negate themselves and in the negation coordinate with me' (p. 69).[6]

When Améry considers how his resentments might be 'settled' at the collective level, 'in the field of historical practice', he invokes this same principle of a moral encounter with the victim's 'logically inconsistent' desire to undo the event. 'Coming to terms with the past' in this sense would mean manifesting through a collective sensibility the same impossible desire that pervades the victim's subjectivity: namely, 'the desire that time be turned back and, with it, that history become moral' (pp. 77–8). Addressing his German audience, he insists that the resentments of Nazism's victims be permitted to 'remain alive', so that they can arouse in all Germans a 'self-mistrust', a refusal to allow German history 'to be neutralized by time' but instead to be claimed as a 'negative possession'.

In a generally sympathetic reading of Améry's resentments, Eugene Goodheart has suggested that we interpet Améry's call for collective 'self-mistrust' on the part of post-war Germans as his way of avenging himself for the loss of 'trust in the world' that he experienced after being subjected to torture by his Nazi captors: 'He would "avenge" himself on the country that bred these torturers by inducing self-mistrust in their descendants.'[7] Yet the demand that post-war German society internalize its own historical memory as self-mistrust will by now be familiar to readers of this book from my earlier discussion of the writings of Jürgen Habermas. Indeed, as we've seen, Habermas makes self-mistrust the very basis of the public memory that he feels must underpin Germany's 'post national' or 'post conventional identity'. Améry's demand that the German 'national community [. . .] reject every-thing, but absolutely everything, that it accomplished in the days of its own deepest degradation' finds a striking echo in Habermas's appeal for a 'critically-examined history' wherein the only German traditions that are retained are those that can withstand a 'suspicious' gaze 'educated by moral catastrophe'.[8] In other words, Améry has once again turned an apparently introspective posture – self-mistrust – into a means for German society to 'externalize' and 'actualize' the 'unresolved conflict' that keeps the victim's resentments alive. Moreover, as I shall argue shortly, if the phenomenological core of the victim's resentments is a memory of abandon-ment and 'loss of trust in the world', Améry is adamant that responsibility for this legacy cannot be laid at the door of Germans alone.

Primo Levi: Resentment and Reason

It is Améry's essay 'At the Mind's Limits' that inspires Primo Levi's chapter on 'The Intellectual in Auschwitz' in *The Drowned and the Saved*. Améry and Levi's incarceration in Auschwitz overlapped for several months (though Levi confesses that despite his 'indelible memory' he can't remember Améry's appearance), and it was their common position of being intellectuals in Auschwitz (and their different responses to this fact) that forms the crux of Levi's reflections.

As mentioned earlier, Levi himself drew a comparison between his and Améry's respective responses to the violence and humiliations each had endured in the camps, both at the time of incarceration and in the retributive demands contained in their testimonial essays. Levi described Améry as someone who learned to 'return the blow' in the Lager – when pushed to his limits of tolerance, Améry punched in the face a Polish criminal who had been persistently assaulting him. Not only was this an act of which Levi felt himself constitutionally incapable, but Levi speculated that this stance of 'trading blows' had been translated into an unyielding and severe disposition in Améry's post-Auschwitz life, with tragic consequences (he committed suicide in 1978). Levi recalled that the one time he had attempted to return the violence of Elias, the robust dwarf who tormented him, Elias had strangled Levi almost to the point of unconsciousness. Levi disputed Améry's claim that he was a 'forgiver', but noted that following this confirmation of his own physical inability to 'trade blows', he had decided 'to delegate punishments, revenges and retaliations to the laws of my country'.[9] It is the putative distinction between Améry's stance of 'trading blows' and Levi's 'delegation of punishment' that merits closer attention.

Several writers have already commented on the deep affinities that unite these two Holocaust survivors, despite evident differences of circumstance and temperament. In introducing the republished edition of *At the Mind's Limits*, Alexander Stille describes Améry as the 'intellectual angel with whom Levi wrestled as he struggled to clarify the ultimate meaning of the Holocaust after the passing of forty years.'[10] Stille confirms the two men's contrasting emotional sensibilities, their different experiences of persecution and incarceration, and the radically incommensurate conditions under which each resumed their post-Auschwitz lives (Améry in self-imposed exile in Belgium, Levi in the nation, region and indeed the very home in which he was born). Yet Stille goes on to make the observation that in fact when Levi 'shifted from autobiographical description to analysis' in *The Drowned and the Saved*, he and Améry were not as far apart in their responses as Levi had suggested in his essay; and Stille cites the following passage, where Levi speaks about the pain of survivors: 'The injury cannot be healed: it extends through time, and the Furies, in whose existence we are forced to believe, rack not only the tormentors, but . . . the tormented.'[11]

The figure of the Furies is taken up in Cynthia Ozick's reflections on the subterranean affinities between the two men. She observes that until *The Drowned and the Saved*, Levi's testimonial voice had been one 'consummately free of rage, resentment, violent feeling, or any overt drive to "trade blows"'.[12] She notes that '[o]f the scribes of the Holocaust, Levi appears to be the one who least troubles, least wounds, least implicates, the reader.'[13] But she also argues that with the publication of *The Drowned and the Saved*, this judgement of Levi must be radically revised. Ozick observes that reading through this book is like following 'the sizzle flying along the fuse'. By the last chapter, 'Letters to Germans', she says, 'the pressure is so powerful, the rage so immense, that "detachment" has long given way to convulsion. What was withheld before is now imploded in these pages.'[14] She continues:

> *The Drowned and the Saved* is the record of a man returning blows with all the might of human fury, in full knowledge that the pen is mightier than the fist. The convulsions of rage have altered the nature of the prose, and – if we can judge by Levi's suicide – the man as well. Almost no one, interestingly, has been disposed to say of Levi's final testimony that it is saturated in deadly anger – as if it would be too cruel to tear from him the veil of the spirit pure. It may be cruel; but it is Levi's own hand that tears away the veil and sets the fuse.[15]

Ozick's explanation for the radically altered tone of Levi's authorial voice supports Stille's contention that it is the shift from description to analysis that partly accounts for, in Ozick's words, Levi's 'surrender to fury'. It is as if Levi's past recourse to the rigours of narrative and exacting description of 'incident' permitted a more detached authorial stance that managed to keep the Furies temporarily at bay.[16] However, without sacrificing his scientific precision in *The Drowned and the Saved*, Ozick believes Levi finally gave in to the 'violated' and accusatory voice of the victim, unleashing a pent-up rage that had hitherto lain dormant, in a state of latency, of mere 'potentiality'. And therein lay the lethal danger: once freed from his own self-imposed restraint – from a self-image, says Ozick, 'of how a civilized man ought to conduct himself when he is documenting savagery' – the floodgates were open to the consuming and self-destructive torments of rage. Ozick laments Levi's seeming equation of rage with self-destruction and the fact that such vehement emotions had not found articulation in Levi's earlier texts. Had they done so, she suggests, the 'insurmountable pressure' of the forces contained in this later text might not have accumulated with such inexorable momentum. She concludes her essay by saying that if Levi was right about Améry – 'that Améry's willingness to trade punches is the key to his suicide – then he has deciphered for us his own suicide as well' (in fact the title of her essay is 'Primo Levi's Suicide Note').[17]

There are certainly risks in this line of interpretation. Ozick's text abounds with metaphors that have a powerful – even overpowering – effect. Levi's earlier emotional sensibility as conveyed by his prose is likened to a 'vessel of clear water'. Invoking an image from Levi's own trade (and reminiscent of his metaphoric incorporation of chemical properties into *The Periodic Table*), Ozick asks us to imagine a lump of potassium being dropped into that water and triggering instant combustion. This, Ozick invites us to speculate, is what happened when the rage released in *The Drowned and the Saved* – 'a book of blows returned by a pen on fire' – encountered the 'unperturbed transparency' that was the quintessential Levi *persona*. But how can Ozick be so sure that the temporality of Levi's affective responses to the Holocaust conforms to metaphoric images of her own invention? Moreover, while conceding at the outset that '[s]uicide is one of the mysteries of the human will, with or without a farewell note to explain it', she nonetheless subordinates this enigmatic dimension of human agency and maps the affective trajectory of his texts directly onto his personal biography.

Goodheart also warns of the dangers of confusing 'fact with metaphor' and admonishes Ozick for failing to distinguish between the 'literal trading of blows' recounted by Améry, and Levi's aggressive prose style in *The Drowned and the Saved*. Goodheart argues for a different understanding of the nature and articulation of Levi's resentments and how they contrast with those of Améry. For a start, he discerns in the earlier Levi a more judgementally-inclined temperament than Ozick allows, one that manifests a combination of 'equanimity' and severity, according to the moral exigencies of the situation he related. Both Levi and Améry, he asserts, 'write from a strenuous moral point of view, springing from the rationalism of the classical Enlightenment'.[18] Both share a 'passionate commitment to moral reason [. . .] and insist upon the discriminations that are the basis for moral judgment'.[19]

However, if Goodheart makes a convincing case for the two men's shared commitment to reason and to using their experiences in order 'to keep alive a kind of moral discourse in response to extremity', he is also concerned to reinstate the divergent sensibilities of Améry and Levi on other grounds. Goodheart cites the contrasts that can be drawn in the 'character of their judgments' – Améry inclining towards a world divided between victim and perpetrator and demanding unequivocal judgement, Levi concerned to explore the 'gray zone' of intermediate behaviours in the camps. Indeed, Levi maintained that since one can never know in advance how individuals will behave in extreme circumstances because, in his words, 'one is never in another's place', immediate judgement must be suspended where victims are concerned (as Goodheart rightly notes, Levi does not extend this tolerant suspension of judgement to the perpetrators).

Goodheart also cites Améry's particular 'experience of extremity' (exile, imprisonment, arrest and torture even before being sent to Auschwitz) as one reason for Améry's avowed preoccupation with death during his incarceration, with *how* he would die, and his later 'self-destructive retaliatory impulses'. By contrast, Levi's youth, his access to a 'cultural memory' that reinforced his sense of Italian-Jewish identity and, by his own admission, his tendency to avoid introspection, were all resources that encouraged Levi to devote himself to the 'aims of life' and above all to practical activity – 'finding a bit of bread, avoiding exhausting work, patching my shoes, stealing a broom, or interpreting the signs and faces around me'. [20]

However, above and beyond these important differences in circumstance, culture and character, Goodheart believes that what primarily distinguished the two men, as revealed in their testimonial accounts, is that Améry 'is driven by the emotion of resentment, Levi is not'.[21]

It would be wrong to give the impression that Goodheart does not empathize profoundly with Améry's insistence on holding onto his resentments; and he vigorously defends both the *legitimacy* and the moral value of these. Yet he does maintain that what Améry has 'in common with the resentful man is the futility of his passion'.[22] And he confirms the Nietzschean view that 'this is an emotion that one does not act upon, it can fester and turn upon the resenter . . .'.[23] I have already argued against Goodheart's view that Améry's appeal for German historical memory to take the form of 'self-mistrust' should necessarily lead to a paralysing collective introspection – or even 'counter-resentment', as Goodheart cautions. Instead, I have proposed that Améry's resentments be understood as his chosen means of externalizing and actualizing the unresolved moral relation between victims and the society from which their persecutors came. I would therefore describe Améry's resentments as the means he uses to transform emotions he had once expressed by literally 'returning the blow' into the moral foundations of a dialogue with the 'enemy'.

When broaching the question of Levi's resentments, which Ozick locates particularly in Levi's essay 'Letter to Germans', Goodheart prefers instead to speak of 'lapses' of anger toward apparently well-meaning Germans. Yet, while one should indeed be wary of confusing 'fact with metaphor', Ozick is right to point out that it is Levi himself who resorts to combative metaphors that evoke an image of him 'trading blows' with an adversary. To consign these responses therefore to deviations from Levi's otherwise balanced moral posture is to deny Levi the expression of resentments that are, like Améry's, active and externally-directed in nature. Indeed, Goodheart himself concedes that, when directed at a 'defeated but still dangerous enemy', Levi's textual 'blows' could be 'an affirmative, life-affirming act'; but he shies away from assigning them the attention they deserve and from elucidating the function they seek to fulfil.

For I think it is precisely in Améry's spirit of insisting on the moral value of his resentments that Levi gives full expression to his own in 'Letters to Germans'. Levi describes how he felt when he learned that *Survival in Auschwitz* [*If This is a Man*] was to be translated into German. He admits that he originally thought he had written the book 'without a specific recipient in mind', simply to 'expel' the memories that dwelled within him. But reflecting upon his reaction to news of the German publishing contract – a 'violent and new emotion of having won a battle' – made him realize that the book had always had a particular addressee in mind. At a general level, Levi could conjure a wide and diverse community of readers for whom the book was intended: 'for Italians, for my children, for those who did not know, those who did not want to know, those who were not yet born, those who, willing or not, had assented to the offense'.[24] But the especially triumphant feeling he experiences and that he describes in the adversarial terms of 'having won a battle' identified for him the book's 'true recipients': the Germans. Continuing the metaphor, Levi states that at that point he knew that *Survival in Auschwitz* was 'aimed like a gun' at the generation of Germans who had been oppressors or indifferent spectators, and '[n]ow the gun was loaded'. Captured by his text, these German readers would find themselves cornered, tied before the mirror of Levi's narrative, from which they could not escape self-recognition.

Almost as if retreating from the sheer locutionary zeal of this confession, Levi then maintains that his motives in this imaginary round-up of German readers were not those of revenge. He claims: 'I had been intimately satisfied by the symbolic, incomplete, tendentious, sacred representation in Nuremberg, but it was fine with me that the very just hangings should be handled by others, professionals. My task was to understand them.'[25] Certainly it might be argued that the very choice of adjectives describing this momentous juridical event – 'incomplete', 'tendentious', 'sacred' – betray ambivalences that belie Levi's professed faith in delegated punishment. (For that matter Améry, too, oscillates between a demand that the Nazi war criminal be juridically 'nailed to his deed' and a scepticism towards what he calls a 'justice that [. . .] could only be hypothetical anyway'.) More revealing, however, is the form that Levi's self-educative endeavour assumes, especially in his essay 'Letters from Germans'.

Here we have, in the form of an epistolary dialogue, an attempt at an 'actualization' or 'externalization' of the relation between victim and perpetrator/bystander that Améry wished to see enacted 'in the field of historical practice'. While Levi states that he can listen to the explanations of his various German interlocutors, and judge them 'without prejudice or anger', this neutral posture is abandoned in the very first letter to which Levi replies – that of Doctor T. H. of Hamburg, who maintains that support for Hitler was virtually inevitable after 1933 when all moderate parties had allegedly disappeared, and that hatred towards Jews in Germany was 'never popular'. Levi comes out of his corner, 'trading blows' with the proponent of these wilful exonerations in a manner not dissimilar to Améry's own mode of address to his German audience. And in the remainder of his exchanges, he maintains this combative stance, asserting time and again against the protestations of those-who-claimed-not-to-know that the collective crime of virtually all Germans of the period was a complicity in silence. Indeed one of his sharpest retorts is directed at M. S. from Frankfurt, who merely asks Levi not to speak of all Germans as a 'single entity'. Levi confesses to a 'perplexity' in answering all these polite and civil interlocutors, and adds 'members of a people who exterminated mine (and many others)'. His rejoinder to M. S.'s plea for a more discriminating judgement of Germans is one that once again follows Améry (and Habermas) in pointing out that while a collective judgement against all Germans is dangerous, it is nonetheless incumbent upon all Germans to examine critically the 'traditions, customs, history, language, and culture' upon which any claim to a German national spirit is based.

Far from being mere 'lapses' of anger directed at 'well-meaning Germans', we can see Levi targeting his resentments not against individual Germans *per se*, but against the memorial *entropy* that their discourses betray, and that Levi, like Améry, perceived to be steadily encroaching upon German historical memory. If Germany remains a 'still dangerous enemy' for both men, it is in so far as its citizens seek from Holocaust survivors a memory that facilitates absolution rather than embracing for their own sakes a public memory steeped in permanent 'self-mistrust'.

The Jewish Nazi Victim

Finally, if both men attempt to 'externalize' their resentments by addressing the German national community, their writings also bear witness to the *internalized* legacy of these resentments – one that profoundly affects the post-Holocaust subjectivity of the survivor. As Levi describes this legacy in 'Memory of the Offence':

> . . . we are dealing with a paradoxical analogy between victim and oppressor, and we are anxious to be clear: both are in the same trap, but it is the oppressor, and he alone, who has prepared it and activated it, and if he suffers from this, it is right that he should suffer; and it is iniquitous that the victim should suffer from it, as he does indeed suffer from it, even at a distance of decades. Once again, it must be observed, mournfully, that the injury cannot be healed . . ."[26]

However, if for Levi it is the ineradicable 'memory of the offence' that affectively grounds his identity as a Holocaust survivor, for Améry the memory formative of his survivor identity is of his prior *social* designation as a Jew. Learning that he was a Jew *in the eyes of the world* was (and remained) for Améry inseparable from an awareness that he was also Nazism's designated victim. Perhaps herein lies the greatest difference between the memories of resentment that constitute each man's post-Holocaust identity.

In the essay 'On the Necessity and Impossibility of Being a Jew', Améry tracks his emerging self-consciousness of his Jewish identity in relation to the biographical coordinates I've outlined above. He recalls himself as a boy at Christmas, 'plodding through a snow-covered village to midnight mass'; hearing his mother 'appealing to Jesus, Mary, and Joseph when a minor household misfortune occurred'. His schoolboy consciousness vaguely apprehended that he was a Jew 'just as one of my schoolmates was the son of a bankrupt innkeeper'.[27] It was while reading the Nuremberg Laws in a newspaper in a Vienna coffeehouse that the young adult Améry knew not only that they applied distinctly to him, that they 'had just made me formally and beyond any question a Jew', but that from then on to be a Jew meant to be a 'dead man on leave [. . .] who only by chance was not yet where he properly belonged' (pp. 85–6). However if this verdict was pronounced by Nazi ideology, Améry is adamant that it was one imposed by society more generally. In a later essay, he notes of his 1940 imprisonment in southern France that whereas he was initially arrested as a *boche* [Hun], following the German occupation of France and the release of *des boches*, he and his fellow refugees were detained as *sales juifs*, thus transformed, he says, from 'the enemy into burdensome aliens and above all: into Jews, now in the full sense of the German racist notion'.[28] (It is instructive in this context to read Hannah Arendt's 1943 essay 'We Refugees' in *The Jew as Pariah*, since Arendt was also detained in Gurs in the same year. Arendt remarks, 'having been jailed because we were Germans, we were not freed because we were Jews'.)[29] Améry is emphatic: 'The Jewish identity imposed on me by society [. . .] was no German phenomenon. It was not only the Nazis who turned me into a Jew. The world insisted that I be one, and I was ready to do what Sartre later called "assumer", freely and inadequately translated, "to take upon oneself." I wrested from myself the feeling of solidarity with *every* Jew' (p. 17).

Thus while 'solidarity in the face of threat' will henceforth bind Améry to his Jewish contemporaries (and to the state of Israel), his identity as a Jew remains one without 'positive determinants' in language, culture or childhood memories. On the contrary, Améry's Sartrean self-description underlines its negative determination: 'I am [. . .] a Jew by the mere fact that the world around me does not expressly designate me as a non-Jew. To be something can mean that one is *not* something else. As a Non-non-Jew, I am a Jew; I must be one and must want to be one' (p. 94). Améry then further specifies his identity as a 'Catastrophe Jew', produced in a 'Holocaust-determined existence' that has simultaneously constituted his identity as a victim. This identity, as we've seen, is above all experienced as abandonment and therefore a loss of 'trust in the world'. He thus describes his ruminations on the question of identity as an 'incessant effort to explore the basic condition of being a victim, in conflict with the necessity to be a Jew and the impossibility of being one . . .' (p. 101).

Resentment or Revenge?

Five years after making his passionate defence of the victim's resentments, Améry wrote an essay entitled 'In the Waiting Room of Death', commemorating the Warsaw Ghetto uprising. Here, Améry, who has witnessed in the intervening years the rise of an 'old-new antisemitism', is no longer concerned to distinguish resentment from revenge, but describes the Ghetto uprising as a 'realization of *human vengeance*', as an 'avenging violence that is intended as the nullification of the oppressor's violence'.[30]

I do not believe there is a single and simple explanation for this apparent inconsistency whereby Améry renounces the motive of revenge in one essay only to celebrate it in another – though this oscillation might be regarded as another defining feature of the memory Améry is trying to elucidate. However, rather than subjecting Améry's defence of the 'existential foundations of the human act of vengeance' (p. 27) to a Nietzschean judgement, in which the desire for revenge would be resentment's pitiless bedfellow, it is worth considering the basis upon which Améry seeks to vindicate this response.

He starts his essay by posing the question: 'who has the right to talk about [the Ghetto fighters]?' His own reply is that once one leaves the terrain of historiography and ventures into the 'phenomenology of the victim's existence in the ghetto', only those who have experienced such events can claim that right. But he justifies his own subsequent reflections by invoking a metaphoric identification between the spatial isolation imposed upon Jewish ghetto existence historically, and the social isolation imposed upon Jews once Nuremberg's racial laws had been promulgated:

'Since the enactment of the Nuremberg Laws the ghetto caught up with every Jew . . .' (p. 21). The only way to break out of that material and existential condition of isolation was to forge a group identity that turned the fact of exclusion and persecution into a force for collective cohesion. Yet, Améry maintains, there was no historical precedent in Jewish history for this form of solidarity, because Jewish identity had been confined to 'the series', to 'the peculiar dialectic of Jewish solidarity', a solidarity that extended 'only to suffering' and did not 'include struggle within its horizon'. However what had emerged in the unimaginable conditions of ghetto life, in the 'Waiting Room of Death', was a form of resistance that freed itself 'from a two-thousand year history', and that did so by forging an identity whose 'group-forming agent' was the 'determination for revenge'.

Thus Améry's sense of solidarity with the Jewish ghetto fighters is determined by three identificatory moments: in the first instance he sees the Ghetto residents as 'companions in fate' by virtue of the death sentence they too faced for being Jews; secondly, he describes 'the phenomenology of the victim's existence in the ghetto', notably the 'total solitude of the Ghetto Jew', as a 'metaphorically extended' iteration of the sense of complete abandonment he endured in the camps; thirdly, in the ghetto fighters' revolt Améry finds affirmation of his own 'determination for revenge'. Anticipating the protest such a claim might provoke, Améry retaliates:

> What an unpopular term is being introduced here! I already hear protests: No, that's not the way it was! An eye for an eye, a tooth for a tooth, *jus talionis*; for God's sake, that is by no means what the Jews wanted who were rousing themselves to resistance! Yes, it is! I believe that is what they wanted. I myself [. . .] wanted just that; and countless comrades along with me (p. 27).

Because Nazism had inflicted on the ghetto a historically unprecedented form of existence – the 'contradictory reality of an anti-world' – its occupants, in Améry's view, were faced with the 'dialectical paradox' whereby 'whoever was to restore morality at all had to include the obviously evil, that is, revenge, in his system' (p. 33).

Finally, he insists that the vengeance guiding the Ghetto uprising was 'singular' and 'irreducible' in relation to all other kinds of revolt against oppression. The ghetto fighters had exercised '*the freedom of choosing death*', thereby rebelling against the death decree of the enemy and enacting on the *victims'* behalf the 'negation of the negation'.

Améry concludes by stating: 'There are concepts that have gained an entirely new meaning because of the ghetto. Revenge. Irreconcilability' (p. 36). But he also attributes to the ghetto uprising the realization on the part of Jews, and of the world more generally, 'the certainty that anything similar can no longer happen because it must not happen . . .' (p. 35).

Conclusion

Nietzsche described the 'man of resentment' as someone who 'cannot get rid of anything [. . .] cannot get over anything [. . .] cannot repel anything – everything hurts. Men and things obtrude too closely; experiences strike one too deeply; memory becomes a festering wound.'[31] We certainly find expressed in the writings of Améry and Levi vividly recounted 'memories of the offence', yet these are not intended to solicit compassion – indeed Améry asserts rather coldly that 'we [victims] don't believe in tears'. Nor in their determination to hold onto resentment (and in Améry's case, revenge) can their memories be characterized as a 'festering wound'. Rather, I have argued that such memories function for both men as an ethical *agency*, or, to borrow the metaphor of Alexander Stille, 'an internal compass in a morally distorted world'.[32] They are there as a counterforce to the 'historical entropy' that Améry acknowledged was an inevitable consequence of 'the silently erosive and transformative effects of time', but whose encroachment should nonetheless be resisted 'with all our power'. They are also there as a permanent reminder that there are still responsibilities to be assumed – and not only by Germany society, but by other European societies that abandoned 'Jewish Nazi victims' to their fate.

But I want to propose by way of a conclusion that the category of resentment as elucidated by these two Holocaust survivors has a wider, contemporary relevance as well.

In 'We Refugees', the 1943 essay cited earlier, Hannah Arendt wrote: 'Refugees driven from country to country represent the vanguard of their peoples – if they keep their identity. For the first time, Jewish history is not separate but tied up with that of all other nations. The comity of European peoples went to pieces when, and because, it allowed its weakest members to be excluded and persecuted.'[33] We have recently witnessed the 'comity of European peoples' once again in disarray because of an inability to protect its weakest members – first, Bosnian Muslims and now Kosovar Albanians. By invoking the contemporary resonance of Arendt's remarks – and indeed the moral imperative that Améry summons as the legacy of the Warsaw Ghetto rising – 'anything similar can no longer happen because it must not happen . . .' – I am not proposing that Nazi genocide be compared with the crimes against humanity committed in the former Yugoslavia. (The *Historikerstreit* or German historians' debate discussed in the previous chapter is a recent reminder of how comparisons can serve neo-revisionist political ends.) And I shall register caution later in this book against the seductions of historical analogy. But as James Young has pointed out: 'Because the suffering of the Holocaust was not like anything else, it became a referent, a standard, by which subsequent suffering would be measured.'[34] Thus even if we resist facile comparison and the temptations of historical analogy, it is nonetheless true that the Holocaust has become the 'guiding figure' (Young's term) by which many Europeans have grasped the logic of persecution in the former Yugoslavia and the sluggish reaction shown by leaders of the New World Order. Yet as a number of observers have pointed out, if this framework of understanding has elicited widespread moral empathy, it has ultimately failed to translate into the kind of action that would spare the countries and their citizens the fate of ethnic cleansing. All signs suggest that this failure to intervene effectively against mass genocide will also be experienced by the victims of these wars as betrayal and a 'loss of trust in the world'.[35]

I don't think that we can even begin to imagine how to 'combat the revenge' that memories of these catastrophes have bequeathed. However, in an article written during the siege of Sarajevo declaring his identification with its beleaguered population, Salman Rushdie relayed an anecdote that offers a profoundly disturbing glimpse of how the victim's resentments were once again being inscribed. A Sarajevan journalist told of a boy whose father was killed, and who subsequently proclaimed, 'Last night I dreamt about my father. I dreamt about him on purpose.' The journalist warned: 'Somebody will one day have to watch out for boys from Sarajevo who dream about their murdered fathers on purpose.'[36]

The victim's resentment, then, is not only a memorial legacy of the Holocaust still to be 'settled', but, I would argue, an ominous foreshadowing of Europe's memorial future.

Notes

1. David Carroll, 'Foreword: The Memory of Devastation and the Responsibilities of Thought: "And let's not talk about that"', in Jean-François Lyotard, *Heidegger and "the jews"* (London: University of Minnesota Press, 1990), p. ix.
2. Sidney Rosenfeld, 'Preface', in Jean Améry, *At the Mind's Limits: Contemplations by a Survivor of Auschwitz and its Realities*, trans. Sidney Rosenfeld and Stella Rosenfeld (New York: Schocken Books, 1990), p. 109.
3. *Radical Humanism: Selected Essays* (Bloomington: Indiana University Press, 1984).
4. 'Resentments', *At the Mind's Limits*. References to this essay appear in parentheses in the text.
5. Améry's remarks on the immorality of natural time are strikingly similar to those made by his contemporary, the Jewish moral philosopher and former French *résistant* Vladimir Jankélévitch, who argued that, because time was a natural process 'without normative value', it could not and should not exercise an 'attenuating action on the insupportable horror of Auschwitz'. Jankélévitch also

defends his resentments in a 1971 essay that seems directly influenced by Améry: 'Car le "ressentiment" peut être aussi le sentiment renouvelé et intensément vécu de la chose inexpiable; il protest contre une amnistie morale qui n'est qu'une honteuse amnésie; il entretient la flamme sacrée de l'inquiétude et de la fidelité aux choses invisible'. See Vladimir Jankélévitch, 'L'Imprescriptible: Pardonner?', in *Dans l'honneur et la dignité* (Paris: Seuil, 1986).

6. Nietzsche's own view was that, as a 'formative activity', justice was the opposite of *ressentiment*. Nietzsche's remarks cited in this essay are drawn from Gilles Deleuze's essay 'From Ressentiment to the Bad Conscience', in *Nietzsche and Philosophy* (London: Athlone Press, 1982). Améry views justice as a necessary, but insufficient condition of the 'externalization' of resentment which is for him the ethical and existential 'actualization' of the relation between perpetrator and victim.

7. Eugene Goodheart, 'The Passion of Reason: Reflections on Primo Levi and Jean Améry', *Dissent*, Fall 1994, p. 522.

8. See Jürgen Habermas, 'On the Public Use of History', in Richard Wolin (ed.), *The New Conservatism: Cultural Criticism and the Historians' Debate*, trans. Shierry Weber Nicholsen (Cambridge: Polity, 1989), p. 234.

9. Primo Levi, *The Drowned and the Saved*, trans. Raymond Rosenthal (London: Michael Joseph, 1988), p. 137. References to this essay appear in parentheses in the text.

10. Alexander Stille, 'Foreword', *At the Mind's Limits*, p. vii.

11. Ibid., p. xv.

12. Cynthia Ozick, 'Primo Levi's Suicide Note', in *Metaphor and Memory* (New York: Knopf, 1989), p. 329.

13. Ibid., p. 334.

14. Ibid.

15. Ibid., pp. 334–5.

16. Though see Byran Cheyette's insightful article, 'The Ethical Uncertainty of Primo Levi', in Bryan Cheyette and Laura Marcus (eds), *Modernity, Culture and 'the Jew'* (Cambridge: Polity, 1998), for a reading that refutes the notion that 'rage and restraint' are two polarities in Levi's writing and foregrounds the 'grey zone' of Levi's memoirs. Sympathetic as I am to Cheyette's more complex reading of Levi, he nonetheless contrasts Levi's determination to 'situate himself outside the violent structures which gave rise to the death camps', with Améry's placement of himself 'firmly within these violent structures', p. 270. My reading of Améry offers an alternative to Cheyette's interpretation.

17. 'Primo Levi's Suicide Note', *Metaphor and Memory*, p. 342.

18. 'The Passion of Reason', p. 518.

19. Ibid., p. 519.

20. Levi, cited by Goodheart, ibid., p. 525.
21. Ibid., p. 521.
22. Ibid., p. 522.
23. Ibid.
24. 'Letter to Germans', in the *Drowned and the Saved*.
25. Ibid., p. 168.
26. 'Memory of the Offence', in *The Drowned and the Saved*, p. 24.
27. 'On the Necessity and Impossibility of Being a Jew', in *At the Mind's Limits*, p. 83. References to this essay appear in parentheses in the text.
28. 'On Being a Jew', *Radical Humanism*, p. 17. Explaining the hierarchy of feelings attached to being persecuted both as a Jew and as a member of the Belgian resistance, Améry notes: 'The Jews were hunted, cornered, arrested, deported *because they were Jews* and only because of that. Looking back, it appears to me that I didn't want to be detained as a Jew but rather as a resistance member. It was my last absurd effort to escape my collective fate', p. 17.
29. Hannah Arendt describes Jewish refugees interned on orders of the French government as 'such loyal Frenchmen they became the first "prisonniers volontaires" history has ever seen'. See 'We Refugees' in Arendt, *The Jew as Pariah: Jewish Identity and Politics in the Modern Age* (New York: Grove Press, 1978), p. 61.
30. 'In the Waiting Room of Death', in *Radical Humanism*, p. 26. References to this essay appear in parentheses in the text.
31. Cited by Gilles Deleuze, 'From Ressentiment to the Bad Conscience', p. 116.
32. Stille, 'Preface', p. xiii.
33. Hannah Arendt, 'We Refugees', p. 66.
34. James Young, *Writing and Rewriting the Holocaust: Narrative and the Consequences of Interpretation* (Bloomington: Indiana University Press, 1990), p. 128.
35. Michael Ignatieff made this point forcefully when, in 1994, he noted that the 'fascination with Sarajevo as metaphor went along with ever more complete disengagement with its actual fate'. Ignatieff is critical of the use of the Holocaust *analogy* with regard to Bosnia, but at the same time he observed: 'Our horror about Bosnia had an amnesiac quality, as if we wished to believe that ethnic cleansing was alien to European traditions.' See 'Hommage to Bosnia', *New York Review of Books*, 21 April 1994.
36. Salman Rushdie, 'Bosnia on My Mind', *Index on Censorship* 23, nos. 1–2, May–June 1994.

-4-

Narrating Perpetrator Testimony

Introduction

Daniel J. Goldhagen's book, *Hitler's Willing Executioners: Ordinary Germans and the Holocaust*, has been described by one renowned historian as a work that has 'already won its place in the history of the memory of genocide'.[1] One could of course mention other texts that have earned a similar place: Raul Hilberg's *The Destruction of the European Jews*, Robert Paxton and Michael Marrus's *Vichy France and the Jews*, Marrus's *The Holocaust in History*, Henry Rousso's *The Vichy Syndrome*, and, certain to follow in this memorial canon, Saul Friedländer's first volume of *Nazi Germany and the Jews*. However Goldhagen's text, like Hannah Arendt's *Eichmann in Jerusalem* before it, has earned this citation not on the basis of the originality or substantiveness of its *historical* contribution, but primarily because of the controversy its claims have generated. Published to thunderous acclaim by the media and a wider public alike, *Hitler's Willing Executioners* was greeted with disparagement and even contempt amongst learned historiographical circles. Expressions of appreciation of the kind voiced by Habermas were few and far between. Indeed, this 'bifurcated reception'[2] between an adulatory public and a hostile scholarly world was so striking that such reactions came to constitute an event in their own right. The Germans spoke of the 'Goldhagen phenomenon' and the French of 'the Goldhagen effect',[3] while American historians devoted a website to the controversy. Omer Bartov maintained that in fact the volatile reception of *Hitler's Willing Executioners* was of greater interest and importance than its value as a scholarly study.[4] In addition to the coverage the controversy enjoyed in the popular press and on television, throughout Europe and North America, special issues of journals and a number of scholarly volumes have already been devoted to dissecting, rebutting and condemning the main claims of *Hitler's Willing Executioners*.[5] This chapter will explore why this book in particular managed to generate the controversy it did and will argue that the issues raised by the Goldhagen debate extend well beyond the historiographical terrain within which they have largely been confined.

The obvious source of the polemic lies in the claims Goldhagen makes about the 'Ordinary Germans' who feature in his title. As is by now well known, Goldhagen's main contention in *Hitler's Willing Executioners* is that anti-Semitic beliefs held by Germans about Jews must be regarded as the 'central causal agent' of the Holocaust. Such beliefs, he alleges, became pervasive by the early nineteenth century and thereafter exercised an enduring grip on German political culture and the belief-system of individuals. He argues that central to this modern German anti-Semitism, and what distinguished it from other European variants, was the casting of Jews as a race apart, as a malevolent force within the body politic and the principal source of all Germany's misfortunes. This mode of anti-Semitism, particularly vilifying in its imagery as well as inciting periodic violence towards Jews, is typified by Goldhagen as 'eliminationist anti-Semitism', because he contends that its logic ultimately implied that only by expurgating Jews from the German body politic would the nation's well-being and integrity be assured. Even the assimilationist path advocated by German liberals does not escape Goldhagen's 'eliminationist' appellation, on the basis that since assimilationism sought the erasure of the visible presence of Jewish cultural difference, under certain conditions these aims could be directed to more sinister ends. In this respect, according to Goldhagen, eliminationist anti-Semitism operated on a continuum between mild and extremist versions, with each of these harbouring a 'genocidal potential' convertible to an exterminationist logic 'in the absence of ethical constraints'. If Hitler and his henchmen were able to pursue their exterminationist goals abetted by thousands of 'ordinary Germans' it was not only because such constraints had been removed, but because the anti-Semitism animating the actions of the perpetrators of genocide had translated into the conviction that 'the Jews *ought to die*'.[6]

After setting out his thesis, the bulk of Goldhagen's book is devoted to an account of three 'face-to-face' settings in which genocide occurred: police battalions, work camps and death marches. For Goldhagen the significance of these sites is not only that they were predominantly peopled by 'ordinary Germans' (rather than exclusively by the SS), but also that by virtue of the close proximity to their victims that these 'artisanal' forms of genocide imposed, a measure of individual voluntarism was required: a desire to kill Jews – or at least a decision not to refuse one's genocidal task. It is this 'willing' mentality that Goldhagen believes he can elucidate with reference to the eliminationist anti-Semitism that he believes was already inscribed in the perpetrator psyche. In implementing orders to kill defenceless men, women and children on racial grounds alone, Goldhagen believes these 'ordinary Germans' had to be convinced that they were fulfilling once and for all the imperative latent in the political culture they had imbibed. Any cognitive dissonance that may have arisen from other human agencies of moral judgement – the claims of conscience or compassion – was overridden by the force of a 'cultural cognitive model' that promoted the obligation to rid the German body politic of its most putatively harmful, alien – and ultimately unassimilable – element: the Jew. Thus

Goldhagen not only asserts the *existence* of a collective, murderous intention towards Jews embedded in German political culture; he finds this intention demonstrated again and again in his analysis of the individual behaviour of the ordinary Germans who carried out their genocidal missions 'under the open sky', whether in mobile police battalions, as guards in work camps or in the 'ambulatory analogue to the cattle car' – the death marches that marked the final throes of the war.

The objections levelled by historians, political scientists and philosophers to Goldhagen's thesis range far and wide. He has been criticized for favouring a 'monocausal explanation' of the Holocaust rather than recognizing a multiplicity of determining elements that together led to the implementation of the Final Solution. Because this monocausality privileges ideological motivation, he has been labelled an 'ultra-intentionalist' who relegates crucial structural determinants embedded in the modern industrial state to a secondary role.[7] His characterization of German anti-Semitism is held to be both inaccurate and reductive, especially his assertion that assimilation, exclusion and physical elimination can ultimately be regarded as 'rough functional equivalents' rather than qualitatively different responses to Germany's Jewish presence.[8] For others, Goldhagen's lack of a comparative perspective means that he fails to explain why non-German nationals participated with such zeal in the genocide of the Jews, why nations with traditions of anti-Semitism every bit as virulent as Germany's did not initiate the Final Solution, and why other categories of the population also became the targets of an exterminationist logic.[9] A number of critics have protested that Goldhagen's choice of these killing sites and neglect of the gas chambers has led him to downplay the industrial and bureaucratic nature of the genocide to which most Jewish victims were subjected – a form that makes the Holocaust both distinctive *and* shows its structural links to modernity's key institutions and everyday routines.[10] Finally, the very fact that Goldhagen posits a confident explanation of *why* the Holocaust occurred is deemed misguided – and even 'obscene'. Critics like the philosopher and filmmaker Claude Lanzmann insist that explanatory schemas drawing upon ideology, economics, sociology or social psychology can at best elucidate some 'necessary but insufficient' conditions of the extermination process and that between these explanations and the *fact* of extermination there is inevitably 'un hiatus [. . .] un salut [. . .] un abîme'.[11]

It is easier to see why the thesis of eliminationist anti-Semitism would provoke the hostility of the scholarly community than it is to account for its endorsement by a wider public, especially in the German context. For even if Goldhagen takes pains to acquit post-war German political culture from the taint of his charges, on the basis that a democratic sensibility has firmly entrenched itself in the body politic, this exemption is not entirely convincing. If the demonic forces that he attributes to pre-war Germany were so pervasively and deeply inscribed in the political unconscious, it is hard to imagine them being conjured away by conscious processes and political will alone. It is far more likely that the huge number of young Germans who counted themselves amongst his fans were attracted in part by a conviction that Goldhagen had touched upon an obscure and resilient ideological chord in *their habitus* that they could now explain as the intangible legacy of eliminationist anti-Semitism. And although its last emanation in lethal form implicated the generation twice removed from their own, in Goldhagen's compelling portrait of their grandparents' compatriots the younger generation of Germans could find justification for an ongoing vigilance that it was their special responsibility to assume. Of course, this same suspicion of an anti-Semitic recidivism haunted their parent's generation, stimulating numerous political debates and inspiring many cultural attempts to 'come to terms with the Nazi past'. However, the warning that issued in subterranean form from the pages of *Hitler's Willing Executioners* seemed to be expressly directed at this younger generation. As François Bédarida perceptively suggested: 'In the end, wasn't the major lesson of the Goldhagen controversy that each generation, rather than profiting from the experience acquired by previous generations, must in its turn, by and for itself, reinvest in the past before it can reinterpret and assume it?'[12]

But why did *Hitler's Willing Executioners* awaken this desire where other political appeals and cultural representations had failed? Ultra-intentionalist though he is, the stridency of his thesis alone does not account for the grip the book exerted on the popular imagination and especially amongst young people. Nor is it explained with reference to the concerted and saturated marketing campaign of the publishers, as much as their tactics may have ensured Goldhagen an international and mass audience. Instead I would contend that, over-long and repetitious though it is, *Hitler's Willing Executioners* is eminently readable in the same manner that *Schindler's List*, despite its length and Spielberg's avowals of continually patrolling the ethical boundaries of what should or should not be shown, is eminently watchable. *Hitler's Willing Executioners* is in many ways the historiographical rival of Hollywood's most popular Holocaust film.

It would be all too easy to use this depiction to bolster the criticisms that many historians have made of the book, and to equate its popular appeal with the public's desire for simple explanations of complex – and ultimately unknowable – events like the Holocaust, or with the voyeuristic instincts lurking within us that its vivid narration arouses.[13] However, these are premature judgements that foreclose not only a more measured assessment of the insights Goldhagen manages to achieve despite, or perhaps because of, the popular form his narration takes, but a more detailed critique of the 'limits of representation' that his historical narration inevitably encounters. For as Omer Bartov concedes (in a remark reminiscent of conclusions many critics drew about *Schindler's List*), *Hitler's Willing Executioners* manages 'to evoke in readers emotions and thoughts that the conventional historical literature fails to stimulate'.[14] If it should be *one* aim of Holocaust historiography to engage a younger generation or wider public in reflections about the Holocaust that are meaningful to their lives, then Goldhagen's success in attracting a mass readership should at least be taken seriously.

The heuristic device I've adopted to explore the book's popular appeal is a comparison of aspects of Goldhagen's account of 'face-to-face' killings with the historian credited with first excavating this historiographical territory: Christopher R. Browning. Browning's book, *Ordinary Men: Reserve Police Battalion 101 and the Final Solution in Poland*,[15] was published to near-universal acclaim by the scholarly community and to an appreciative – though far more muted – public reception. This comparison is partly prompted by the fact that reviewers of Goldhagen repeatedly invoke Browning's *Ordinary Men* as the by-far superior explanation of the voluntarism displayed by German perpetrators and the more judicious 'thick description' of face-to-face killings. However, few critics go beyond an assertion of their preference, and even those who are inclined to give more credit to Goldhagen's emphasis on the anti-Semitic motivations governing the behaviour of the men of Reserve Police Battalion 101 do not delve into the distinguishing features of the psychological profiles each author attempts.[16] I'm not concerned to challenge these critics' preference for *Ordinary Men* so much as to explore in more detail why Goldhagen's version in particular has aroused such vehement distaste and dismay.

For their accounts of Reserve Police Battalion 101, both authors draw on the same archival sources: the judicial documents that constitute the pre-trial interrogations of members of a Hamburg reserve police unit indicted for war crimes in the 1960s.[17] In first reading these documents, Browning was struck by the fact that some testimonies revealed that in the first stages of the genocidal mission carried out by Reserve Police Battalion 101 in Poland in 1942, the unit's leader had offered the older men the opportunity of withdrawing from their killing assignments, yet it was apparent that relatively few had chosen to take up this offer. As the mass murder unfolded in earnest, and in the most gruesome of circumstances, still very few asked to be relieved of their duties. And while in the aftermath of their 'initiation to mass murder' the men reacted with repugnance and anger to the experience they had undergone, they nonetheless continued their murderous activities without protest. Disgust soon gave way to habituation and in some cases to an enthusiasm for killing. After analysing his sources, Browning concluded that, while a combination of factors could explain this initial reluctance to demur, peer pressure and group conformity constituted the strongest motives. Moreover, Browning did not believe that these men commenced their missions harbouring murderous intentions toward Jews, but only developed this resolve as they grew increasingly inured to their grisly task. The emphasis in Browning's account, then, is on the capacity of human beings to act in dehumanized and brutal ways when subjected to a specific set of circumstances that induce conformist behaviour as a defensive – but all too human – reaction.[18] In this respect, he is a 'functionalist' who views anti-Semitism as a necessary but insufficient condition of the features of the Holocaust he attempts to elucidate.

Goldhagen takes strong issue with Browning's interpretation of these sources and, not surprisingly given his thesis of ideological causation, with Browning's emphasis on the situational and social-psychological factors that smoothed the path to genocide. He conducts this polemic in a point-by-point refutation of many of Browning's claims in footnotes that accompany the very different account he renders of the behaviour and responses of these same reserve policemen during their genocidal tour of duty in Poland.[19] These are too lengthy to recapitulate, but even a selective discussion of the most salient objections raised by Goldhagen suggests that more is at stake than different explanatory paradigms, and that how each author *represents* perpetrator behaviour and psychology is an equally contested domain.

Perpetrator Memory and Testimony

Browning acknowledges that the first obstacle encountered in dealing with the testimony of this category of perpetrators is the problem of sources, and especially the absence of documents contemporaneous with the events in which Reserve Police Battalion 101 took part. These men, he reminds us, were not the 'desk murderers' so starkly unmasked by Raul Hilberg, who 'left a lengthy paper trail behind them'.[20] Nor did they show the same compulsion as their *Einsatzgruppen* superiors to boast of their murderous exploits in diaries, letters or reports. The documentation from which the activities of Reserve Police Battalion 101 has to be charted derives primarily from the interrogations of a number of these men conducted some two decades later in the context of judicial proceedings against them. Thus not only is the historian confronted with multiple memories of, and perspectives on, the same set of events, but with accounts extracted in the full knowledge that certain versions of events would lead to criminal indictment, while others would spare the testifier from prosecution. Faced with a powerful incentive either to admit to having been offered a choice and not shooting Jews, or to shooting without being given a choice, Browning concedes that 'not only repression and distortion but conscious mendacity shaped the accounts of the witnesses' (p. xviii). Assessing the reliability of any given account became not only a matter of cross-checking and other verification procedures, but of exercising 'purely instinctive judgments' – deciding when testimonials had, in Browning's words, 'a "feel" of candor and frankness' about them (p. xvii). In Browning's view, however rigorous the procedures of corroboration, the subjective judgement of the historian was inevitably involved in making decisions about what credence to lend to individual statements. Moreover, the subjective quotient was further raised by limitations inherent in the information elicited. Designed to adduce evidence about criminal acts allegedly committed by particular individuals, the interrogators' questions were not concerned with 'the broader, often more impressionistic and subjective facets of the policeman's experience' (p. xviii) – foremost among which for Browning's purposes was the men's state of mind as they became habituated to their genocidal duties. It fell to the historian to make the testimonial material yield this social-psychological dimension.

Goldhagen, like Browning, wishes to draw from this material (and as we shall see from other sources as well), an explanation of the mentality that was willing and complicit in Jewish massacres. However, he is adamant that a convincing account of motivation and action can only emerge from these judicial documents by discounting '*all* self-exculpating testimony that finds no corroboration from other sources' (p. 467). Goldhagen is even more distrustful than Browning of the selectivity of the men's memories in the light of their powerful legal motives to dissimulate, and the censure any admissions of guilt would provoke from a 'now disapproving society'. To lend credence to any exonerating testimony that was otherwise unsubstantiated is, in Goldhagen's view, tantamount to being taken in by the criminal's repeated proclamations of innocence despite the most damning evidence. Indeed, Goldhagen argues that the yawning gap between the large number of Jewish victims that the men themselves recalled, and the tiny number who confessed to actually killing anyone in their battalion's actions, proves just how disingenuous their exculpatory claims were. For the same reason, he regards as highly implausible Browning's estimation that at the outset up to 20 per cent of Reserve Police Battalion 101 disapproved of the killing or did not become killers themselves.[21]

Whether one is inclined to agree with Browning that even the exonerating testimony, if read with a wary eye, can offer 'texture and differentiation' to a portrait of the willing perpetrator,[22] or to share Goldhagen's suspicions about its irredeemably mendacious character, clearly the limitations of this testimonial material both in relation to the historical reality of which it speaks and the memories it purports to transmit pose a formidable hermeneutic challenge. Yet both men *do* make considerable interpretative use of the relatively sparse amount of material that passes their respective selection criteria.[23] Sometimes differences arise from conflicting accounts of the same event by different individuals: for example, whereas the testimonials cited by Browning paint a picture of uniform repugnance as the men recall their reaction to the first massacre, Goldhagen includes one policeman's memory of his colleagues laughing at his uniform, which had become spattered with the remains of a victim (p. 219). As we shall see, since much of the burden of demonstrating whether battalion members fulfilled their genocidal duties with reluctance or zeal hangs on the meaning and significance ascribed to such statements, the particular compendium of statements upon which their narratives rely is of tremendous interpretative consequence.[24] But more often than not, discrepancies in their accounts of the massacres arise from the different meanings they confer on statements offered by the same individuals.

A striking example of this comes from the testimony of a policeman who recalled that on the night before the massacre at Józefów, Poland in July 1942, whips were handed out to his unit, leading men to surmise that a *Judenaktion* was to take place the next day. Browning reports this statement, but notes that it found no corroboration from other battalion members (p. 56). Goldhagen seizes upon the same statement and the *lack* of corroborating testimony as indicative of its likely factual status. Goldhagen argues that because the 'bearing and use of whips is precisely the sort of detail that the members of the battalion would be biased against presenting', the reseacher should treat as credible this man's emphatic assertion that he can 'remember clearly' the distribution of 'genuine ox-hide' whips. He also suggests that Browning's dismissal of its significance is conditioned by his belief in the men's initial aversion to violence, whereas 'the image of men going to round up women and children armed with ox-hide whips is one that is hard to square with the claim that they were acting reluctantly or unwillingly'. Finally, Goldhagen points out that whips are manifestly in evidence in photographs that were taken during the round-ups and deportations that followed on the heels of Józefów, and this alone should have alerted Browning to the possibility of their alleged distribution for use in Józefów – 'namely from the beginning of their genocidal operations'.[25]

This dispute over details is important not only because, as we shall see later, such details furnish Goldhagen with images with which to embellish his narration of massacres, but because it highlights the extent to which, even prior to their respective reconstruction of events, each author is engaged in a difficult interpretative exercise regarding the status of the testimony *as memory*. In his introduction to *Ordinary Men*, Browning had acknowledged that, in light of the considerable degree of subjective judgement required in the interpretation of these testimonials, '[o]ther historians looking at the same materials would retell these events in somewhat different ways' (p. xix). But when Goldhagen did precisely this, and ventured a very different exegesis in *Hitler's Willing Executioners*, it was clear from the negative reactions that his account drew that considerably more was at stake than showing, in good postmodernist fashion, the relativist's tolerance toward competing representations of the past.

Narrating Massacres

On the basis of the testimonial material they examined, both Browning and Goldhagen reconstruct several key massacres in which Reserve Police Battalion 101 played a major role. These include: the massacre of 1,500 Jews – mostly women, children, the ailing and the elderly – from the Polish town of Józefów on

July 13, 1942; a second massacre of 1,700 Jews at Łomazy one month later; the deportation of 11,000 Jews from Międzyrzec to Treblinka one week after Łomazy, in the course of which close to a thousand people were shot; and the 'Jew Hunts' that took place throughout autumn 1942 and spring 1943 in pursuit of Jews remaining in the battalion's security zone who were not in transit ghettos.

There is a minimal descriptive consensus on what occurred across this genocidal trajectory, but it is apparent nonetheless that two very different narratives of Reserve Police Battalion 101's participation in this murderous itinerary emerge from *Ordinary Men* and *Hitler's Willing Executioners*. These cannot be examined in detail here; but I would like to draw from their respective accounts of what transpired at Józefów – the men's 'initiation' in face-to-face mass killing – certain salient features that put into stark relief the different manner in which the day's events are told and interpreted.

Again, in prescient fashion, Browning anticipated this possibility when, drawing on events at Józefów to reflect on the problems in writing perpetrator history, he made the observation that:

[e]ven if different historians did agree on a long list of facts or particular events that occurred that day in Józefów, they would produce neither the same narrative nor the same interpretation. They would not structure their retelling of those events in the same ways; they would not find identical meaning and importance in those events.[26]

Browning was responding to Hayden White's axiom that historical narration be treated as a mode of 'emplotment' of events that in themselves possess no necessary coherence or inherent meaning. In agreement with White that specific modes of emplotment support particular interpretative stances, Browning nonetheless insisted that a prior set of questions and 'moral concerns' ultimately provided the impetus and 'set the parameters' for his emplotment of what took place at Józefów on 13 July 1942. These questions revolved primarily around how to interpret the men's reactions to the choice that was presented to them by Major Wilhelm Trapp early on that day. Had another type of question about the day's events been formulated, Browning contended, a very different story would have emerged.[27]

However, precisely because Goldhagen's narrative is driven by the same question concerning the men's state of mind as the events of that day unfolded, a comparison of their respective 'emplotments' of the same horrific events can help to highlight not only the interpretations that divide them, but how these dictate the kinds of historical narratives each author constructs.[28]

The reconstruction of the day's main events at Józefów, based on the testimonies by individual battalion members of which each author has availed himself, yields the following broad chronology: Several days before the operation, Major Wilhelm Trapp received an order to kill all the Jewish residents of Józefów except males of

, working age. The night prior to the action, he related this order to the battalion's officers. One officer declined to participate in the killing and was reassigned the task of transporting the men to a work camp. Although the rest of the men were not officially informed that evening, some had gleaned from their officers' words or behaviour that a major action was to take place the next day. Early on the morning of 13 July 1942, the men were driven from their barracks in Biłgoraj to Józefów. Upon arrival, Trapp assembled the men, explained his order and made an offer that older men[29] could step out if they did not feel up to the task. Some ten to twelve men came forward and were reassigned, despite angry protests from one captain. Instructions for the day's operation were then issued: men of working age were to be separated out and sent to a work camp and the remainder of the inhabitants were to be taken to the market square; anyone resisting arrest or unable to walk was to be shot on the spot. A brutal round-up began as the men evacuated private and public buildings, including a hospital, in the course of which a considerable number of Jews were shot. At the marketplace, the men were separated from their families and taken away. One contingent of battalion members was given instructions on how to shoot the victims with fixed bayonets and was then transported to a forest at the edge of the town. When groups of Jews began to arrive, the men paired off individually with a victim and followed a path into the woods. At a designated point, their victims were made to lie face down and were then shot at close range. The men returned to the arrival point and paired off with another victim. This gruesome method of killing went on all day and into the evening. As the day progressed, other battalion contingents arrived and the killing reached even more grisly proportions as new recruits fired without fixed bayonets. The clothes of the shooters became 'besmirched' with the 'blood, brains and bone splinters' of victims. Throughout the day, a number of men had their requests to be reassigned granted; others evaded their duties. The vast majority continued their mission until all the Józefów Jews were killed. On return to barracks that evening, the men appeared depressed and perturbed by the day's events.

Browning's narration of the harrowing events at Józefów (and other massacres he recounts in *Ordinary Men*) has been likened to a *chronicle* – a discursive form that, by resisting the figuration and stylization endemic to other narrative modes, can offer a more 'literal' account of the inexpiable event, and is therefore less likely to impose external meaning on it.[30]

Thus Browning's account of what happened when the Józefów Jews were transported to the forest's edge begins:

> When the first truckload of thirty-five to forty Jews arrived, an equal number of policemen came forward and, *face to face*, were paired off with their victims. Led by Kammer, the policemen and Jews marched down the forest path. They turned off into the woods at a point indicated by Captain Wohlauf, who busied himself throughout the day selecting

the execution sites. Kammer then ordered the Jews to lie down in a row. The policemen stepped up behind them, placed their bayonets on the backbone above the shoulder blades as earlier instructed, and on Kammer's orders fired in unison (p. 61).

Arguably, only the emphasis given to the descriptive term 'face-to-face' orients the reader's attitude to the scene depicted. Compare this 'spare' narrative style to Goldhagen's introductory passage on the same moment of arrival:

> A squad would approach the group of Jews who had just arrived, from which each member would choose his victim – a man, a woman, or a child. The Jews and Germans would then walk in parallel single file so that each killer moved in step with his victim, until they reached a clearing for the killing where they would position themselves and await the firing order from their squad leader (p. 217).

Whereas in Browning, the agents of the crimes in progress are 'policemen', in Goldhagen they are 'Germans' and 'killers'. In Browning, the men are 'paired off' with their victims; in Goldhagen, this apparently passive form of assignation becomes an active matter of a perpetrator choosing 'his' victim – the latter now further delineated as a Jewish man, woman or child. As policeman and victim march down the forest path in Browning, military connotations give way in Goldhagen to the far more sinister image of a 'killer' keeping exact pace with *his* victim.

If it is one aim of Browning's 'clinical'[31] descriptions of the actual killings in the woods to let these iniquitous events speak for themselves rather than impose authorial meaning on them, Goldhagen's rhetoric is aggressively in keeping with the central thesis of his book – namely, that Germans were willing executioners. And while this rhetorical mode may be no less controversial than the claim it embodies, there is no doubt that it effectively evokes aspects of anti-Semitic ideology to which perpetrator testimonies contained in both texts give explicit expression. Consider this most harrowing verbatim testimonial, cited by both Browning and Goldhagen, of one *August Zorn,[32] who recalls dragging an elderly Jew to the execution site whereupon

> . . . *my Jew* threw himself on the ground and remained lying there. I then cocked my carbine and shot him through the back of the head. Because I was already very upset from the cruel treatment of the Jews during the clearing of the town and was completely in turmoil, I shot too high. The entire back of the skull of *my Jew* was torn off and the brain exposed [my emphasis] (*Ordinary Men*, pp. 66–7; *Hitler's Willing Executioners*, p. 540, n. 61)

As this example shows, Goldhagen's adoption of the first-person possessive form for his narrative articulates the proprietorial manner in which this perpetrator regarded the elderly Jewish man whom he allegedly found it so difficult to dispatch.

Historians may prefer Browning's manner of recounting because of what Bartov describes as his 'conscious detachment and intentional separation between victims and perpetrators',[33] but because Goldhagen's rhetorical artifice is so transparent, it at least has the virtue of offering the reader immediate access to the interpretative stance that subtends it.

Even more controversial than his rhetorical style, however, are Goldhagen's repeated narrative digressions wherein he purports to explore the psychology of perpetrators in the very throes of their murderous conduct. The most notorious example of these follows directly on from the above-cited passage, which has the 'German' and Jew keeping step down the forest path:

> The walk into the woods afforded each perpetrator an opportunity for reflection. Walking side by side with his victim, he was able to imbue the human form beside him with the projections of his mind. Some of the Germans, of course, had children walking beside them. It is highly likely that, back in Germany, these men had previously walked through woods with their own children by their sides, marching gaily and inquisitively along. With what thoughts and emotions did each of these men march, gazing sidelong at the form of, say, an eight- or twelve-year-old girl, who to the unideologized mind would have looked like any other girl? In these moments, each killer had a personalized, face-to-face relationship to his victim, to his little girl. Did he see a little girl, and ask himself why he was about to kill this little, delicate human being who, if seen as a little girl by him, would normally have received his compassion, protection, and nurturance? Or did he see a Jew, a young one, but a Jew nonetheless? Did he wonder incredulously what could possibly justify his blowing a vulnerable little girl's brains out? Or did he understand the reasonableness of the order, the necessity of nipping the believed-in Jewish blight in the bud? The "Jew-child," after all, was mother to the Jew.
>
> The killing itself was a gruesome affair. After the walk through the woods, each of the Germans had to raise his gun to the back of the head, now face down on the ground, that had bobbed along beside him, pull the trigger, and watch the person, sometimes a little girl, twitch and then move no more . . . (p. 218).

How should we evaluate this notorious extract and others like it that have been the object of much critical scorn but little analytic commentary?[34] Is Goldhagen's transgression the fact that he offers a full-blown *mise-en-scène* of 'face-to-face' slaughter that he endows with both visual and auditory dimensions? In the case of the walk in the woods at Józefów, he invites the reader to *hear* the lighthearted gait of a father and daughter on a forest romp, and to compare it with the unison marching of the perpetrator and his victim toward the killing sites, to *visualize* the compassionate glance of a father at his little girl and compare it to the hate-filled gaze of an anti-Semite at a 'Jew-child'. Finally he confronts us with his most disturbing 'sensurround' image of all: the exploding skull of a young female victim. Indeed, Goldhagen's rhetorical strategy in this passage, which begins by invoking a generalized image of the Józefów victim but ends with the specific image of a prostrate little Jewish girl etched in our minds is reminiscent of the ghetto round-up scene in *Schindler's List*, where the uniquely colourized image of the little girl in the red coat ensures the spectator's attention is focused on this one victim to the virtual exclusion of all around her. And if Goldhagen's image, like Spielberg's before it, could be criticized for establishing a hierarchy of victims in the reader's mind, it could equally be defended for reminding us that Holocaust victims, though counted in millions, were all individuated beings whose specific fate deserves commemoration. However, Spielberg is careful to elide the moment of the little girl's death – we merely see from a distance the red coat in a mound of bodies being carted away – whereas Goldhagen insists upon conjuring a close-up perspective of the exact manner of her execution as well. Why and to what effect?

In an otherwise critical commentary on *Hitler's Willing Executioners*, Omer Bartov concurs that this kind of narration may not deserve historiographical respect, but nonetheless concedes Goldhagen's

> is the only such study that demands and elicits direct and immediate empathy for the victims, by means of its rhetoric, through its obsession and fascination with horror and the resulting kitsch that fills its pages, and by dint of the author's voyeuristic fantasies of the victims' suffering and the perpetrators' pleasure at causing and observing them . . .[35]

But can we be as sure as Bartov that the effect of Goldhagen's macabre dramaturgy is to arouse in us unequivocal empathy for the victim? In a scathing review in *Les Temps Modernes*, Liliane Kandel argued very differently, claiming that the very features of Goldhagen's 'theatre of cruelty' that Bartov credits with producing empathy with the victims instead permit a vicarious identification with the perpetrator's perverse pleasures. The book's 'true obscenity', in Kandel's view, is that its mode of narration *authorizes* each reader to put him/herself in the exact position of the executioner – his words, thoughts, deeds and even his 'eye riveted to the rifle's sights' – and yet to 'virtuously deny' that any such identification has taken place.[36]

Faced with the dilemma of arbitrating between these two contrasting views of the identificatory position the reader is induced to adopt within these execution scenes, it might be more useful to shift the debate away from whether the reader experiences either '*exultant revulsion* or *infinite pity* for those whose fate is displayed',[37] to consider instead whether these ambivalences produce a 'crisis of identification' *in* the reader because it has implicated us in what Gillian Rose describes as an 'emotional economy which we cannot project and disown'.[38] Here it is useful once again to refer to another example from *Schindler's List*: the notorious shower scene at Auschwitz-Birkenau. This scene was controversial because it raised the spectre of representing an event – the inside of a gas chamber – that should render any attempt at depiction both impossible and obscene. In this respect, one critic has argued that the horror aroused in the audience by this scene has less to do with the events themselves, than with 'the thought that absolutely nothing is going to be left unshown in this film'.[39] But another critic has posed the question of whether in this scene these two kinds of horror are in fact in competition with each other:

> What if feeling horrified by the 'actual events' does not compete with the thought that 'nothing is going to be left unshown', but, instead, is augmented by it? For a related thought may be: even if it is obscene to show too much, it is *only by showing too much* that the film can show the actual events – events which, being much too obscene, are otherwise impossible to represent. According to this line of thought, the film's obscenity is justified because the film brings to these events their actuality for the audience. It offers the audience a fantasy of being able to 'bear witness' to the actual events, at the cost of being horrified – and this being horrified becomes a measure of the film's authenticity.[40]

It seems to me that this describes very precisely the circular logic that informs Goldhagen's mode of narration: on the one hand, there is the presumption that his lurid depictions of massacres are legitimate because they stand in mimetic relation to the obscene events they reference; on the other hand, if these close-up reconstructions arouse dismay and horror in the reader they will have confirmed their representational proximity to the historical reality they are attempting to document. But what if a mass public, and especially young readers, have found Goldhagen's accounts of face-to-face killing readable and credible – but not all that horrifying – precisely because they conform to the idioms of violence in the public domain with which they are already very familiar? Thanks to the 'invasive technological gaze' of contemporary news reporting, the public is now on visually intimate terms with scenes of genocide, including those whose victims include children.[41] And while Hollywood's codes of taste may stop short of representing the slaughtered child, readers of Goldhagen would recognize in his manner of representing scenes like Józefów – close-up images and sounds, the 'psychologization' of the criminal's actions, the unflinching gaze at skulls shattered by the impact of close-range executions – the very conventions that are now common if not dominant in popular culture forms. As Omer Bartov argued with respect to *Schindler's List*,

> the problem of audience familiarity with graphic violence means [. . .] that there exists an inherent tension between exposure to the sheer brutality of the event and its trivialization, between complete ignorance of its course and scope and the dangers of partial or distorted knowledge, between a total distancing which breeds indifference and false objectivity, and a false familiarity which breeds an erroneous sense of understanding,

between the abhorrence evoked by human degradation and suffering, and a perverse, pornographic curiosity about the limits of human depravity . . .[42]

In his presumption that the idioms of violence he deploys will produce *only* a horrified reaction, Goldhagen disavows the 'inherent tension' to which Bartov refers and shortcircuits the reader's confrontation with the ambivalent emotional economy that his 'historical simulacrum'[43] arouses.

By now we have broached the matter of whether Goldhagen's mode of narration ultimately – notwithstanding his indisputable desire to 'bear witness' to the Józefów victims and the horrific manner of their deaths – breaches the ethical 'limits of representation' of the Holocaust. Goldhagen himself compellingly argues throughout *Hitler's Willing Executioners* that the genocidal intention of eliminationist anti-Semitism strove to ensure that there would be 'no true witnesses' to the implementation of the Final Solution. Would it therefore not be more in keeping with this fundamental truth of the Holocaust to resist the temptation to give the scenes of Józefów and other massacres this embellished representational form and instead to seek ways to represent the testimonial absence that is at their very core?[44] Browning's 'clinical' reconstruction, which for the most part limits itself to relating what the perpetrators claimed to witness, at least does not try to fill in this testimonial gap. Goldhagen's narrative digressions, by contrast, by putting the reader into the massacre scene, offer a 'fantasy of witnessing' what took place in the woods of Józefów – a position to which neither he nor his readers are morally entitled.[45]

Finally, if historians would point out that, whatever ethical issues are raised by Goldhagen's chosen mode of historical narration, the fundamental flaw is that he resorts to acts of psychological projection that have no place in historiographical discourse, then Browning should not escape this criticism either. For although Browning's descriptive language and speculative imagination are restrained by comparison with Goldhagen's, by his own admission Browning's ambitions for his historical narration exceed the mere chronicling of the actions in which Reserve Police Battalion 101 took part. Although we are encouraged to read the narrative trajectory of genocide as unfolding *in tandem* with the men's increasingly dehumanized responses, it is only by embracing a psychological dimension that Browning can convince the reader of this connection. In Browning's narrative of the Józefów massacre, although we remain external observers to the scenes depicted we are given an 'insider's' point-of-view on their alleged psychological consequences. In this respect, Browning leaves the terrain of the chronicle and embraces the conventions of more traditional narration. As Hayden White has observed in another context, this transition from chronicle to narration is marked by a discursive shift, which 'at once personalizes (humanizes) and generalizes the agents and agencies involved in those events. Such figuration personalizes by transforming those agents into the kind of intending, feeling, and thinking subjects with whom the reader can identify and empathize, in the way one does with characters in fictional stories.'[46] In Browning, this transition occurs almost imperceptibly in a passage where he recounts the men's return to barracks at the end of their day of killing at Józefów:

> When the men arrived at the barracks in Biłgoraj, they were depressed, angered, embittered, and shaken. They ate little but drank heavily. Generous quantities of alcohol were provided, and many of the policemen got quite drunk. Major Trapp made the rounds, trying to console and reassure them, and again placing the responsibility on higher authorities. But neither the drink nor Trapp's consolation could wash away the sense of shame and horror that pervaded the barracks. Trapp asked the men not to talk about it, but they needed no encouragement in that direction. Those who had not been in the forest did not want to learn more. Those who had been there likewise had no desire to speak, either then or later. By silent consensus within Reserve Police Battalion 101, the Józefów massacre was simply not discussed. 'The entire matter was a taboo.' But repression during waking hours could not stop the nightmares. During the first night back from Józefów, one policeman awoke firing his gun into the ceiling of the barracks (p. 69).

It is clear from the footnotes accompanying this passage that this version of events has been reconstructed from testimonies in which the men of Reserve Police Battalion 101 recall their alleged remorse about what transpired at Józefów. But the issue here is not the trustworthiness of their exonerating claims, but the fact that Browning's attribution of 'shame' to these men, a condition of psychological interiority, is entirely a function of an omniscient narration into which is woven a confident depiction of the perpetrators' psychology with its attendant emotions, capacity for volition, and unconscious psychic mechanisms.[47] This emplotment is perfectly consistent with Browning's contention that at the time of the Józefów massacre, these reserve policemen were not already the 'willing executioners' of Goldhagen's title, but sentient beings capable of a range of humanly-recognizable responses and therefore deserving of the historian's empathetic understanding – if not forgiveness.[48] And it will be the aim of his subsequent account and explanation of events to establish the reasons for the men's descent from this state into one of indifference toward their own brutality and barbarism. But it is important to see how this interpretative conviction authorizes a speculative entry into the men's post-massacre state of mind – an act of psychological projection that Browning integrates seamlessly into his emplotment of events. It is true that Browning limits such speculation to the men's thoughts and emotions *after* they have committed their murderous deeds, while Goldhagen shows no hesitation in sketching the interior monologue that he believes the perpetrators were most likely to have conducted *during* the killing process. And while I have argued that in Goldhagen's case purporting to transcribe their innermost thoughts fosters the presumption of witnessing their deeds, it is arguably at least as problematic on Browning's part to *ascribe* contrition to men who have just committed the most heinous crimes against humanity.[49]

Goldhagen, equally convinced that the men arrived in Józefów as already dedicated anti-Semites, constructs a narration, couched in speculative psychological rhetoric, that merely confirms this profile. Though he purports at the outset the need to delve into the perpetrators' 'phenomenological reality' in the hopes that ' imagining ourselves in their places, performing their deeds, acting as they did, viewing what they beheld' (p. 21) will divulge the obsessions which drove them, this 'difficult enterprise' he sets himself in fact functions as a narrative ruse for a succession of scenes entirely of his own devising.

Mementoes of Genocide

However, there is another dimension to Goldhagen's aspiration to give full representational dimension to the events in which Reserve Police Battalion 101 was involved that is deserving of more critical attention than it has received thus far.

In the late 1980s, a book was published in Germany entitled *'Those Were the Days' (Schöne Zeiten)*.[50] The title refers to a caption in the photographic album of Treblinka commandant Kurt Franz, below which appears several photographs of the camp itself. The book charts the unfolding of the Final Solution as recorded in the photographic and written records kept at the time by German witnesses to it – in their role as either perpetrators or bystanders. There are several reports written by reserve policemen,[51] but the majority are by regular soldiers, members of the Einsatzgruppen, SS officers or civilian functionaries on military assignment. In his introduction to the English edition, Hugh Trevor-Roper (Lord Dacre of Glanton) contends that such records, and especially photographs, were strictly forbidden at the time because the SS considered their very existence jeopardized 'the security of the Reich'. However, despite this prohibition, and the risk of prosecution, photographs continued to be taken and, in Lord Dacre's view, now possess an indisputable evidential status. In this book, they are captioned with simple descriptions and juxtaposed with verbally-transcribed or written records deriving from a number of sources: post-war interrogations, official documents and private diaries and letters. As Dominick LaCapra has aptly pointed out; this visual and textual material is particularly disturbing 'for the way its documents mingle extreme cruelty with kitsch sentiment [. . .] and for the elated, carnivalesque atmosphere that often surrounds the killing of Jews, for both perpetrators and bystanders'.[52]

It is instructive to compare this text and the meanings that LaCapra draws from its photographic material with Browning's and Goldhagen's treatments of the photographs pertaining to the activities of Reserve Police Battalion 101 that each of their books include.

Ordinary Men includes a small number of photos from two 'actions' in which Reserve Police Battalion 101 was engaged: the liquidations of the Łuków ghetto in late 1942, and of the Międzyrzec transit ghetto between August 1942 and July 1943. In the first Łuków photo, which also adorns the cover of the 1992 paperback edition, a group of Jewish men are assembled in the background, many elderly and many with their hands raised in the air. In the foreground, kneeling, are two elderly men in prayer shawls, also with their hands raised. Framing them are several policemen who pose for the camera, two of them grinning (Figure 1). The second Łuków photo shows one of these older men still kneeling, now without his hat; several policemen stand immediately behind him, one continuing to look at the camera (Figure 2). The second set of photos from Międzyrzec show the Order Police guarding or marching the town's Jews prior to their deportation. A set of four photos from Międzyrzec show battalion members assembled in front of the ghetto's 'undressing barracks' followed by images of Jewish residents being subjected to strip searches. One caption relates that while in other deportations Jews were instructed to take a few belongings with them on the pretext that they were being resettled, these strip searches signified to both policemen and Jews alike that this pretence was no longer being maintained. In Browning's text, these photos, disturbing as they are, appear as supplemental information to his account of the clearing actions that the Order Police organized in 1942–3.

Both Browning and Goldhagen concur that these round-ups were particularly ferocious, but for fundamentally different reasons. In Browning's narration, which, as we've seen, aligns the trajectory of the battalion's genocidal mission with the men's progressive dehumanization, Międzyrzec stands out because even though the men were by now 'increasingly numbed and callous participants' in their genocidal tasks, the vivid recollections of the testimonies suggest that its particular brutality, partly driven by a shortage of manpower available to conduct the round-up, left 'a singular imprint' on the men's memories (p. 95).[53] For Goldhagen, the brutality demonstrated at Międzyrzec had its impetus not in a practical circumstance, nor even in the perpetrators' determination to implement their duties efficiently and callously, but in the desire to ensure that in the course of that implementation the victims would experience the full force of the perpetrators' power over, and contempt for, them. Goldhagen integrates his interpretation of the photographs the book includes *into* his narration, and what lends his account considerable force are the rituals of humiliation that he explicitly foregrounds and that he argues constitute the psychological bedrock of what transpired during the Łuków and Międzyrzec round-ups.

In the light of the prohibition that seemingly surrounded the taking and circulation of photographs of Jewish persecution, it is extremely interesting to note that, in his section on Police Battalions, Goldhagen not only includes more photographs in which Reserve Battalion 101 feature than appear in *Ordinary Men*, but draws on a

Figure 1

Figure 2

testimonial by a battalion member, not referred to by Browning, that recalls their very public display and circulation. Goldhagen contends that these photographs should not be seen merely as the company's records of events, but as 'keepsakes' of the men's tour of duty in Poland – virtual memorial trophies and 'not private mementos, furtively taken, guarded, and husbanded by individuals' (p. 246). Indeed, he cites a battalion member who recalls that anyone could order copies of the photographs on display, whether or not he had participated in the events depicted.

That photographs had this memorial as well as documentary status is not Goldhagen's original insight. Indeed, just before his book had reached the German bookstalls, a controversy had been ignited by a photographic exhibition entitled the 'Crimes of the Wehrmacht' (*Vernichtungskrieg: Verbrechen der Wehrmacht 1941 bis 1944*) that began touring Germany in 1995. Part of the controversy stemmed from the fact that the photographs offered, especially to those Germans still in denial of this fact, irrefutable proof of Wehrmacht participation in the massacres, hangings and tortures of Jewish men, women and children. However, there was another 'scandal' that the exhibition invited the public to contemplate – namely, that the majority of these photographs had been taken by Wehrmacht soldiers themselves out of an evident desire to record for posterity and even in some cases for their own family albums the historic deeds they were enacting.[54] Goldhagen insists that we should treat the photographs taken by Reserve Police Battalion 101 also as a distinct kind of evidence both of the events they record and of the mentality their existence betrays. On the one hand, he maintains that these photographs were indicative of the men's desire to 'adorn their photo albums with images from their genocidal operations'; on the other hand, he alleges that they show these men not as unwilling or disapproving agents of the actions in which they are engaged (*pace* Browning), but as unperturbed and, in many instances, 'in poses of pride and joy as they undertake their dealings with their Jewish victims' (p. 247).

Thus Goldhagen's reading of the same two photos of the elderly Jewish men of Łuków is not only more extensive than Browning's, but offers a significantly different interpretative inflection. Rather than treating these photographs as documentation of a moment in the ghetto's liquidation caught by the unit's photographer, Goldhagen proposes that we see this event as *staged for* the camera's eye. The photograph is taken, Goldhagen's caption tells us, in order to serve as a boastful reminder – a 'photographic memento' – of the humiliation suffered by these elderly Jews before being sent to their deaths. What supports this reading, according to Goldhagen, is the absence of the man's hat in the second photo, 'presumably knocked off' by an act of aggressive mockery that took place between the two shots (p. 259).

Photographs that accompany Goldhagen's account of the massacre at Łomazy on 17 August 1942, following Józefów by a matter of weeks, also lend themselves to similar interpretative purposes. On that day, the men of Reserve Police Battalion 101 were ordered to clear the Jewish quarter at Łomazy and assemble the Jews in a school sports field. A group of young Jewish men were issued with shovels and spades and driven to the woods, where they were ordered to dig a mass grave. The remainder of Łomazy's Jews waited for hours on the pitch. When groups were finally transported from the town to the killing site, they were told to undress and to lie face down. They were then chased to the mass grave, where they were shot by Trawnikis[55] expressly recruited by the battalion's officers for these purposes, allegedly to spare the men of Reserve Police Battalion 101 from a repetition of the Józefów carnage and its demoralizing effects. Even prior to the shooting, and under orders from a battalion officer, a number of elderly Jewish men were forced by an officer to undress and crawl on the ground in front of the gravesite, before being viciously beaten.[56]

Despite their conflicting interpretations of what the Łomazy massacre represented in the men's psychological itinerary and their habituation to killing,[57] both Browning and Goldhagen emphasize the component of humiliation integral to this most horrific of massacres.[58] However, in addition, Goldhagen's account refers to four photographs taken at difference stages of the Łomazy massacre from which he draws the conclusion that we should see the rituals of humiliation to which the Łomazy Jews were subjected not as aberrant exploits condoned by a single officer, but on a continuum with a cruelty toward Jewish victims that had become the norm for the ordinary battalion member.[59] In the first photograph, an Order Policemen stands in front of the second row of assembled Jews on the sports field, holding a folded whip. This is a pose, suggests Goldhagen, that betrays the policeman's eager compliance with the photographer's mission of recording the day's events for posterity: 'That he stood momentarily with his back to the Jews under his guard, squarely facing the photographer, suggests that he was proud of his actions, wanting not to conceal the image of him participating in a genocidal operation, but to preserve it for posterity' (pp. 224–25). Like the photograph of the Łuków Jews, Goldhagen's treats this image not as a discrete documentary moment but as a freeze-frame from a filmic scenario that needs a 'before' and an 'after' in order to be meaningfully reconstituted. Or, to put it another way, Goldhagen reconstructs his interpretation of these photographs not only from what they contain but from the acts that he alleges they elide: a policeman's *cuff* of an elderly Jew who crouches before him in terror, a policeman's *turn toward* the camera to preen in front of his captured quarry.

It could be argued that Goldhagen takes too much interpretative license with images into which we can read nothing more than the fact of their own, 'having-been-there' quality. But if a photograph depicts both 'a scene *and the gaze of the spectator*',[60] a dynamic space of interaction, then it seems important to attempt to describe not only the scene in the frame but other dimensions that surround its existence. Another two shots from different angles and camera distances show the Łomazy Jews waiting on the sports field. In the fourth photo, Jewish men up to their knees in water are shown digging their own grave. An inscription on the back reads: 'Jews constructing a mass grave/Lomartczy 18 August 1942/1600' (p. 226). The number, Goldhagen informs us, refers to the photographer's tally of Jews killed that day. To be sure, we don't know who the photographer was nor why exactly he took the photos, but it is unlikely, as Goldhagen suggests, that they were taken to create a photographic record that would incriminate himself and his colleagues. (As Goldhagen points out, there were not even handed over by the photographer with this exonerating explanation.)[61] If, then, we can accept Goldhagen's proposition that these photographs stem at the very least from the photographer's desire to declare his presence at the grisly events that unfolded before him, to affirm his bird's-eye view of a mass grave being dug by Jewish victims, then do not these, as well as photographs that show perpetrators as willing objects of the camera's gaze, tell us *something* about the individual psyches habituated to scenes whose murderous outcome was not in doubt?

It is this 'something' in the perpetrator psyche that perhaps ultimately confounds the explanatory paradigms of both Browning and Goldhagen. Browning's account of the men's habituation to violence does not pay particular attention to the question of why, for example, after the strip search at the 'undressing barracks', the men of Reserve Police Battalion 101 only allowed the victims to put their underclothes back on before boarding the deportation trains (as his caption to the photograph tells us), or why these photographers even decided it necessary to take pictures, especially of female victims, in this state of undress. Goldhagen has an answer to such questions: that integral to the eliminationist anti-Semitism displayed by the 'Ordinary Germans' of Reserve Police Battalion 101 was the desire to inflict prior humiliation on the victims they would then proceed to slaughter without remorse. But photographs in *'Those Were the Days'* show scenes of mass murder carried out by Lithuanian civilians that are as distressing as anything found in *Hitler's Willing Executioners*. The report of a German soldier who photographed one such scene in Kovno described 'unbelievable' scenes of a Lithuanian executioner standing on the corpses of the Jewish victims he had clubbed to death and playing the national anthem to the singing and clapping of the crowd.[62] Could Goldhagen draw a meaningful distinction on *national* grounds between the hateful passions that clearly fuelled this carnivalesque 'theatre of cruelty' and those he so powerfully conjures from the photographs in his text?

In his own attempt to explain some psychological dimensions of perpetrator behaviour, Saul Friedländer has appealed to an 'independent psychological residue' that embraced radical anti-Semitism but whose full psychic dimensions were not exhausted by it. Friedländer draws on a 1943 speech by Himmler to a Posen audience of fellow elite Nazis to suggest that a 'core motivation' of perpetrator psychology may be attributed to the element of *Rausch* or 'elation', the kind of hallucinatory rapture that was induced by knowing that with the ever-greater masses of Jews killed, perpetrators were fulfilling the Führer's will and thereby consolidating their own *Führer-Bindung* ('Führer-Bonding').[63] But Friedländer also cautions against assuming that in the face of an 'amorality beyond all categories of evil', such psychology will ever be truly knowable, and for this reason the historian may have to bow to an 'unease' that stems 'from the noncongruence between intellectual probing and the blocking of intuitive comprehension'.[64] In the photographs of the men of Reserve Police Battalion 101 engaged in their genocidal mission, Goldhagen claims to have glimpsed something akin to this element of *Rausch* or 'elation' within perpetrator psychology to which Friedländer refers, although in contrast to the incomprehension that Friedländer ultimately concedes, Goldhagen is confident that he *can* fully explain these demonic psychical forces with reference to the ideology of eliminationist anti-Semitism specifically embedded in the German mind-set.

Conclusion

Reflecting upon Goldhagen's success with the mass public in Germany, Dan Diner commented that '. . . the reading public took the historian's [*sic*] representation of the Holocaust to be what it unmistakably was, as defined by its narrative framework: a veritable writ of accusation, necessarily coming from the *outside* and presented to the Germans from the victim's perspective'.[65] Indeed, Diner recasts the intentional/functionalist controversy as a conflict between two 'judicially shaped structures of narration with opposing orientations'. On one side of his hypothetical courtroom are the functionalists, entering the plea of culpability for crimes committed by the Nazi state and its institutional representatives with reference to the 'principle of negligence' – a kind of 'guiltless guilt' according to Diner; on the other side are intentionalists who insist that the same mass crimes were 'an expression of culpable action'. Widening this perspective beyond the confines of scholarly discourse, Diner suggests that memories of the Holocaust embraced by specific communities also assume the form of juridically-shaped narratives by virtue of the questions they ask and the approach to historical representation their questions dictate: 'The "German" Holocaust memory thus tends to foreground the *circumstances* leading to the crime; the "Jewish" memory is concerned with the *motives* that informed it. Likewise, researchers who lack any direct or indirect affiliation to the collectives involved with the crime tend to *universalize* its meaning.'[66] Though Diner doesn't explicitly declare himself a Goldhagen fan, I read his typology and the critique of 'genocide studies' that follows as a limited endorsement of Goldhagen's attempt to redirect historical attention to the question of the 'why' vs the 'how' of the Final Solution. For his part, Diner contends that a further elaboration of the 'why' question would have to include consideration of the Nazi determination to exterminate the Jews as an ethnic community *constituted by a common memory*. 'In the case of genocide', argues Diner, 'what is truly at stake is not simply the number of victims, but the attempted or actual extermination of a *"mnemonic entity"*. The objects of genocidal extermination are not simply members of an ethnic entity, but of an entity that is both bearer and subject of a historical – hence specifically collective – memory.'[67]

Goldhagen might well decline Diner's qualified defence on the grounds that neither has he issued a 'writ of accusation' nor is his text primarily concerned with historical memory or representation. As we've seen, Goldhagen tends to see his contribution as an explanatory transcription of certain events of the Holocaust and as an equally transparent exposé of the 'phenomenological reality' of its perpetrators. But however Goldhagen would characterize his achievement or his critics berate it, I have argued that *Hitler's Willing Executioners* has now firmly secured its place within the 'history of the memory of genocide' precisely because of a representational strategy that encourages readers to claim this accusatory voice as their own.

Notes

1. This is Philippe Burrin's description in his very critical review of Goldhagen, 'Il n'y a pas de peuple assassin!' in *L'Histoire* no. 206, January 1997.
2. The term is A. D. Moses's in his cogent article 'Structure and Agency in the Holocaust: Daniel J. Goldhagen and his Critics', *History and Theory*, vol. 37, no. 2, 1998.
3. See the German references cited by Moses, ibid., Josef Joffe, 'Goldhagen in Germany', *New York Review of Books*, 28 November 1996, and the chapters by Geldbach, Gerlach, Jäckel and Mommsen in Franklin H. Littell (ed.), *Hyping the Holocaust: Scholars Answer Goldhagen* (Merion Station, PA: Merion Westfield Press International, 1997) for a sampling of German reaction and *Les Temps Modernes*, no. 592, Feb.–Mar. 1997, for a sampling of French responses.
4. Omer Bartov, 'German Soldiers and the Holocaust', *History and Memory*, vol. 9, nos. 1/2, Fall 1994.
5. See Littell (ed.), *Hyping the Holocaust: Scholars Answer Goldhagen*; R. R. Shandley (ed.), *Unwilling Germans?: The Goldhagen Debate* (Minneapolis: University of Minnesota Press, 1998); and *Le Débat*, no. 93, Jan.–Feb. 1997.
6. Daniel J. Goldhagen, *Hitler's Willing Executioners: Ordinary Germans and*

the Holocaust (New York: Knopf, 1996), p. 14. See in particular his 'Introduction' and 'Part 1: Understanding German Antisemitism: The Eliminationist Mind-Set'. References to this book appear in parentheses in the text.

7. I draw this term from François Bédarida, 'Le peuple allemand, l'antisémitisme et le génocide', *L'Esprit*, nos. 3–4, Mar.–Apr. 1997. Almost every reviewer refers to the intentionalist/functionalist debate in their comments on Goldhagen, and a very lucid and full discussion of these opposing historiographical approaches can be found in A. D. Moses, 'Structure and Agency in the Holocaust'.

8. Goldhagen writes: 'All these "solutions" are but variations, enormously different as they may be, on the eliminationist mind-set. From the antisemites' perspective, though not from that of the Jews, these "solutions" were, with their remaining differences, rough functional equivalents. They emanated from the common belief that German society must be de-Jewified, made *judenrein*, one way or another. The eliminationist mind-set was the logical and actual product of this belief' (p. 70). Of the many critiques of Goldhagen's characterization of German anti-Semitism, two stand out: in his scathing review 'The Goldhagen Phenomenon', *Critical Inquiry*, no. 23, Summer 1997 (first published in *Les Temps Modernes*, 592), Raul Hilberg pointed out that at the turn of the century 'German anti-Semitism . . . was not only weaker than the eastern European variety, but by 1914 it began to decline.' Yehuda Bauer also addressed this issue at length, disputing the eliminationist character of liberal assimilationism and other German anti-Semitic platforms. However, Bauer does insist that Goldhagen is right in saying that 'by 1940–41 the general German society had become a reservoir for willing executioners . . .' and credits Goldhagen with at least redirecting scholarly attention to this issue. See 'Goldhagen's View of the Holocaust' in *Hyping the Holocaust*. In 'Le peuple allemand', Bédarida claims that France at the time of the Dreyfus affair was more intensely and pervasively anti-Semitic than Germany. Readers are referred to Chapter 7 for an account of the radical anti-Semitism of the late nineteenth-century French *colon*, which undoubtedly had an eliminationist component.

9. This is the main force of Hilberg's critique in 'The Goldhagen Phenomenon'. See also Christopher Browning's review, 'Daniel Goldhagen's Willing Executioners' in *History and Memory*, vol. 8, no. 1, Spring/Summer 1996. As we shall shortly see, Browning, author of a seminal study of a Hamburg reserve police battalion engaged in a genocidal mission in Poland, does not share Goldhagen's view of the role played by a specifically German anti-Semitism, and uses the example of the Luxembourg contingent within this battalion as a 'controlled experiment' in how men of different cultural and national backgrounds reacted to the 'same situational factors'.

10. Again see Hilberg, 'The Goldhagen Phenomenon', who accuses Goldhagen of shrinking the Holocaust, 'replacing its intricate apparatus with rifles, whips,

and fists' (p. 727). In 'La Lettre volée de Daniel J. Goldhagen', Liliane Kandel claims that by relegating the gas chambers to the margins, Goldhagen plays into the hands of the negationists who deny their very existence. In 'Notes Ante et Anti Eliminationnistes', Claude Lanzmann contends that by not giving primacy to the gas chambers, Goldhagen 'exonerates' the perpetrators by turning them into a common kind of killer and negates the Holocaust's uniqueness: 'Massacre à grande échelle, mais massacre, donc précédent. L'humanité à l'habitude des Saint-Barthélemy' (p. 12). All three broadsides are in the special issue of *Les Temps Modernes* devoted to the controversy. Jean-Charles Szurek defends Goldhagen's emphasis on killings 'under the open sky', pointing out not only the frequency with which Goldhagen refers to gas chambers and crematoria, but the fact that his detailed account of round-ups in places like Łuków in Poland make clear that the Jews there were destined for Treblinka. See Jean-Charles Szurek, 'Goldhagen, Vrais et Faux Enjeux', *Les Temps Modernes*, no. 592, Nov.–Dec. 1997. Hilberg estimates that 1,300,000 Jews died by shootings.

11. Lanzmann, 'Notes Ante et Anti Eliminationnistes', pp. 13–14.
12. Bédarida, 'Le peuple allemand'. My translation.
13. Hilberg is a typical exponent of this position, referring to its 'appeal to a large number of book buyers, who cannot do research but who have wanted an explanatory statement for a long time, one that appears to be sufficient, and for that reason satisfying as well'. See 'The Goldhagen Phenomenon', p. 726. The functionalist historian Hanns Mommsen criticizes Goldhagen for indulging in a voyeuristic portrayal of sadism and brutality compared to which, in Mommsen's view, '"Schindler's List" gives an impressive look into the multiple brokenness of the psychological-ideological concept of most of the executioners.' See his 'Conditions for Carrying Out the Holocaust', in *Hyping the Holocaust*, p.42. Mommsen is famous for his 'cumulative radicalization' thesis: namely, that the Final Solution was not the consequence of a single order by Hitler, but imposed itself cumulatively in measures initiated by local SS authorities and in response to a chain of spectacular failures that the German war effort suffered.
14. Omer Bartov, 'German Soldiers and the Holocaust', p. 180.
15. Christopher R. Browning, *Ordinary Men: Reserve Police Battalion 101 and the Final Solution in Poland* (New York: HarperPerennial, 1993). References to this book appear in parentheses in the text.
16. Yehuda Bauer is a case in point: his assessment of the strengths and weaknesses of Goldhagen's book is very measured, but on the issue of any comparison with Browning, he confines his remarks to pointing out that Goldhagen's examples are 'repetitions of what Browning has already shown in *Ordinary Men*'. See 'Goldhagen's View of the Holocaust'.

17. These are located in the town of Ludwigsburg in the Central Agency for the State Administrations of Justice (*Zentrale Stelle der Landesjustizverwaltungen*). See Browning, *Ordinary Men*, p. xvi, Goldhagen, *Hitler's Willing Executioners*, pp. 525–6, n. 13.

18. A key component of Browning's analysis is his use of the Milgram findings, based on experiments conducted by an American psychologist, Stanley Milgram, in the 1970s. Subjects were instructed to administer an escalating series of fake electric shocks to 'victims' whose responses to the alleged pain were registered in programmed voice feedbacks. Milgram was interested in the conditions under which individuals would resist or comply with instructions. Following different variations on the experiments, he concluded that individuals would comply most readily with non-coercive authority because of a socialization process that promoted a tendency toward conformity and need for peer approval. The Milgram experiment is discussed at length in Browning's final chapter and related to the circumstances of the men of Reserve Police Battalion 101, especially in the first stages of their killing activity in Poland. See also Zygmunt Bauman, 'The Ethics of Obedience (Reading Milgram)' in *Modernity and the Holocaust* (Cambridge: Cambridge University Press, 1989).

19. In 'Il n'y a pas de peuple assassin!', Burrin describes this method of criticism as 'obsessive guerilla warfare'. For a summary statement of Goldhagen's criticisms of Browning, see *Hitler's Willing Executioners*, p. 534, n. 1.

20. See the 'Preface' in *Ordinary Men*, and 'German Memory, Judicial Interrogation, and Historical Reconstruction' in Saul Friedländer (ed.), *Probing the Limits of Representation: Nazism and the "Final Solution"* (London: Harvard University Press, 1992).

21. See Goldhagen's review of *Ordinary Men*, 'The Evil of Banality', *The New Republic*, 13–20 July 1992.

22. Browning's terms in his review, 'Daniel Goldhagen's Willing Executioners'.

23. Ruth Bettina Birn takes Goldhagen to task for the small evidentiary base upon which he draws, though the same criticism would presumably apply to Browning. Birn's is a thorough and harsh methodological critique that has clearly been endorsed by a wide community of historians. While it is essential to be aware of the grounds of this criticism, my chapter hopes to demonstrate that it doesn't invalidate other critical approaches to *Hitler's Willing Executioners*, especially in so far as they illuminate issues concerning representation and narration that often go unexamined by historians. See Birn's 'Revising the Holocaust', *Historical Journal*, vol. 40, 1997, and her book, co-authored with Norman Finkelstein, *A Nation on Trial: The Goldhagen Thesis and Historical Truth* (New York: Henry Holt and Co., 1998).

24. In 'Revising the Holocaust', Ruth Bettina Birn in turn highlights as significant Goldhagen's exclusion of a testimonial cited by Browning in which she discerns

an expression of shame and guilt coupled with self-incrimination. The statement explains how a battalion member runs away from the shooting site at Józefów after killing three Jews but missing the fourth victim: 'It was simply no longer possible for me to aim accurately. I suddenly felt nauseous and ran away from the shooting site. I have expressed myself incorrectly just now. It was not that I could no longer aim accurately, rather that the fourth time I intentionally missed' (pp. 68–9). I would take issue with Birn's characterization of this example as self-incriminatory. While the first form of the statement claiming inaccuracy is an admission of culpability, the second, in which the shooter claims to have intentionally missed, is clearly self-exculpatory whether this 'secondary revision' is true or not.

25. See *Hitler's Willing Executioners*, pp. 536–7, n. 19, for this critique of Browning.
26. Browning, 'German Memory, Judicial Interrogation, and Historical Reconstruction: Writing Perpetrator History from Postwar Testimony'.
27. Hayden White, a leading theorist of history-as-narrative, has expounded his position in many texts, but the most important is *The Content of the Form: Narrative Discourse and Historical Interpretation* (Baltimore: Johns Hopkins University Press, 1987). In this instance, Browning is responding to White's essay, 'Historical Emplotment and the Problem of Truth' in *Probing the Limits of Representation*, an essay that serves as the volume's controversial centre-piece. For a full exploration of White's position in relation to Holocaust narrative, which is beyond the scope of this essay, see Jeremy Varon, 'Probing the Limits of the Politics of Representation', *New German Critique*, no. 72, Fall 1997. See also Edith Wyschograd, 'Historical Narrative' in *An Ethics of Remembering* (Chicago: Chicago University Press, 1998).
28. I am aware that not only does my own recapitulation endow the events at Józefów with narrative meaning, but that I run the risk of treating this irreducible reality as if it were *merely* a narrative. I have no answer to this quandary; but it seemed to me necessary to the analysis that follows to attempt this broad overview.
29. Goldhagen disputes Browning's claim that only older men were given the choice of stepping out, and cites testimonies where it is evident that younger men thought the offer applied to them as well.
30. I am drawing here upon Saul Friedländer's suggestion, in his 'Introduction' to *Probing the Limits of Representation*, that Hayden White might consider Browning's account within the category of the chronicle.
31. This is Goldhagen's term, which he doesn't ascribe directly to Browning, though the implication is unavoidable; but it is also a familiar description of Browning's style by many reviewers. For example, in 'Goldhagen in Germany', Josef Joffe compares Goldhagen's 'stark and enthralling narrative' to Browning's 'academic treatise with no explicitly moral voice', p. 20.

32. This name has been asterisked to indicate that it is not the testifier's real name.

33. Omer Bartov, 'German Soldiers and the Holocaust', p. 180. Yehuda Bauer is one of the few historians who maintains that 'the details and the way [Goldhagen] describes the attitude of the murderers is powerful and convincing'. See 'Goldhagen's View of the Holocaust', p. 70.

34. Goldhagen's rhetorical ploy is to open these psychological digressions with interrogatives. A few examples: 'With what emotions did the men of Police Battalion 309 gaze upon this sacrificial pyre to the exterminationist creed?' (p. 190); 'With what emotions did [the men of Police Battalion 65] gaze upon the transport disappearing into the death camp?' (p. 199); 'What did they say to each other upon reading that another operation in the ongoing destruction of the Jews was in the offing . . .' (p. 201).

35. Omer Bartov, 'German Soldiers and the Holocaust', p. 180.

36. Liliane Kandel, 'La Lettre Volée de Daniel J. Goldhagen', p. 53.

37. The phrase is Gillian Rose's in 'Beginnings of the Day', in Bryan Cheyette and Laura Marcus (eds), *'Modernity, Culture and "the Jew"'* (Cambridge: Polity Press, 1998). In this typically penetrating analysis, Rose argues that in approaching films like *Schindler's List*, a distinction should be made between the 'representation of Fascism' (which *Schindler's List* attempts) and the 'fascism of representation' (which she believes the novel *Schindler's Ark* manages to evoke).

38. Ibid., p. 250.

39. Bryan Cheyette, 'The Uncertain Certainty of *Schindler's List*', in Yosefa Loshitzky (ed.), *Spielberg's Holocaust: Critical Perspectives on Schindler's List* (Bloomington: Indiana University Press, 1997), p. 232. Cheyette also makes compelling use of Rose's distinction between the 'representation of Fascism' and the 'fascism of representation'.

40. Gary Weissman, 'A Fantasy of Witnessing', *Media, Culture and Society*, vol. 17, no. 2, April 1995, pp. 300–1.

41. See Geoffrey H. Hartman's 'The Cinema Animal', in *Spielberg's Holocaust*, p. 63.

42. Omer Bartov, 'Spielberg's Oskar', in *Spielberg's Holocaust*, p. 52.

43. The term is Hartmann's in 'The Cinema Animal', p. 65.

44. Claude Lanzmann's film *Shoah* is often brought in at this point as an 'answer' to this representational quandary. While I think *Shoah* should not be held up as the last word on Holocaust representation – indeed it engenders its own problematics of representation – Lanzmann does make an insightful point in his critique of Goldhagen: 'Le récit chronologique, parce qu'il n'est rien d'autre qu'une plate succession d'avant et d'après, est antitragic par essence et la mort, lorsqu'elle survient, le fait toujours à son heure, c'est-à-dire comme

non-violence et non-scandale. Les six millions de Juifs assassinés ne sont pas morts à leur heure.' 'Notes Ante et Anti Eliminationnistes', p. 15. For an intrepid critique of *Shoah* that runs against the critical grain, see Dominick LaCapra's 'Lanzmann's *Shoah*: "Here There Is No Why"' in *History and Memory after Auschwitz* (Ithaca: Cornell University Press,1998). In 'Beginnings of the Day', Gillian Rose also contends that *Shoah* is 'not self-referentially sceptical about its own means and form of representation' (p. 247).

45. In 'Revising the Holocaust', Ruth Bettina Birn criticizes the 'position of the intermediary' that Goldhagen adopts, insisting that '[W]e, i.e. people without acute personal involvement – be it as members of the second or third generation – have to resist both the temptation to assume the voice of survivors and the moral authority that goes with it.' However, Birn seems to assume that only a historical discourse of the kind enunciated by Browning surmounts these problems.

46. Hayden White, 'Historical Emplotment and the Problem of Truth', in *Probing the Limits of Representation*, pp. 44–5. White is here recapitulating Berel Lang's defence of the chronicle as the most appropriate manner of relating the facts of genocide. See Lang's *Act and Idea in the Nazi Genocide* (Chicago: University of Chicago Press, 1990).

47. This is a criticism of Browning forcefully made by Goldhagen. See *Hitler's Willing Executioners*, p. 540, n. 68.

48. Browning is adamant that his attempt at an empathetic understanding of the men of Reserve Police Battalion 101 does not imply forgiveness of their crimes. See both *Ordinary Men*, and his essay, 'German Memory, Judicial Interrogation, and Historical Reconstruction', in Friedlander (ed.), *Probing the Limits of Representation*.

49. To repeat: I am not taking issue here with Browning's *analysis* of the men's state of mind following Józefów, but only with the manner in which this analysis infiltrates his narrative. Goldhagen, however, does take issue with this interpretation in a long footnote in which he argues that visceral disgust, of a kind familiar to soldiers 'sampling for the first time the grisly offerings of real battle', rather than shame, is the more plausible description of the men's reactions. See pp. 540–1, n. 68.

50. Ernst Klee, Willi Dressen, and Volker Riess (eds), *'Those Were the Days': The Holocaust as Seen by Its Perpetrators and Bystanders* (London: The Free Press, 1991). The American edition has the title *'The Good Old Days'*.

51. These are in a section 'Quite happy to take part in shootings: Forced to obey orders – the myth', and each report confirms that reserve policemen were not disciplined for refusing to take part in shootings.

52. Dominick LaCapra, 'History and Memory: In the Shadow of the Holocaust', in *History and Memory after Auschwitz*, p. 31. I owe to LaCapra's text the

insight that Goldhagen's 'haunting' depictions of face-to-face killings might usefully be read in the light of *'The Good Old Days'*.

53. Międzyrzec also stood out because of the presence of several officers' wives during the round-ups, notably a Frau Wohlauf, on honeymoon with her new husband Captain Wohlauf. Browning claims that battalion members recalled feeling indignation and outrage 'that a woman was brought to witness the terrible things they were doing' and he adds: 'The men of First Company, if not their captain, could still feel shame', p. 93. Goldhagen once again hotly disputes Browning's attribution of shame, and says the men's emphasis on Frau Wohlauf's pregnant condition, and the 'possible damage to her sensibilities and person' that witnessing the round-up in this condition might have inflicted, was the more likely cause of their offence. Goldhagen insists that '[T]heir objections bespeak no shame at what they were doing, no desire to conceal from others their contribution to mass annihilation and torture, but rather a sense of chivalry and propriety that Frau Wohlauf's presence violated, particularly since this ghetto clearing was, even by their own standards, unusually brutal and gruesome . . .' (pp. 242–3 and p. 546, n. 16). Ruth Bettina Birn also weighs into this dispute, claiming that German women's witnessing these round-ups did not make them 'participants', as Goldhagen insinuated. See 'Revising the Holocaust'. Goldhagen's term is that the women were 'party to' the round-ups; however, the general issue about whether the men shared their murderous exploits with their wives is clearly worthy of further investigation and debate.

54. See Omer Bartov, 'German Soldiers and the Holocaust', for a discussion of this exhibition.

55. 'Trawnikis', sometimes known as 'Hiwis' (a shortened form of '*Hilfswilliger*', meaning 'willing helper') were 'eastern Europeans, mainly Ukranians, who worked as German auxiliaries in the mass extermination.' See *Hitler's Willing Executioners*, p. 224, and p. 542, n. 78, and *Ordinary Men*, p. 52.

56. Here I am drawing a schematic outline from the accounts of Łomazy given by Browning and Goldhagen.

57. Browning highlights the fact that the men recalled Łomazy with much less horror than Józefów because of the use of the Hiwis, the more depersonalized method of killing (even when the battalion members had to step in there was rapid rotation, and the killing was not face-to-face), habituation and the fact that they were not offered a choice to withdraw: '[T]herefore, those who shot did not have to live with the clear awareness that what they had done had been avoidable' (*Ordinary Men*, p. 86). Goldhagen disputes Browning's interpretation at considerable length, concluding that at Łomazy '. . . they carried out their duties well, not because they had no choice (at least formally), but because they saw no reason to do otherwise', p. 543. Like other interpretative disputes

between Browning and Goldhagen, a full discussion of this example is beyond the scope of this chapter, but extremely relevant to an appreciation of how widely their readings and recountings of the same events differ.

58. Both authors give an excruciating account of the Lomazy Jews' being herded to the massacre site inside a large rope that they were made to carry and that was supposed to ensure that they shuffled in orderly fashion to their deaths.

59. Goldhagen charges Browning with underplaying and misinterpreting the wanton cruelty that accompanied the battalion's genocidal itinerary in favour of 'instrumental' explanations. See also Goldhagen's discussion of a photograph of a man from Reserve Police Battalion 101 grinning as he snips the beard of an elderly Jew – a 'personal desecration' performed for the camera's eye, 'ensuring that the victim's shame would be displayed to people for years to come'. The caption on the reverse side, Goldhagen tells us, translates as: 'He should work, but he must be clean-shaven' (p. 246).

60. Victor Burgin, 'Looking at Photographs', in *Thinking Photography* (London: Macmillan, 1982), p. 146.

61. *Hitler's Willing Executioners*, p. 542, n. 80.

62. *'Those Were the Days'*, p. 23. This scene is cited by LaCapra as well as evidence that 'elation' at killing Jews wasn't confined to German perpetrators. See *History and Memory after Auschwitz*, p. 31.

63. See Friedländer's extremely compelling essay, 'The "Final Solution": On the Unease in Historical Interpretation', in *Memory, History and the Extermination of the Jews of Europe* (Bloomington: Indiana University Press, 1993). Once again, I am indebted to LaCapra's text for signalling the importance of this essay and the concepts that Friedländer develops therein.

64. 'On the Unease in Historical Interpretation', p. 111. It is significant that Browning refers to this essay and Friedländer's doubts about the possibility of undertaking an 'intuitive *Verstehen*' of the perpetrator in 'German Memory, Judicial Interrogation, and Historical Reconstruction'. However Browning maintains that he cannot apply the concepts of 'elation' and *Führer-Bindung* to the reserve policemen who carried out the massacre at Józefów: 'I find no *Führer-Bindung* in a situation in which the commanding officer, openly before his men, disassociated himself from the orders he had received from above. I find no "elation" in a situation in which the overwhelmingly predominant reaction of the men – both those who killed that day and those who refused, evaded, or stopped – was sheer horror and physical revulsion at what they had been asked to do' (p. 36). Again the moot point is whether the men's reactions are ones that can be safely deduced from the testimonials and Browning's narrative of these, or whether they should be clearly posited as part of his interpretative hypothesis.

65. Dan Diner, 'On Guilt Discourse and Other Narratives: Epistemological Observations regarding the Holocaust', *History and Memory*, vol. 9, nos. 1–2, Fall 1977, p. 307. Goldhagen is in fact a political scientist.

66. Ibid., p. 309. It is interesting that in a footnote to this statement, Diner notes that this 'universalist message is also conveyed by Browning in *Ordinary Men*' (p. 319, n. 15). The reader is again referred to the article by A. D. Moses, 'Structure and Agency in the Holocaust', for a lucid discussion of how the intentionalist/functionalist dispute bears on the question of guilt and why *Hitler's Willing Executioners* should be read as a response to the functionalist 'decentering of Jewish victimhood' (p. 206).

67. Ibid., pp. 316–17.

–5–

Memory on Trial in Contemporary France

'The Nazi crimes, it seems to me, explode the limits of the law; and that is precisely
what constitutes their monstrosity.'

– Hannah Arendt in a letter to Karl Jaspers, 17 August 1946[1]

Introduction

After a trial lasting six months, the longest in French legal history, Maurice Papon,
former Secretary General of the Gironde prefecture during the Occupation, was
convicted on 2 April 1998 of complicity in crimes against humanity. Essentially,
Papon had been accused of lending active assistance (*concours actif*) to arrests,
internments, deportations and murders or attempted murders during the German
implementation of the Final Solution on French soil. Close to 1,600 Jews had been
deported in ten convoys from the Bordeaux region to Drancy and on to Auschwitz,
and the charges against Papon implicated him in eight of these. The civil plaintiffs
represented 72 victims who had been rounded up and deported in these operations.

At the trial's outset, the prosecution case rested on several central claims: (1)
that Papon, in complying with the anti-Jewish dictates of the Germans, had personally ordered actions – particularly arrests and imprisonments – that confirmed his
individual responsibility for these crimes; (2) that he acted with knowledge of the
eventual fate of those who were apprehended and deported; (3) that he had had
authority over the administrative bodies – especially the local *Service des questions
juives* – that had aided the Nazis in compiling lists and carrying out round-ups of
local Jews; and (4) that constraints on functionaries like him had not been so
overwhelming as to abolish a certain liberty of action on his part.

The trial was a mass-mediated event of an unprecedented scale in France,
enjoying daily newspaper coverage and regular television, radio and magazine
commentary. For the more voracious consumer, a glut of information related to
the trial could be accessed through hundreds of sites on the World Wide Web. At
one point a tally noted that 146 accredited journalists had attended the trial; 1,413
scholars had abandoned lessons or libraries to witness History-in-the-making, and
8,827 members of the general public had been admitted.[2] With this kind of saturated
media and public attention, there was the attendant expectation that Maurice Papon's

trial would yield lessons of a pedagogic, historical and symbolic nature for French society as a whole.

The trial also began in a public climate that confidently anticipated that Maurice Papon would be found guilty of crimes against humanity and that the courtroom would merely provide the setting for the juridical *mise-en-scène* of his culpability, and by extension the culpability of the entire Vichy administration. At the time of the trial's commencement, *Le Monde* writer Laurent Greilsamer summed up the prosecution's case against Papon in the following manner: 'He signed what he shouldn't have signed, carried out what he shouldn't have carried out, organized what above all he shouldn't have organized.'[3] Greilsamer also observed that while political will and public pressure had combined to bring Papon to trial, the evidence in departmental archives would prove more decisive to the prosecution's case.

But as this juridical drama moved toward a conclusion, the verdict was no longer a foregone conclusion. The evidence that the civil parties claimed to be in possession of, which would link Papon directly to acts of complicity in arrests, internments and deportations, was sparse and controvertible.[4] The risk of an acquittal was mooted, and the civil parties were divided amongst themselves as to both the nature and degree of Papon's complicity in crimes against humanity, and the appropriate punishment for these.

In the event, Papon was convicted of complicity in arrests and internments – but not complicity in murder – and sentenced to ten years' imprisonment. The verdict was greeted with general acclaim. The civil plaintiffs, though unhappy that Papon was not also found guilty of complicity in murder, expressed their satisfaction that he had been held individually responsible for the tragic fate of their families and loved ones. Others saw in the verdict a wider and contemporary symbolic significance. By condemning a former Vichy functionary for implementing orders that had criminal consequences, the verdict, some maintained, sent the signal that no longer could any public functionary take refuge in the defence of obeying orders from higher authorities. The Papon verdict, declared *Libération* editor Serge July, 'also speaks to the present'. It was a 'salutary shake-up' in a country where public officials had been virtually exempt from the laws that held ordinary individuals accountable for their actions. 'The Bordeaux verdict', declared July, 'puts an end to the untouchables, ultimately responsible but never culpable.'[5] Finally, political observers hailed the trial as the historic moment when France, after decades of disavowal, had finally faced up to the shameful reality of *les années noires* and accepted national responsibility for the crimes of the Vichy state.

Amidst such acclamations of the multiple symbolic functions fulfilled by the trial and verdict, the ambiguities and dissonances that had characterized the judicial process seemed quickly forgotten. Only a few discordant voices were heard. The most vociferous of these was that of Henry Rousso, renowned author of *The Vichy Syndrome*, the highly influential account of the memory of Vichy in post-war France, and co-author with Éric Conan of *Vichy, un passé qui ne passe pas*, a polemical text that criticized the 'memorial militancy' that had accompanied the growing obsession with Vichy of recent years.[6] In an interview with *Le Monde* in the week after the verdict's pronouncement, Rousso disputed both the trial's pedagogic function and its value in helping France to 'assume' the Vichy past. Contrary to those, like Serge July, who hailed the trial as the moment when 'the France of 1998 has accepted to look at [. . .] the France of the 1940s for what it was . . .', Rousso declared that the trial in fact marked a 'regression' in terms of the historical knowledge of the period that it had solicited.[7]

The reasons for Rousso's misgivings stem from his conviction that trials cannot serve the needs of history, memory and justice simultaneously.[8] This is a position that warrants close consideration, especially in political cultures where the courts have increasingly become, to evoke Pierre Nora's term, important *lieux de mémoire*.[9] The larger issue raised by Rousso's critique of the Papon trial, then, is whether these juridical *lieux de mémoire* serve memory well – either the memories for which victims and their families seek juridical redress, or consensual representations of the past that a larger public has come to embrace as a 'national' or 'collective' memory. While much ink has been spilled – and will continue to be spilled – on various aspects of the Papon trial, this chapter will limit itself to the vexed relationship between law, memory and history that is the focus of Rousso's critique. The following analysis also acknowledges its own dependency on – to borrow Rousso's term – 'the virtual trial' – i.e. the trial that was represented in media reporting and commentary, rather than the one that occurred behind the closed doors of the courtroom.

'Juridical Acrobatics'[10]

As the Papon trial got under way, journalist and historian Éric Conan cited a candid remark that had been made by one of the lawyers representing the civil plaintiffs: 'Magistrates don't change: under the Occupation, they did what Pétain asked of them: today, they do what public opinion demands of them. But what matters is that Papon should be brought before an Assizes Court (*cour d'assises*).'[11] There was no doubt that public sentiment, by late 1997, was registering a desire to see Maurice Papon in the dock. Any doubts that were expressed largely invoked the accused's advanced age, the problem of evidence after more than fifty years, or the regret that higher Vichy functionaries – like former police chief René Bousquet or his henchman Jean Leguay – had not lived to face the same legal fate. Civil plaintiffs had been lobbying for this outcome since the early 1980s, and in the intervening years, public opinion had not only rallied to this campaign, but the demand that Papon face his accusers in court had become the latest focus of the 'memorial militancy' that had gripped France since the early 1990s. Fuelled by the Touvier trial of 1994, Mitterrand's public pronouncements about his wartime activities, President Chirac's *Vél d'Hiv* speech of 16 July 1995, which accepted French responsibility for crimes committed by the Vichy state, and many other ongoing revelations and controversies relating to the Vichy era, Papon's name had become a clarion call in the ongoing battle over how France should deal with Vichy's role in the Final Solution.[12] The few voices that expressed reservations about the use of the courts for these symbolic, pedagogic or commemorative purposes tended to be drowned out in the louder clamour for a legal showdown. But doubts that this trial would also accomplish 'the application of the law, the dispensation of justice and the punishment of the guilty' proved to be well-founded.[13]

Perhaps it could not be otherwise in light of the legal footsteps in which the Papon case was treading. Many media reports leading up to the trial rehearsed the legal vicissitudes of the definition of crimes against humanity since its incorporation into French law in December 1964. The broad narrative of these is by now well known, but some details need to be restated in order to appreciate the particular legal parameters – and aberrations – of the Papon trial.[14]

In the trials of Vichy functionaries of the immediate post-war period, the French courts and military tribunals relied primarily on Articles 75 to 83 of the 1939 Penal Code, which designated as major crimes treason, collaboration with the enemy, attacks on the laws of the Republic and 'acts harmful to national defence'. Crimes relating specifically to anti-Semitic persecution tended to be subsumed within one of these Articles. An ordinance of 26 August 1944 did specify the additional crime of 'national indignity' for espousing racist views; but this offence referred only to a person's ideological position and not to acts committed by them, and in any case incurred the relatively light sentence of 'national degradation'. Thus, when the actions for which Vichy functionaries were tried directly related to their participation in the Final Solution, the legal terms of reference did not allow their specifically genocidal character to be foregrounded. It was this legal anomaly, itself the reflection of a widespread perception that treason and collaboration constituted more serious crimes against the nation than Vichy's anti-Jewish measures, that later gave rise to the feeling that post-war trials had failed France's victims of anti-Semitic persecution and genocide. Successive amnesties for French collaborators only reinforced this retrospective sense of *malaise*.[15]

. Moreover, although France had participated in drafting the war crimes legislation adopted by the Nuremberg Tribunal to prosecute key Nazi figures and had pressed into service a 1944 edict to deal with war crimes committed by them on French soil, domestic legislation lacked any specific codification of crimes against humanity. The application of France's statute of limitations would have made impossible the prosecution of any more suspected Nazi war criminals after the expiry of the twenty-year time limit. However, in December 1964 the French National Assembly voted unanimously to abolish the statute of limitations for crimes against humanity as defined by the Charter of the Nuremberg Tribunal and ratified by the UN in 1946, thereby incorporating this category of offence into French law for the first time. The definition of crimes against humanity, basing itself on clause 6(c) of the London Charter, encompassed 'murder, extermination, enslavement, deportation, and other inhumane acts committed against any civilian population, before or during the war, or persecutions on political, racial or religious grounds'.[16] By contrast, in 1967, France applied the statute of limitations to war crimes, leaving all future prosecutions of culpable individuals to be pursued as crimes against humanity alone.

The 1964 law was voted by the French parliament with Nazi war criminals exclusively in mind, and so when attempts were made in the 1970s to apply this law to French nationals Paul Touvier and Jean Leguay, they were met with obstacles and protracted delays. The law was only put to the test in the 1980s in the course of proceedings against former Gestapo chief Klaus Barbie, extradited from Bolivia to face charges relating to his role in the implementation of the Final Solution in France, and specifically for deporting forty-four Jewish children in hiding at Izieu. But Barbie was also responsible for the death of the martyred Resistance hero Jean Moulin, who had died under torture in one of Barbie's prisons, and probably at Barbie's hands. Even though Barbie had been convicted *in absentia* in the 1950s for war crimes, the statute of limitations had subsquently come into effect, thus preventing the application of this charge to other crimes committed by Barbie against the Lyons Resistance, including his role in the death of Moulin. The court at first held firm to the distinction between war crimes and crimes against humanity, with the result that associations representing former members of the Resistance who had joined the trial as civil party plaintiffs were 'reduced to silence'.[17] But the media coverage and public controversy outside the courtroom clearly highlighted the pressure the court was under to make Barbie answerable for a war crime so indelibly inscribed in national memory.

Meanwhile, Barbie's lawyer, Maître Jacques Vergès, raised the spectre of drawing legal parallels between the crimes cited in the indictment and crimes committed during France's decolonization *débâcle*. Nurturing particular resentment towards former Resisters who had supported the cause of *l'Algérie française* during the Algerian War of Independence, Vergès also supported the inclusion of charges relating to Barbie's anti-Resistance activities within the indictment, since the media attention this drew allowed him to stir up the allegation that Moulin had been betrayed by his own Resistance comrades at a time when 'partisan political passions' had prevailed over internal loyalties. The Supreme Court of Appeal (*Cour de cassation*) yielded to these combined pressures by issuing a new ruling that succeeded in both tightening and loosening the extant definition of crimes against humanity. On the one hand, it restricted the 'inhumane acts and persecutions' constitutive of a crime against humanity to those 'committed in the name of a State practising a politics of ideological hegemony'. This thereby excluded from legal consideration crimes committed by the post-war French state in other arenas of conflict. But the court expanded the category of victims designated by the existing law to include not only civilians but combatants or 'adversaries of this politics [of ideological hegemony] regardless of the form of this opposition'.[18] This allowed the civil parties to add several charges to the indictment that treated Barbie's inhumane treatment of former Resistance activists as crimes against humanity.

Barbie was eventually convicted on charges of crimes against humanity; but it is important to register how the evolving legal parameters of his trial affected the historical memories that were in play. Memories of the Final Solution found themselves competing with (divisive) memories of the Resistance. Certainly this subordination was rooted in the deferred recognition of the genocidal consequences of French collaboration, as Rousso and others have shown. However, the inclusion of certain offences within the category of crimes against humanity that would previously have been designated as war crimes, and the attention both inside and outside the courtroom that was subsequently devoted to Barbie's persecution of the local Resistance, contributed to the hierarchy of French memories that the trial established. Meanwhile, this same redefinition excluded from legal consideration the possibility that crimes against humanity might have been committed in other arenas of conflict in the post-war period, and presaged the difficulties that would arise should the French state be impugned for such infamies committed in *its* name.

These were precisely the legal stakes of the protracted proceedings against Paul Touvier, former Vichy *Milicien*, accused of crimes against humanity. In 1992 a division of the Court of Appeal (the *Chambre d'accusation*) examining the Touvier dossier declared a *non-lieu* – 'no grounds' – on the basis that the charges could not be applied to a servant of Vichy, since Vichy was not a regime that practised a policy of ideological hegemony. Later that year, and in the wake of public outrage at such a blatant exculpation of the Vichy regime, the Supreme Court of Appeal overturned this decision. It declined the historical vocation that the judges of the lower court had assumed by sidestepping entirely the issue of Vichy's criminal character, but instead declared that, consistent with the Nuremberg Charter, French law regarded as complicit in, or the authors of, a crime against humanity those 'acting in the interests of the European Axis countries'. Touvier, the court alleged, fulfilled this criterion, since one of the charges against him – the murder of seven Jewish hostages at Rillieux-la Pape in 1944 – had been pursuant to a German order. In 1994, Touvier was convicted of crimes against humanity, though the existence of such an order remained unproven. On the contrary, the deeper the Assizes Court probed this matter, the more it seemed likely that Touvier had acted on his own initiative out of the 'anti-dreyfusard' passions that governed the murderous and brutal behaviour of the *Milice*, and that the Vichy regime actively cultivated. As

Tzvetan Todorov commented shortly after the verdict: it was the 'strange definition of crimes against humanity fashioned by the *Cour de cassation*' that dictated that 'the same acts are crimes if they are committed by Germans or anyone in their service, but cease to be so if their authors are French, acting for the sake of the French state or French institutions'. Todorov considered the Touvier trial a major setback for the principle of equality before the law, because it had deployed the definition of crimes against humanity in order 'to meet the political objective of the moment, instead of allowing it to judge individual cases according to unchanging criteria'.[19] In *Vichy, un passé qui ne passe pas*, Henry Rousso and Éric Conan also analysed this legal decision as one that had achieved its political aim – the conviction of Paul Touvier – not only at the expense of historical truth but by circumventing a legal reckoning with the autonomy of Vichy and a distinctly French responsibility for war crimes and crimes against humanity.[20]

Many had predicted that, legal definitions notwithstanding, these issues could not have been avoided had the trial of René Bousquet taken place. Bousquet was a former head of the Vichy police and the signatory of the Bousquet–Oberg accords of July 1942, which guaranteed the help of the French police and administration in the round-up and deportation of foreign Jews. Bousquet had led a successful post-war career until his name came up in a 1978 *L'Express* interview with Darquier de Pellepoix, a virulent anti-Semite and former minister of the *Commissariat général aux questions juives* under Vichy. Darquier de Pellepoix named Bousquet as the organizer of the infamous *Vél d'Hiv* round-up of 16 July 1942, which had resulted in the arrest, imprisonment and deportation of nearly 13,000 Jewish men, women and children. Bousquet had been tried for treason in 1949, but had pleaded the defence of *double jeu* (playing the 'double game'). He had been convicted on the lesser charge of 'national indignity' and sentenced to five years' loss of civil rights – a punishment immediately commuted for the services that the court accepted he had rendered to the Resistance. In 1989, Serge Klarsfeld, the historian of French Jewry and famous Nazi-hunter, who (with his wife Beate) had tracked down Klaus Barbie in Bolivia, brought charges against Bousquet for crimes against humanity relating to his role in the round-ups of thousands of Jewish families in the summer of 1942. But the legal contrivances that followed his initiative made it clear that political forces were putting pressure on the courts to delay juridical proceedings against Bousquet. Indeed, it became one of the persistent reproaches against President Mitterrand that not only had he enjoyed a past friendship with Bousquet, but he had aslo personally intervened to postpone Bousquet's trial indefinitely. Following the public outcry over such suspected politico-juridical collusion, a division of the Court of Appeal (the *Chambre d'accusation*) finally decided to hear the case in 1991 and indicted Bousquet on charges of crimes against humanity. The indictment cited in particular Bousquet's complicity in arresting foreign Jews and turning over Jewish children to the Germans (in the latter case without being compelled by the Germans to do so). Further charges were added in 1992 by the Bordeaux courts as a result of investigations into the wartime role of Maurice Papon. In June 1993, three days before Bousquet was to be tried, he was murdered by a deranged publicity-seeker, Christian Didier, in his Paris apartment.

With Bousquet's death, Maurice Papon became for many the remaining living symbol of a French functionary who had been complicit in crimes against humanity. However, writing for *L'Express* in the week the trial opened, Éric Conan noted that the case of Maurice Papon had posed new legal challenges for a juridical system that had hitherto proved itself so malleable in its definitional strictures and so prone to political and public pressure alike.[21]

Papon had assumed his position as Secretary General of the Gironde prefecture in June 1942 and remained in this post until the end of the war. Praised (like Bousquet) for lending aid to the Resistance, he was promoted at the Liberation and enjoyed an illustrious post-war career that included the positions of police prefect of Paris under de Gaulle in 1958–66 and budget minister under President Valéry Giscard d'Estaing in 1978–81. In 1981, in a highly controversial media exposé by *Le Canard enchaîné*, he was accused of crimes against humanity for having participated, while Secretary General, in the deportation of Jews from Bordeaux. The same year, a special *Jury d'Honneur* investigated the Resistance credentials Papon claimed for himself and ultimately confirmed these, though it also noted that Papon should have resigned his Vichy post in July 1942. Following further action by civil plaintiffs, Papon was indicted for crimes against humanity in 1983, investigations followed, new indictments were issued and in 1991 Papon held a press conference demanding that he be judged or acquitted of the charges against him. The *non-lieu* handed down in 1992 in the course of the proceedings against Touvier provoked a new set of indictments against Papon, and Touvier's conviction in 1994 inspired renewed demands from the civil plaintiffs for the trial of Maurice Papon finally to take place.

It had generally been acknowledged that, unlike Touvier's, the crimes of which Papon was accused were not motivated by ideological conviction, nor anti-Semitism, nor even by the desire that had obsessed Bousquet of reinforcing Vichy autonomy in relation to the Germans. Papon, it appeared, had acted primarily out of opportunistic career self-interest. In other words, Papon's *intentional* complicity with an Axis power in its bid for ideological hegemony, which was required by the 1994 Supreme Court of Appeal ruling, could not be confidently supposed. What therefore accompanied the preliminary legal stages during which Papon's dossier was reviewed was a series of interpretative manoeuvres and political directives bent on ensuring that Papon would not slip through the wide holes that now appeared in a legal net that had been designed to catch different and bigger fish. Conan recounted that no lesser a figure than the Justice Minister Jacques Toubon had issued the order to the public prosecutor's office of Bordeaux that they should resolve the legal quandaries in which the case was immersing them and 'sort things out' to ensure it was brought before an Assizes Court.[22]

The General Public Prosecutor (*le procureur général*) therefore attempted in December 1995 to establish complicity by asserting Papon's guilt by association with anti-Jewish measures instigated by the German occupiers, since, the Prosecutor maintained, Papon would have known that one of their aims was deportation of Jews to the East. While the Prosecutor conceded that in all likelihood Papon had remained ignorant of the Final Solution, the fact that he had taken up the post of Secretary General of the Gironde prefecture, armed with the knowledge he already had of German objectives, allegedly indicated an attitude of tacit approval toward German policy. In the next stage of investigation in September 1996, the division of the Court of Appeal showed itself far less reticent in pronouncing upon the nature of Papon's knowledge of the fate awaiting deportees. It alleged that from the time of taking up his prefectural duties, Maurice Papon had had 'a clear, reasoned, detailed and continuous knowledge of the plan formulated by the Nazis to take the lives of these people'.[23] From this moment on, the die was cast and the question of Papon's knowledge of the fate of deportees, of the Nazi policy of extermination and of the means to achieve this would subsequently become central and necessary to the prosecution case. It would become the testimonial burden of many witnesses – historians and former Resistance members foremost among them – to establish or disprove that Papon's knowledge contained this intentional element.

However, in a last-ditch effort to forestall the inexorable momentum toward committal to trial that the case had gathered, Papon's defence lawyer, Maître Jean-Marc Varaut, an expert on the Nuremberg trials,[24] submitted that these various legal pronouncements had still not demonstrated a motivation consistent with the law's stipulation that the accused be complicit with an Axis power practising a policy of ideological hegemony. In January 1997, the Supreme Court of Appeal, feeling itself 'cornered' (to use Conan's term)[25] by the accumulated legal and political pressures, then issued the ruling that it was not necessary for the accomplice of a crime against humanity to have adhered to the policy of ideological hegemony of its principal authors. Whereas in Touvier's case criminal agency required complicity in the ideological hegemony promulgated by the German occupiers, now there was no need to demonstrate even this attenuated intentional element in order to establish complicity. In one sense this was a return to the Nuremberg emphasis on crimes against humanity understood primarily as culpable acts against particular categories of victims. But French law had progressively modified the terms of the Nuremberg statutes precisely to lay greater stress on complicity in the ideologically-motivated and systematic criminal policy of the Nazis. Faced with an apparent absence of ideological motivation on Papon's part, but the political and public determination to see him stand trial, the legal definition of crimes against humanity was once again modified. With this deeply unsettling instrumentalization of the law, the imperative issued by the civil lawyer was fulfilled and Papon was ordered to stand trial at the Bordeaux Assizes Court.

Maurice Papon's Tears and the Question of Knowledge

Establishing Papon's complicity no longer required the element of intentionality, but the terms of the indictment referred – albeit in a vague and inconsistent manner – to his knowledge of the fate of deportees. But could intention be separated from knowledge? Paul Thibaud argued prior to the trial that,

> in effect, anyone who would have participated in a crime against humanity, in full knowledge of the aims and actions of the principal authors, would have shown, except in the case of unbearable constraints, at least a certain tolerance of the criminal intention [. . .] In fact, the question of shared intention can't really be separated from that of knowledge of the undertaking to which one is contributing.[26]

For the prosecution, then, the challenge was not only to prove Papon's participation in the criminal acts cited in the indictment, particularly in arbitrary and illegal arrests and internments, but to establish that he had acted 'in full knowledge' of the larger schema to which such acts contributed.

At the beginning of the trial, the prosecution case alleged that Papon's knowledge had been both broad and general and local and specific. The term *en connaissance de cause* came to designate a knowledge that may not have extended to the death camps or the technical means of the Final Solution, but nonetheless implied full apprehension of the certain death for which deportees were destined. Not long after the trial opened, Papon recalled Christmas of 1943, and tears he had shed in the wake of a convoy that had departed on 23 December. Why would he shed tears, one civil lawyer asked, unless he already knew of the fate awaiting the deportees?[27] However, several civil lawyers placed more emphasis on the fact that Papon had been complicit in crimes against humanity by virtue of remaining in post while knowing of the degrading conditions of treatment that existed in the detention camp of Mérignac where Jews of the region were detained, and on the transport trains that took them to Drancy. This knowledge of the 'cruel fate' (*le sort cruel*) endured by women, children and the elderly, it was argued, was in itself constitutive of a crime against humanity. Had the prosecution confined the question of Papon's knowledge to this local context, and the criminal complicity it represented, the trial might not have embarked on the more questionable path of appealing to historical expertise or the experience of historical actors to prove (or in the defence case disprove) the kind of knowledge Papon had possessed of the Final Solution.[28]

Outside the courtroom and in the wider historiographical arena, the issue of what was known about Hitler's plans for the destruction of European Jewry, by whom and when, is one that continues to be investigated and remains hotly disputed.[29] But in the Bordeaux Assizes Court, renowned historians of Vichy were called upon, not to interpret and assess the range of informed historical opinion on this question, but to testify about the likely knowledge possessed by a single Vichy functionary. Indeed, one *Le Monde* journalist proclaimed at the trial's conclusion that what had been rehearsed throughout the proceedings concerning the state of Papon's knowledge had already been previously resolved by a French historiography that had shown '. . . that the genocide of the Jews had been known practically in real time'.[30]

In the aftermath of the Touvier trial, which had also called historians to the witness stand, Henry Rousso and Éric Conan posed the question of whether it was even possible for 'historical truth' to find proper expression in a courtroom, given the necessary differences between juridical discourse (the law), judiciary discourse (the court), the historian's discourse and testimony. They maintained that the historian could not describe 'what had happened', but only attempt, on the basis of available traces and navigating 'between islands of established truths in an ocean of uncertainty', to reconstitute a plausible account of events. By contrast, justice demanded to know exactly 'what had happened' in order to make judgements based on the balance of evidence. The hypotheses developed by historians, they argued, are not of the same nature, nor do they have the same consequences, as the 'intimate convictions' of a jury. Thus in Touvier's case, historians could speculate about whether he was likely to have acted alone or only on German orders according to a range of plausible historiographical interpretations of the degree of agency of a high-ranking *milicien*. But the prosecution needed to convince the jury that despite the evidentiary absence of such an order, its material existence at the time was the incontrovertible reason for Touvier's actions. Without this, Touvier could not be convicted within the terms of the existing law on crimes against humanity: complicity in the criminal acts of an Axis power.[31]

A similar tension between historical opinion and juridical imperatives was soon to insinuate itself into the Papon proceedings in a variety of guises. When historians summoned to testify either for the prosecution or the defence ventured *hypotheses* about the nature and degree of Papon's knowledge of the Final Solution, these were treated by both sides as assertions of fact to be added to the evidentiary balance sheet. When historical actors of the period, notably former members of the Resistance, denied knowing about the Jewish genocide as it was occurring, civil lawyers often reminded them that radio broadcasts and other official and non-official dispatches had referred to Germany's policy of extermination at least since December 1942. Thus, one after another, former Resisters, who were called by the defence primarily to attest to Papon's reputed Resistance credentials, felt compelled to speak to their wartime awareness of the extermination process as if their own belated apprehension of the Final Solution was also on trial.

On one level, both the accusatory stance of the prosecution lawyers and the defensive posture adopted by some former Resisters are understandable from the perspective of a post-Holocaust society still haunted by the trenchant accusation that Allied governments and anti-Nazi movements failed to act early enough on the information they were acquiring about the genocide of Europe's Jews. However, such an important and controversial issue cannot be resolved in a legal standoff, but deserves a hearing in another public forum where the historical investigation and argumentation it demands are not subordinated to the court's more overriding goal of establishing legal certainties. But apart from these objections, the legal treatment of this issue was bound to ride roughshod over more profound ethico-philosophical concerns about formulating the question of knowledge of the Final Solution in positivist terms at all. As Rousso observed: 'The Prosecution and the majority of civil parties wanted at all costs to establish that the accused "knew", even though this question cannot be formulated in this manner. What does "knowing" mean? At what level? One could very well be in possession of the information and not assimilate it.'[32] For Rousso, then, the issue was not only one of acknowledging the incommensurability between historical and legal discourses, but of recognizing that apprehension of the Final Solution was ultimately something upon which neither law nor history could – or should – make confident pronouncements.

Interviewed in *Le Monde* about the verdict, Claude Lanzmann, director of the highly-regarded film *Shoah*, deepened Rousso's critical insight when he declared that while he had no doubt that Papon's complicity in criminal acts had been established, the court's manner of posing the question of Papon's knowledge of the Final Solution had failed to grasp the inner logic of the event. This, Lanzmann insisted, was the Nazi determination to ensure that there would be no witnesses to the extermination process, and to this end to erase the traces of their crimes even as they committed them. Inasmuch as the Shoah could thus be defined as 'an event without a witness, an event whose scheme is, historically, the literal obliteration of its witnesses',[33] the question of what it meant to be 'a contemporary of the Shoah', with knowledge of its unfolding, had to be posed in radically different terms. Moreover, even if, as Lanzmann believed, it was legitimate to reflect upon whether Papon might have acted differently had he known about the gas chambers, it was still necessary to ask: 'what do we mean by "knowing"'? For Lanzmann, such knowledge could not signify an apprehension of the meaning of the Shoah coincidental with its occurrence – 'in real time' as the *Le Monde* journalist would have it – but 'a split in consciousness', a *necessary disjunction* between knowledge and cognition imposed by the lethal logic of the event.[34]

Clearly one is on territory here that legal minds bent on securing a conviction might regard as a diversion at best and a form of exculpation at worst. But precisely because broaching the question of knowledge of the Shoah raises issues of an ethico-philosophical order, one should be suspicious of an appeal to historiography alone to explain how such a singular event was apprehended by, and integrated into the consciousness of an individual – or indeed of the larger collectivity.

The Tribunal of History

But if historians and other witnesses could not shed decisive light on a question as complex as Papon's knowledge of the Final Solution, might they nonetheless illuminate Papon's character as historico-political agent? In other words, could the trial fulfil a pedagogic function by showing the extent to which Papon was representative of a Vichy functionary – or alternatively, the extent to which his case was a singular one? And how should such historical disclosures inform the 'intimate conviction' of the jury faced with the specific charges against Papon? Since French legal procedure prevented the historians called to the witness stand from having access to the historical documents that made up Papon's hefty file, their testimony was expected to address only the wider historical context and issues raised by his case.[35]

The very fact that, following Bousquet's death, Papon remained the only living symbol of the Vichy regime whose conviction for crimes against humanity was actively and persistently sought, suggested that his case was exceptional in important respects. As previously noted, the *milicien* Touvier – right-wing Catholic, pro-Nazi, dedicated anti-Semite and opponent of the Resistance – was not the functionary Papon, whose pre-war biography revealed more left political leanings with no apparent anti-Semitism, and who ended the war in the Resistance camp. And while civil plaintiffs and a wider public had stepped up the campaign for both men's committal to trial on crimes against humanity throughout the 1980s, as Vichy historiography expanded and garnered increasing media attention over this same period, each man came to stand for a different type of reckoning with the Vichy past. Touvier's trial, however ineptly handled in legal terms, emphasized the existence of an ideologically-driven complicity in the Final Solution in the larger context of *la guerre franco-française*. Maurice Papon's trial, by contrast, would represent a very distinctive moment in the appraisal of the Vichy regime by providing an opportunity to scrutinize the role played by Vichy's *administrative apparatus* in the implementation of the Final Solution. While Papon's unsavoury character had been the subject of investigation since the *Canard enchaîné* exposé, and his culpable role as Paris police prefect during the Algerian war added to his alleged criminal inventory,[36] it was only when Vichy historians increasingly focused their attention on the issue of the 'continuity of the State' that his political trajectory could be placed in its specific context.

It is well known that the path-breaking work of the American historian Robert Paxton prepared the ground for French historians of Vichy to focus on the key role that functionaries like René Bousquet had played in the implementation of the Final Solution. In particular, Paxton's research showed that the motives of figures like Bousquet, who zealously carried out anti-Jewish measures, did not arise primarily out of an ideological sympathy with anti-Semitism, but were the consequence of the desire of high functionaries to ensure French autonomy in police matters and thus to reinforce Vichy's authority in relation to the Germans.[37] Called to testify at the Papon trial by the civil plaintiffs, Paxton reiterated that Vichy's obsession to negotiate more autonomous responsibilities for the police and administration had constituted *l'engrenage fatal* – the fatal point of getting caught up in the Nazi policy of extermination.[38] But if historians like Paxton understood their role at the trial as one of only illuminating the context within which Papon's alleged crimes had been committed, how could the generality of their discourse resist the snare necessarily set by the juridical exigency of establishing Papon's guilt or innocence?[39]

In the footsteps of Paxton, French historiography of Vichy has witnessed a proliferation of studies of the civil service culture – *la culture fonctionnaire* – that prevailed during the final years of the Third Republic and into the Vichy period. The most influential of these are several major studies of the Vichy administration by Marc-Olivier Baruch. In the lead-up to the trial, media analyses bestowed even wider attention on Baruch's central claims, and to a certain extent these came to lend a certain historiographical authority to the juridical proceedings to which the civil lawyers referred – albeit more implicitly than explicitly.

In its main outline, Baruch's work cautions against any sweeping generalizations concerning the administrative attitudes or conduct of Vichy officialdom. His studies show that on the eve of the war, the French administration was by no means a monolithic entity but embraced a wide range of professions – munitions workers, teachers, ministerial employees, prefects and so on. Moreover, he highlights that in the late years of the Third Republic, the political inclinations of the majority of functionaries tended to be moderate or even radical-socialist, and manifested a high trade-union consciousness. With the defeat of 1940, a large number of these civil servants resigned; with the armistice many, especially amongst the young, became German prisoners-of-war. Others were replaced in the specific purge of Jewish functionaries in late 1940 and in the general purge of the administration that continued into 1941. The ageing, right-wing composition of the Vichy regime reflected this early upheaval.

Despite this change of personnel and retrenchment of political perspective, Baruch locates the element of continuity between the late Third Republic and Vichy in the insular 'culture of obedience' that prevailed notwithstanding the administration's structural overhaul during the Occupation years. It was this culture that survived the defeat, the armistice and the subsequent purges intact and that would be decisively manipulated by Pierre Laval upon his return to power in April 1942. Laval sought to secure the obedience and loyalty of Vichy functionaries not by issuing ideological appeals on behalf of the National Revolution, but by using the system of professional rewards and punishments as a veritable 'currency of exchange'. The disaffection and dissent toward the regime that did surface was as much the product of internal divisions caused by these manoeuvres and by government interference in a world traditionally protective of its autonomy. Such was the case, for example, with the regime's creation of new departments like the *Commissariat général aux questions juives* (CGQJ), which provoked discontent within the administrative ranks not primarily on ideological grounds but amongst those who felt bypassed either in decision-making or in the more favourable professional advances this ministry offered its employees. Ultimately, however, such dissent as did exist – and Baruch's own research reveals isolated acts of bureaucratic revolt – did not inhibit the administration's efficiency nor provoke significant rebellion from within.[40]

Clearly this historiographical perspective has an enticing relevance to Papon's specific circumstances. It suggests that Vichy functionaries were inclined to implement rather than resist orders of a morally reprehensible or even criminal kind not only because the administration became increasingly politicized, but because they were already immersed in a long-standing culture of obedience. The fact that more resolute forms of revolt – resignation, and anti-German or pro-Resistance activity within the administration – were extremely limited only reinforces how prevalent this quiescent administrative culture was. Also summoned to appear for the civil parties at the trial, Baruch expounded on the scope for disobedience that Vichy's administrative structures provided for the ordinary functionary – 'there was always a way', he maintained – but that was not by and large exploited because of an evident lack of political will.[41]

In another setting, this compelling historiographical framework could be used as a focal point for considering the extent to which Maurice Papon was a representative figure of this culture of obedience. Locating Papon's scrupulous discharge of duties – from signing the order to stamp 'Jew' on ration and identity cards to writing *comptes-rendus* of Jewish persecution – within the context of the aspirational career culture, which survived the change of political regimes intact, puts into different critical perspective his own justifications about remaining in post in order to soften the effects of Vichy's collaborative activities. Like Touvier, who was a product of an indigenous anti-Semitic tradition, Papon emerges as a figure whose willingness to engage in 'routine' forms of collaboration sanctioned by the Vichy regime was evidently nurtured by a long-established reward system within the state administrative apparatus. It was but one step from such 'routine' collaboration – activity Papon referred to only as *la régularisation administrative* – to collaboration with the murderous dictates for which Papon was being tried. As the flamboyant civil lawyer Arno Klarsfeld, son of Serge Klarsfeld, put it after the trial: 'One calls oneself a spectator when one is already a protagonist.'[42]

Klarsfeld had pressed this point on several occasions during the trial, most notably during an examination of the convoy that had left Bordeaux on 12 January 1944, including French Jews amongst its prisoners. While documents produced by the court showed that Papon and other high functionaries in the Bordeaux prefecture had written to Pierre Laval questioning this action as contrary to the terms of the Bousquet–Oberg accords, the order had been confirmed.[43] With this convoy, Klarsfeld proclaimed, not only had Vichy abandoned French Jews, but in the light of the illegality of its actions, it rendered all those who complied with its orders complicit in crimes against humanity. Klarsfeld therefore put to Papon the following question: 'To voluntarily participate in something one knows to be a crime – doesn't that amount to being complicit in it, even without having desired the consequences?' To which Papon, keenly aware of the legal knot into which his case had been tied, simply replied: 'In law or in morality?'[44]

In the emphatic words of Éric Conan: 'On the plane of History and morality, the condemnation of Maurice Papon is indisputable.'[45] And as reactions to the verdict made clear, the decision to convict Papon of complicity in crimes against humanity, despite evidential gaps in the prosecution case, was a clear articulation of the jury's *moral* condemnation of his failure to extricate himself from this 'chain of responsibility' and to exercise the right to disobey orders. In this respect, the resonances of the verdict may well be a salutary lesson for today's functionary, who, as the historian François Bédarida noted, is increasingly enmeshed in complex administrative systems that have a tendency 'by virtue of the compartmentalization of functions and tasks, to dilute personal responsibility and to develop an entirely administrative and professional logic – technical, even technocratic – as if acts were deprived of meaning within a soulless mechanical apparatus'.[46] Contemporary societies, Bédarida continued, must make it their urgent task to define the duty to disobey faced with certain orders, just as the individual must learn how to assume moral responsibility for his or her acts rather than hiding behind the excuse of impersonal administrative authority. But if these are undoubtedly moral imperatives for the present and future,[47] how do they square with the legal task of the Bordeaux Assizes Court, which was to judge Papon for specific past acts of which he was accused? On the one hand, the fact that the jury found Papon guilty in arrests and sequestrations relating to four out of eight convoys cited in the indictment suggests that the balance of evidence implicated him directly in the fate of the individuals whom the civil plaintiffs represented.[48] And on this basis, it seems right that he should be convicted. On the other hand, if the assertion of *Libération* editor Serge July is also true – that Papon 'has just been condemned [. . .] for his actions as an authoritarian high functionary, efficient and indifferent to the consequences of his actions . . .',[49] then one cannot help agreeing with Michael Marrus's post-trial observation that, from this perspective, thousands of ordinary functionaries escaped justice. Echoing Henry Rousso's reservations about celebrating the trial's symbolic function, Marrus maintained that 'the goal of a trial is to seek justice, not history [. . .] I don't think that the Papon trial was a vehicle for historical explanation.'[50]

But the attempted elucidation of Maurice Papon's historico-political agency at the trial was not limited to his status and role as a Vichy functionary. Several analysts readily located Papon's professional profile within the larger social category of what has become known as the *vichysto-résistant*, someone who passed from collaboration to the Resistance out of political or – as is more likely in Papon's case – careerist motivations.[51]

The 'belated conversion' to the Resistance that Papon appeared to have undergone was already familiar from the wartime biography of François Mitterrand, who had worked from early 1942 in Vichy's civil administration before going over to the Resistance in the spring of 1943. When Mitterrand's wartime profile became a matter of general public knowledge and media debate in the early 1990s, Rousso and Conan seized the occasion in order to assert that a wider social constituency than is generally admitted, both inside and outside the Resistance, adopted a position similar to that of the youthful Mitterrand.[52] This position, known as *maréchalisme* after the eulogizing of Marshall Pétain's First World War heroism, was hostile to the German occupation, to Nazi ideology, and even to the fully-fledged *pétainisme* represented by the National Revolution. Yet *maréchalisme* was supportive of elements of collaborationist policy, especially 'tactical' accommodation with the German occupiers. Such was the 'typicality' and social acceptability of this ideological position, that one could be a *maréchaliste* before becoming a *résistant*, or even remain one after entering the Resistance. However de Gaulle's assertion of an early, massive and unequivocal commitment to the Resistance denied legitimacy to this narrative of evolving and ambivalent allegiances, and for the historical actors who had pursued this latter course, it had since become, in the words of Rousso and Conan, an 'encumbering secret'.

Le Monde journalist Nicolas Weill proclaimed after the trial concluded that the 'incapacity to assimilate the hybrid notion' of *vichysto-résistant* had become a source of considerable discomfort – not to mention of outright hostility – during the trial precisely because of the prospect that it could be stretched to include a figure like Maurice Papon.[53] But to what extent was this discomfort a reflection of the category's hybrid nature and to what extent was this indicative of the unsuitability of the courtroom to ascertain its applicability to Papon? For if Papon's administrative career warranted unequivocal condemnation on a moral plane, his transfer of political allegiances represented a not uncommon wartime trajectory. Thus by the time former Resisters were called to the stand to testify about Papon's Resistance credentials, a great deal more seemed to be at stake than merely confirming whether or not their networks had benefited from his 'belated conversion'.

Former *résistants* testified in several stages of the trial – in the early stages as character witnesses primarily on behalf of the Papon they had come to know in his illustrious post-war career, and at a later point when the events of the Liberation were under examination. As would be expected, those called by the prosecution disputed Papon's claims to have assisted Resistance networks, whereas defence witnesses – more numerous – recalled how Papon had given information and material provision from spring 1943 onwards, including to a Jewish *résistant*, and confirmed the high regard in which he was held by de Gaulle's commissioner Gaston Cusin, who awarded Papon with a prefectural post at the Liberation. As their facts and opinions accumulated, and the authenticity of Papon's aid to the Resistance became harder to deny, several civil lawyers seemed to imply by their aggressive stance towards these witnesses that an affirmation of such transferred loyalties on Papon's part was tantamount to a declaration of total exoneration for his wartime behaviour. This tension mounted when the testimonies of several Resisters raised, only to leave in suspended animation, the issue of the extent to which the trajectory of the *vichysto-résistant* implied an adherence to Vichy's anti-Jewish measures, or at least general indifference to the fate of the Jews.[54]

Caught on the defensive and clearly wanting to give vent to their pent-up resentment, a number of ex-Resisters (and right-wing Gaullists) used the occasion of the trial to condemn as anti-Gaullist and a besmirching of Resistance memory, President Chirac's *Vél d'Hiv* speech of 1995, which acknowledged French responsibility for the crimes of the Vichy state. For some commentators, the atmosphere of confrontation during these testimonies, which followed on the heels of the examination of the convoys in which Papon was implicated, reactivated memories of the Barbie trial, where disputed memories of Resistance betrayals competed with the crimes against humanity that were the trial's ostensible juridical preoccupation. But now the stakes were different and greater: it was not a question of relegating national memory of the Final Solution to the margins, but of accusing Resistance memory of harbouring an alleged war criminal and masking deep ambivalences toward the Jewish genocide.[55]

Were these tensions and outbursts the product of new revelations about the 'true nature' of the Resistance, or a situation, induced by the setting and needs of the trial, where the sum of the parts assembled did not add up to an unambiguous broader picture? Rather than eliciting the need for a 'revisionist' reading of the Resistance, the controversies surrounding the testimonies of ex-Resisters perhaps only demonstrated once again Rousso's contention that there was a basic and irresolvable contradiction between treating these issues in all their historical complexity, and the juridical certainties sought by both the prosecution and defence. Moreover, as Conan remarked, whether or not Papon was 'a Resister just a little, a lot or not at all', ultimately had no relevance for the key legal issue finally before the courts: 'how to describe in penal terms the attitude that was his – that of a functionary who remained at his post?'[56]

It is worth reflecting upon why Rousso's position, anticipated and reinforced by Éric Conan's coverage of the trial for *L'Express*, did not receive a more sympathetic hearing amongst the trial's more astute reporters and commentators. Even those respectful of historical contextualization remained unconvinced that the achievements represented by the verdict should be overshadowed or diminished by considerations of complexity. Indeed, following the trial, Nicolas Weill criticized proponents of complexity for not recognizing the exonerating implications of their stance. In a thinly-disguised polemic against the authors of *Vichy, un passé qui ne passe pas*, Weill argued that while the verdict represented an unequivocal condemnation of Vichy, the constant appeal by certain historical experts to 'nuances' and 'subtleties' ran the risk of making Vichy historiography vulnerable to a kind of political apologetics. As a case in point, Weill cited the tendency of some historians of Vichy to focus on distinctions, rather than culpable continuities, between Vichy's anti-Semitic legislation and the Nazi process of extermination. How could one be sure, asked Weill, 'that this *malaise* wouldn't one day rebound in a part of Vichy historiography'?[57]

With that broadside, one is tempted to speculate that the Papon trial succeeded in provoking amongst those concerned with the history of Vichy their very own 'historians' debate'. After all, in the German *Historikerstreit*, however different the issues, the charge of revisionism was also levelled at several of its protagonists. But if the Papon trial managed to sow the seeds of dispute, this manifested itself as a dispute not so much *within* historiographical circles as between historians of Vichy and those in the wider public who consider themselves specialists of Vichy and its memorial legacy. Historians certainly differed on the question of whether to testify at the trial,[58] but they did not disagree to any significant extent about the responsibilities to be laid at the door of the Nazis as opposed to the Vichy government regarding the persecution of French Jews.[59] However, as the occasional critical stabs in *Le Monde* made clear, this consensus did not extend to a number of their journalist counterparts. The charge of creeping revisionism within Vichy historiography, hinted at by Weill, who prefers to speak instead of Vichy's 'co-authorship' of the Final Solution, of a 'logic of extermination' practised by the regime rather than one of 'apartheid',[60] indicated a determination to flag publicly this ideological divide.

'We Hope To Become Living People'

Finally, after all the doubt cast on the trial's symbolic and pedagogic functions, shouldn't the verdict ultimately be considered from the standpoint of those who had most to gain from seeing Papon brought to trial: survivors or the families of victims? Is not the single most important and legitimate function of war crimes trials, as Jean Améry declared, to 'nail the criminal to his deed', by making the perpetrator directly answerable to survivors and families for their suffering and losses?[61] And for survivors and victims' families, is not the judicial process, with all its flaws, a forum for 'bearing witness' to the inexpressible experience one has had or the losses one has endured? Primo Levi likened the need to 'bear witness' to the Holocaust to an elementary *physical* need for survivors. Understood in this way, testimony is not only an act of narration – not only the telling of the event – but a form of survivorship. Child survivor and psychoanalyst Dori Laub has remarked: 'The survivors did not only need to survive so that they could tell their story; they also needed to tell their story in order to survive. There is, in each survivor, an imperative need to *tell* and thus to come to *know* one's story . . .'. For Laub, testimony entails this more elaborate and complex psychical process by which the survivor 'comes to know' his or her own story of survival and by so doing is able ideally to achieve the therapeutic goal of 'repossessing the act of witnessing'.[62]

Can this form of testimony take place in a court of law? Is the act of 'bearing witness' in order 'to come to know one's story' or speak to one's losses compatible with the aims of testimony in its juridical sense? Did the trial of Maurice Papon, however flawed, not only render the verdict needed by survivors and victims' families, but also facilitate a process of transmission in order for them to 'repossess the act of witnessing'? Compared to the volatility provoked by the testimonies of former members of the Resistance, those of survivors and of the families of victims constituted, according to Éric Conan, a kind of 'sacred ceremony', listened to in a silence that seemed temporarily to suspend the trial's relentless juridical progression.[63] In an extraordinary act of commemoration for a legal forum, photographs of the victims were projected onto a large screen in the courtroom and their names were read out. One lawyer contended that the simple fact of holding the trial had an 'assuaging value' for the civil parties. And one survivor testified in court: 'We have been survivors, we hope to become living people'[64] – voicing in vivid terms the hope that transmission would eventually achieve a release from survivorship. Finally, testimony after testimony regarding individual victims confirmed the role of the local Bordeaux administration and its ancillary services in the implementation of the Final Solution. Surely establishing this historical truth in a court of law – a truth fudged in the Paul Touvier trial – was a symbolic precondition of that renewal process.

Such questions lead inevitably to another: was it possible to separate the reclamation of the act of witnessing from the goal of the prosecution case – securing Papon's conviction? The issue arises not least because however much survivors' testimonials helped to decipher the sequence of events in which they or their families were ensnared and the culpable activities of the local bureaucracy, and to evoke the moral dereliction of the Vichy regime, the court also expected these testimonials to speak *unequivocally* to the issue of the accused's guilt. But as Éric Conan remarked, 'the victims are not the best testifiers to the facts'.[65] And not only because most of those who appeared to give testimony were mere children or adolescents when caught up in the events for which Papon was held responsible. More salient was the fact that, as Rousso pointed out, when the trial took on the function of a 'commemorative ritual', it became evident that such a ritual 'was sometimes ill suited to the judiciary ritual'.[66]

The testimonies of survivors and victims' families given at the Papon trial primarily spoke to another truth – the truth of their experience of the Holocaust – but these truths were of a moral, ethical or even historical order rather than ones that lent themselves to juridical certainties. These were testimonies of traumatic separations of family members, of unspeakably tragic losses, of lives shattered and never fully repaired. Called by the civil parties to pay tribute to three functionaries of Papon's rank who had saved Jewish children, Samuel Pisar used the occasion to recount his own memory of the last days with his family before the evacuation of the Polish ghetto where they were living. His mother, he recalled, anguished over whether he should wear short pants or long trousers when the moment came to depart, since in the first case he might be allowed to stay with the women, but in the latter he would join the men.[67] In this *image intime* as he called it – a mother calculating her son's life chances on the basis of an item of clothing – Samuel Pisar certainly testified to the truth of the event: the arbitrariness of survival for most Holocaust victims. Or consider a case read to the court from a civil party deposition – that of Irma Reinsberg, a young woman deported from Bordeaux in the convoy of 26 August 1942 who threw herself off the train. She was arrested and, suffering head injuries, was taken to the hospital in Orléans. A telegram was sent to the Gironde prefecture asking to which camp she should be sent. The reply, signed by 'adviser to the prefecture', was: 'To Drancy.'[68] Here was the irrefutable truth of collaboration and cold indifference on the part of a Bordeaux functionary. But such ethical and historical truths did not speak directly to the actions of which the former Secretary General of the Gironde prefecture was accused.

In elaborating how the process of repossessing the act of witnessing occurs for Holocaust survivors in the therapeutic context, Dori Laub made the following observation:

> In the process of the testimony to a trauma [. . .] you often do not want to know anything except what the patient tells you, because what is important is the situation of *discovery* of knowledge – its evolution, and its very *happening*. Knowledge in the testimony is, in other words, not simply a factual given that is reproduced and replicated by the testifier, but a genuine advent, an event in its own right.[69]

This is not to suggest for a moment that the witnesses appearing for the civil parties at the Papon trial confused the courtroom with a therapeutic setting, but merely that if their testimonies facilitated the process of repossessing the act of witnessing, in few cases did they also fulfil the juridical function the court expected of them. In fact in several instances, the failure to fulfil this specific function must have severely hampered that passage from survivorship to 'living people' that the above-mentioned survivor so fervently hoped for. At least two examples exemplified in a heart-rending manner these tensions and contradictions between juridical testimony and bearing witness in Laub's sense.

Perhaps the most well-known case the court heard was that of the Slitinsky family, represented at the trial by Michel Slitinsky, a civil plaintiff, author of a book on Papon, and the first person to initiate the process of bringing Papon to trial in the immediate post-war period. His father and sister were rounded up in Bordeaux in October 1942; Michel, seventeen at the time, escaped arrest. His father was deported to Drancy and then to Auschwitz, where he was gassed. His sister protested against her internment at Mérignac, the local internment camp, on the basis that she had French nationality. She was released in December 1942. Papon had always claimed he was responsible for saving Alice Slitinsky; the family had always contested this claim and had accused the *Service des questions juives*, over which Papon allegedly had authority, of delaying her release. The court dossier indeed contained documents addressed to Alice's mother and signed by Papon, relating his interventions with the Germans on Alice's behalf. The presiding judge, Jean-Louis Castagnède, examined these, as well as a letter by SS officer Dober-schutz (submitted for the first time by the defence and thus presumably unknown to Michel Slitinsky), making explicit reference to Papon's intervention. Castagnède then confirmed publicly and for the court record the veracity of Papon's claim. As a journalist observed at the time of the hearing, here was irrefutable evidence of 'an intervention of the accused on behalf of the sister of his principal accuser'.[70] Slitinsky's own testimony on the following day, clearly under the effect of these devastating revelations, crumbled into a meandering testimony that was criticized by judge Castagnède – solicitously, but with evident impatience – for saying so little about the facts concerning the convoy of his father that was under examination.

The original indictment cited Papon's complicity in the arrest, illegal sequestration and murder of a doctor of Egyptian origin, Sabatino Schinazi, in November 1943. Father of nine children, son of a Catholic mother and with a Catholic wife, Schinazi was arrested on German orders by French police, interned at Mérignac and deported to Auschwitz. He died at Dachau in 1945.[71] According to the terms of the Bousquet-Oberg accords of July 1942, because he was married to an Aryan, Schinazi should have been exempted from the arrest list. In any event, faced with lack of evidence to substantiate Papon's complicity in Schinazi's fate – notably Papon's signature on the deportation order for Schinazi's convoy – the questioning against Papon by the civil lawyers focused on his failure to save the doctor from this illegal sequestration and his inaction during the period when Schinazi was interned at Mérignac. This *inaction*, the civil lawyers maintained, could on occasion be qualified as a crime against humanity. Papon invoked the defence that at the time of Schinazi's internment, not only had prefects had no power over those interned on German orders, but the Germans, suspicious of prefectural sabotage of the round-ups, had also been dealing directly with the regional police. But the details of his defence aside, Papon demanded that the court prove his culpability for the convoy that had deported doctor Schinazi by producing the signature referred to by the indictment. The civil parties were unable to satisfy the accused's demand. Meanwhile civil lawyers had introduced into the proceedings the new charge of Papon's 'non-assistance to victims of crimes against humanity' – a covert retreat from the charge of active complicity and a crucial shift in juridical discourse that the defence was quick to seize upon.[72]

The exception to the above cases was that of Léon Librach. Librach was a twenty-six-year-old French Jew who had been imprisoned in the military prison of Fort-du-Ha in Bordeaux in spring 1942 (for reasons that remain unclear, since at that time French Jews were not by and large the target of German measures). In June 1942 the Germans ordered him transferred to Drancy. Papon issued an order to transfer Librach to Mérignac even though the Germans had not ordered this intermediary measure (the court saw Papon's order, bearing his signature, projected onto a large screen in the courtroom). Librach was duly transferred from Mérignac to Drancy and then in September 1942 to Auschwitz, where he was exterminated. Papon excused himself for his actions on the basis that he had only just arrived in Bordeaux to take up his prefectural duties and was inexperienced, and that his reasons for initiating this order were now 'lost in the densest fog'.[73] However, despite the fact that this one case appeared to prove beyond a doubt Papon's complicity in a crime against humanity, the jury ultimately decided that Papon was not guilty of complicity in Léon Librach's death.

Notwithstanding its probative value, this case took place at the very outset of the examination of the convoys, when the climate of the proceedings was very much to Papon's disadvantage. And it was not followed – as the case led one to anticipate – by further evidence from the civil plaintiffs showing Papon's signature on arrest, deportation or requisition orders. This left the prosecution stranded with a new legal conundrum: without hard evidence of Papon's active agency, they were obliged to switch their focus to Papon's *passive* criminal agency. As the prosecution sought to reconfigure the legal terms of Maurice Papon's culpable agency during the remainder of the trial, the solitary figure of Léon Librach tended to fade from view.

In fact in the summing-up phase of the last few weeks of the trial, the singularity of Léon Librach's dossier played a lesser role than would have been expected in the light of its evidential status. The most influential civil lawyers recalibrated their original accusations to focus on the responsibility and criminal culpability attendant upon the fact that Papon had remained in his prefectural post.[74] To have done so knowing that crimes against humanity were being committed superseded the charge of direct and active complicity. One civil lawyer, Michel Zaoui, contended: 'it wasn't the signature which demonstrated responsibility', but Papon's implication 'in the chain of responsibility of the crime's implementation' and he spoke of 'an administrative crime', an 'office crime'.[75] This meant, as we have seen, asking the court to judge Papon not so much for his individual acts against the victims represented by the civil plaintiffs, but for his representative and culpable *function*. And the jury, exercising its 'intimate conviction', appears to have complied with this injunction.

But the understandable satisfaction and jubilation amongst all the civil parties following the verdict's announcement does not erase completely from view the figure of Michel Slitinsky, who, after over fifty years of seeking juridical redress for the arrest and deportation of his father by *French functionaries*, was reduced to silence by an impatient court. The fact that in his distracted state Michel Slitinsky was precisely testifying to the *failure* of the judicial process to fulfil its paramount function – to personalize responsibility for his father's fate – had to be consigned to irrelevancy by the court. It is this poignant image that raises a doubt as to whether the trial facilitated – *or could have facilitated* – for witnesses the act of repossessing the act of witnessing. That judgement, however, is for survivors and victims' families alone to render.

Notes

Unless otherwise stated, translations from the French are my own.

1. Lotte Kohler and Hans Saer (eds), *Hannah Arendt–Karl Jaspers Correspond-ence, 1926–1969*, translated by Robert and Rita Kimber (New York: 1992), p. 54. Cited by Dan Diner, 'On Guilt Discourse and Other Narratives', *History and Memory*, vol. 9, nos. 1–2, Fall 1997, p. 319, n. 9.
2. *L'Express*, 22 January 1998.
3. *Le Monde*, 9 October 1997.
4. Apart from the scarcity of direct evidence, the indictment can also be faulted for omitting from legal consideration two convoys for which Papon allegedly requisitioned the assistance of gendarmes. Since no civil parties represented victims of these convoys, details relating to them could not be dealt with by the court.

5. *Libération*, 3 April 1998.

6. See Henry Rousso, *The Vichy Syndrome: History and Memory in France since 1944* (London: Harvard University Press, 1991), and Éric Conan and Henry Rousso, *Vichy, un passé qui ne passe pas* (Paris: Fayard, 1994). See also my review of the latter in 'Memorial Militancy in France: "Working-Through" or the Politics of Anachronism?' in *Patterns of Prejudice*, vol. 29, nos. 2–3, 1995, pp. 89–103.

7. July in *Libération*, 3 April 1998; Rousso in *Le Monde*, 7 April 1998.

8. Rousso elaborated this point further in an interview conducted just before the Papon verdict: 'Justice sets itself the task of deciding whether an individual is guilty or innocent; national memory is the result of an extant tension between memorable and commemorable recollections and forms of forgetting that permit the survival of the community and its projection into the future; history is a project of knowledge and elucidation.' See Henry Rousso, *La hantise du passé (entretien avec Philippe Petit)*, (Paris: Les éditions Textuels,1998), p. 97.

9. Pierre Nora (ed.), *Les Lieux de mémoire* (Paris: Gallimard, 1984, 1986, 1992).

10. I borrow the term *des acrobaties juridiques* from an article in *Le Monde*, 25 March 1998, by historian Georgette Elgey during the week in which the verdict was originally expected.

11. *L'Express*, 2 October 1997.

12. See the illuminating interview with Pierre Nora, 'Tout concourt aujourd'hui au souvenir obsédant de Vichy', *Le Monde*, 1 October 1997.

13. These are Tzvetan Todorov's words in relation to the trial of Paul Touvier, but they equally apply to the Papon trial. See his 'The Touvier Trial' in Richard J. Golsan (ed.), *Memory, the Holocaust and French Justice: The Bousquet and Touvier Affairs* (Dartmouth: University Press of New England,1996), p. 173.

14. The following account relies largely on articles assembled in *Memory, the Holocaust and French Justice* and my own 'Crimes or Misdemeanours?: Memory on Trial in Contemporary France', *French Cultural Studies*, vol. 5, 1994, pp. 1–21.

15. See Henry Rousso's very detailed and acute analysis in 'Une Justice Impossible: L'épuration et la politique antijuive de Vichy', *Annales ESC*, no. 3, May–June 1993, pp. 745–70; and 'Did the Purge Achieve its Goals?' in Golsan (ed.), *Memory, the Holocaust and French Justice*, pp. 100–4. Rousso argues that it is anachronistic to expect from these trials a coherence based on contemporary morality, and that the laws reflected the 'collective perception of magistrates, of juries, of resistance fighters, even of victims themselves, who at the time, in the great majority of cases, did not demand a special punishment for crimes resulting from anti-Semitism in these trials' (p. 103).

16. Golsan (ed.), *Memory, the Holocaust and French Justice*, p. 18.

17. See Rousso's account of the Barbie trial in *The Vichy Syndrome*.

18. Golsan (ed.), *Memory, the Holocaust and French Justice*, p. 19.
19. Todorov, 'The Touvier Trial', p. 175.
20. See 'Touvier: Le dernier procès de l'épuration?' in *Vichy, un passé qui ne passe pas*, pp. 109–72.
21. The following account of the legal intricacies of Papon's case is indebted to Conan's 'Le casse-tête juridique', *L'Express*, 2 October 1997.
22. Toubon's phrase was 'de se débrouiller pour conclure au renvoi', *L'Express*, 2 October 1997.
23. *Le Monde*, 16 October 1997.
24. Varaut had also been lawyer for General Challe at the trial of the *putchistes* during the Algerian War and was an ardent defender of *l'Algérie française*.
25. Conan, 'Le casse-tête juridique'.
26. Paul Thibaud, 'Un temps de mémoire?', *Le Débat*, no. 96, Sept.–Oct. 1997, p. 170. In this article, Thibaud disputes the trial's anticipated value for national memory or justice, believing instead that it was responding to the 'anachronistic' demand of subsequent generations who use memory as 'pure retrospection' rather than as a guide to present action.
27. *Le Monde*, 17 October 1997.
28. Papon claimed that only after receiving a report about Drancy in August 1942 did he have 'no illusions' about the fate of the deportees. If this was naïve, then, said Papon, he confessed to committing 'the crime of naïveté'. Ibid., 7 January 1998.
29. See, for example, Walter Laquer, *The Terrible Secret* (London: Weidenfeld, 1980); Martin Gilbert, *Auschwitz and the Allies* (London: Michael Joseph, 1981); William D. Rubinstein, *The Myth of Rescue: Why the Democracies Could Not Have Saved the Jews From the Nazis* (London: Routledge, 1997); Stéphane Courtois and Adam Rayski (eds), *Qui savait quoi? L'Extermination des Juifs, 1941–1945* (Paris: La Découverte, 1987).
30. *Le Monde*, 3 April 1998.
31. See Conan and Rousso, 'Touvier: Le dernier procès de 'épuration'?', p. 159.
32. *Le Monde*, 7 April 1998. See also Saul Friedländer on 'the simultaneity of considerable knowledge of the facts and of a no less massive inability or refusal to transform these facts into integrated understanding' in '"The 'Final Solution": On the Unease in Historical Interpretation', *Memory, History and the Extermination of the Jews of Europe* (Bloomington: Indiana University Press, 1993), p. 107.
33. *Le Monde*, 1 April 1998. Lanzmann is here citing Shoshana Felman and Dori Laub, whose book *Testimony: Crises of Witnessing in Literature, Psychoanalysis, and History* (London: Routledge, 1992) contains an influential chapter on *Shoah*.
34. Ibid.

35. See Rousso's highlighting of the paradox that historians could not speak to the very documents that it was normally their professional *métier* to analyse. Only the magistrates, lawyers, civil parties and Papon himself had access to these. Nor was the expertise of historians regarding these documents sought at an earlier investigative stage, as it was in the Touvier case with the Commission on Touvier and the Church headed by René Rémond. *La hantise du passé*, p. 103. As this book was going to press, Rousso's critique had ignited a further round of debate about the differences between juridical and historical 'truth'. See 'Vérité judiciaire, vérité historique', *Le Débat*, no. 102, Nov.–Dec. 1998.

36. On 17 October 1961, over 200 Algerians were allegedly killed in the aftermath of a demonstration against a curfew imposed on Algerians living in Paris. According to Jean-Luc Einaudi, author of *La bataille de Paris: 17 octobre 1961* (Paris: Seuil, 1991), Papon's responsibility for this massacre, as Paris police prefect, was 'direct, personal, overwhelming' (*Le Monde*, 17 October 1997). The incident became the subject of testimony and volatile debate in the first month of the trial. However valuable the revelations and actions that followed (especially the government's decision to open the police archives on this matter), Varaut was right in declaring that this constituted a 'trial within a trial'. See also Richard J. Golsan's 'Memory's *bombes à retardement*: Maurice Papon, crimes against humanity, and 17 October 1961', *Journal of European Studies*, no. 28, 1988. There has been a subsequent government report by state adviser Dieudonné Mandelkern that puts at 32 the number of demonstrators killed that night. See *Le Monde*, 5 May 1998.

37. See Robert O. Paxton, *Vichy France: Old Guard and New Order, 1940–1944* (New York: Knopf, 1972) and, co-authored with Michael R. Marrus, *Vichy France and the Jews* (New York: Basic Books, 1981).

38. *Le Monde*, 2–3 November 1997.

39. This argument that the historians who testified were 'prisoners of the mode of interrogation' forms the basis of Rousso's critique of their 'instrumentalization' by the trial: 'A historian does not illuminate a context without direct links to legal interrogation: from the moment the question becomes one of determining an individual's culpability, any argumentation is going to revolve – whether consciously or not – around whatever purports to provide an answer . . .'. See *La hantise du passé*, p. 100. See also Éric Conan, 'L'heure des historiens', *L'Express*, 6 November 1997, for a critical perspective on the role of historians during the trial.

40. See especially Marc-Olivier Baruch, *Servir l'État français. L'administration en France de 1940 à 1944* (Paris: Fayard, 1997), and the interview in *Le Monde*, 1 October 1997. See also Denis Pechanski's article written at the time of the Touvier trial, 'Was There Massive Collaboration of Top Administrative Officials?' in Golsan (ed.), *Memory, the Holocaust and French Justice*, pp.

87–90. Pechanski notes that altogether 'there were 36 prefects and assistant prefects who died because of deportation or their participation in the Resistance. Thirty-five others who were deported returned' (p. 89).

41. *Le Monde*, 7 November 1997.

42. Ibid., 3 April 1998.

43. A number of commentators focused on the revealing attitude implied by Papon's use of the term *juifs intéressants* in his letter to Laval to designate those on whose behalf he had intervened. Historian Pierre Vidal-Naquet for one found this usage encapsulated the essence of Papon's attitude: 'One indeed wants to save some Jews, on the understanding that one shows indifference to the fate of the rest.' Papon, as if to prove this point, claimed that the term was 'a keyword incorporated into the language of the times which alluded to persons on behalf of whom there was an interest to intervene'. Ibid., 2 April 1998.

44. Ibid., 11 February 1998.

45. *L'Express*, 22 January 1998.

46. *Libération*, 4–5 April 1998.

47. It was not lost on some commentators that the Papon trial drew to a close at the very moment when the Front National was making substantial and alarming gains in regional elections in France. See in particular, Patrick Prado in *Le Monde*, 28 March 1998. Prado expressed his incredulity that the Front National could garner such support when the public was being reminded on virtually a daily basis of the historical antecedents of the nationalist ideology it espoused. Prado also noted the similarity between the former functionary being judged in Bordeaux and the 'ideological and psychological profile' of many Front National adherents.

48. In French law, the jury need not give reasons for their judgement; but it was speculated that the strongest case bearing on Papon's administrative complicity concerned some 20 children, sheltered by families after their parents' arrest in July 1942, but then deported to Drancy one month later for reasons that Papon could not explain. No document proved that he signed the order for the children to be removed, but two taxi receipts addressed to the *Service des questions juives* were deemed by civil lawyers to indicate subprefectural involvement.

49. *Libération*, 3 April 1998.

50. Ibid.

51. See especially Éric Conan, 'Un vichysto-résistant parmi d'autres', *L'Express*, 2 October 1997.

52. See 'Génération Mitterrand' in *Vichy, un passé qui ne passe pas*, pp. 173–207. See also *La hantise du passé* (p. 121), where Rousso argues that the evolving allegiances of Mitterrand and Papon are not significant for their 'exemplarity' but because they raise important questions concerning the 'porous nature' of the regime and the 'composite nature' of the Resistance.

53. *Le Monde*, 3 April 1998.
54. This is an issue deserving extended treatment elsewhere. See Nicolas Weill's article, ibid., 1–2 March 1998, which cites important examples of anti-Semitism amongst Resisters and the contrasting perspectives of Paul Thibaud, 'Un temps de mémoire?' and Zeev Sternhell, 'Maurice Papon n'était pas seul', *Le Monde*, 24 September 1997, on whether the patriotism of the Resistance discouraged or nurtured anti-Semitic prejudices.
55. See Éric Conan, 'Procès Papon Résistance', *L'Express*, 5 March 1998.
56. Ibid.
57. Weill's title is significant: 'Une contribution ambiguë à l'historiographie de Vichy', *Le Monde*, 3 April 1998.
58. See Henry Rousso, *La hantise du passé*, p. 98. Despite his critique of the role of historian-as-witness, Rousso is adamant that there were no hard feelings between those who agreed or declined to testify. If historians of Vichy are divided on any single issue at the moment, it is probably the public role that they are now expected to play regarding controversial issues. See *La hantise du passé* for a discussion of the 'Aubrac affair', a controversial roundtable discussion, sponsored by *Libération*, with former Resisters Lucie and Raymond Aubrac and renowned Vichy historians.
59. At the trial, Jean Pierre Azéma and Philippe Burrin explicitly emphasized the distinction between Vichy's politics of exclusion and the Nazi policy of extermination, echoing the arguments of Rousso and Conan in *Vichy, un passé qui ne passe pas*.
60. See Nicolas Weill, 'Premières leçons du procès Papon', *Le Monde* 12 June 1998. Deliberately evoking Goldhagen, Weill referred to the 'eliminationist' anti-Semitism existing in France from the Dreyfus affair to the 1930s.
61. See Jean Améry, 'Resentments', *At the Mind's Limits: Contemplations by a Survivor of Auschwitz and Its Realities*, trans. Sidney Rosenfeld and Stella Rosenfeld (New York: Schocken Books, 1990), p. 72 and Chapter 3 of this book.
62. Felman and Laub, *Testimony*, p. 78. See also Primo Levi's, *If This Is A Man/The Truce* (London: Abacus, 1987), p. 15 for his description of testimony as a physiological need.
63. Éric Conan, 'Cérémonies sacrées', *L'Express*, 25 December 1997.
64. Cited in ibid.
65. Ibid.
66. *Le Monde*, 7 April 1998.
67. Ibid., 5 March 1998.
68. Ibid., 22 January 1998.
69. Felman and Laub, *Testimony*, p.62
70. *Le Monde*, 23 January 1998. Despite this intervention on Papon's part, he had

not 'saved' 130 Jews, as he had alleged during the trial. A *Libération* exposé published in the week following Papon's claim showed that he had merely struck off the 'Jewish file' (*fichier des israelites*) those who were not Jews according to the *Statut des juifs*. According to *Libération*'s investigation: 'He only applied conscientiously Vichy's racial laws, dividing "Ayrans" from Jews, thus condemning the latter to deportation but "saving" Catholics whom the Germans never had the intention of deporting – or killing' (3 December 1997). Papon maintained later in the trial that by 'the simple application of the *Statut des juifs* then in force', letters to the German authorities, warnings to families, and other similar measures he had saved hundreds of persons. *Le Monde*, 18 February 1998.

71. *Le Monde*, 29 January 1998.
72. See Éric Conan, 'Il faut en finir!' *L'Express*, 22 January 1998, for an astute analysis of this turn in the trial.
73. *Le Monde*, 11 December 1997.
74. Arno Klarsfeld is the notable exception. Klarsfeld concentrated on the case of the children deported in August 1942. He also incurred the wrath of other civil party lawyers by demanding an exemplary sentence rather than imprisonment for perpetuity – a move supported by the Public Prosecutor but decried by other prosecution lawyers as the *minimalisme klarsfeldien*. The role of the Klarsfelds during the trial warrants extended treatment in its own right. Rousso describes their approach as one that constantly attempted to 'force the hand of the court', so that, by its verdict, the court would 'write the history they wanted'. See *La hantise du passé*, p. 113.
75. *Le Monde*, 18 March 1998.

–6–

Colonial Nostalgia and *Le Premier Homme*

Introduction

Writing in *Le Nouvel Observateur* in 1978, journalist and editor Jean Daniel commented with great force and passion on a 'recourse to Camus' that was then making itself felt in French intellectual culture. Daniel himself was not an indifferent chronicler of this perceived 'Camusian' turn: fellow *pied-noir* from Algeria, and friend of Albert Camus's since a 1953 collaboration on Daniel's journal *Caliban*, he spoke of a 'reparation' that had been anticipated for some time by Camus's loyal followers – a making of amends, in his words, '. . . where Camus's loyal followers, and they alone, would render the justice due to him'.[1] Daniel was of course referring to the progressive decline in Camus's stature – at least among left intellectuals – consequent upon his famous rupture with Sartre in 1952, after *Les Temps modernes* published Francis Jeanson's scathing review of *L'Homme révolté*.

In the next decade, another appeal for a 'return to Camus' could be heard, though this time inspired by very different political contingencies. In the mid-1980s, on the occasion of a colloquium 'Camus et la politique', journalist Paul Thibaud argued that, once again, recourse to Camus could provide a point of departure for a critical, 'non-Manichaean' reappraisal of the past. However this time the past invoked was not the French left's embrace of Marxism, and of a view of History, in Camus's words, considered 'as a totality' and 'without a value to transform it',[2] but the positions and allegiances claimed by French intellectuals during the Algerian war. And it is Camus's writings on Algeria, and the path which led him in 1958 to pledge silence on the subject of the war, that are proposed as the vital source of this reflection. Though they were long considered by the left as a testimony to Camus's failure to transcend his primal loyalties to Algeria's *pied-noir* community, and to the impasse of a reformist solution faced with demands for independence, the seminar subjects Camus's writings on Algeria to a new reading. This reading emphasizes Camus's early awareness of nascent nationalist sentiments, his conviction that the policies of metropolitan France were fuelling these and thwarting the necessary reform, and his belief that the nationalist cause was being appropriated by the authoritarian socialist variant represented by the FLN. An appreciation of the complexity of Camus's positions, it was argued, and even their own prophetic

– 143 –

nature – the successive FLN cliques that had ruled independent Algeria retained power thanks to systematic political repression – implicitly turned the spotlight on the French left's own very partial understanding of the dynamics of the Franco-Algerian conflict.[3]

In the 1990s, there have been signs in France of yet another 'return to Camus'. A conjunction of factors seems to be responsible for this latest revival. The murderous intensification of Algeria's civil war has compelled many to delve deeper into Camus's writings on Algeria, not in the hopes of finding a panacea for Algeria's current troubles or even to vindicate the positions adopted by Camus, but in order to recall some features of his analysis and initiatives (including his unsuccessful appeal for a 'civil truce' *(trêve civile)* during the height of the Algerian war) that might contain relevant insights for the present.[4] Meanwhile, as French intellectuals are increasingly accused of sacrificing their moral principles on the altar of media adulation, Camus's 'moral authority' continues to be cited as one of the few sources of inspiration for an ethically oriented politics.[5]

But perhaps the most tangible sign of his continuing and imposing presence in the contemporary intellectual landscape is the tremendous success of his novel *Le Premier Homme*, published thirty-four years after his death. An avalanche of reviews hailed *Le Premier Homme*'s publication (in spring 1994 in France, followed a year later by the English edition) as the year's literary event. Indeed, many reviewers declared the book to be nothing short of an unfinished masterpiece – an estimation rendered all the more compelling by the circumstances surrounding its publication. Not only was the manuscript's very existence of dramatic import (it was found in Camus's muddied briefcase at the scene of the fatal car crash in 1960), but tantalizing hints as to its content were revealed in Herbert Lottman's extensively documented biography of Camus in 1979. Lottman opened his biography with a discussion of the importance Camus attached to this work-in-progress: as a return to the creativity that had eluded him for so long, Camus joked to his friends that the book represented no less than his *War and Peace*.[6] The long delay in publication, defended by his daughter Catherine Camus in the English edition as a decision taken in order not to give further 'ammunition to those who were saying Camus was through as a writer',[7] only intensified among the book's champions the sense that the justice invoked by Jean Daniel some twenty-five years earlier had finally been rendered. As one reviewer perceptively noted, the appearance of *Le Premier Homme* was an 'editorial and quasi-sociological phenomenon', betraying

> an emotional burden which extends considerably beyond the boundaries of the literary field: the result of curiosity, of nostalgia, of Camus's intact fame, of regret for an *oeuvre* that was never written and that one wanted to be even more beautiful, an *hommage* to someone loved and detested, who is today respected. One celebrates the myth of a brilliant life, transformed by accidental death into a destiny, a sign from beyond the grave, a reproach for the days when French literature counted for something . . .[8]

Amidst such emotionally overdetermined reasons to defend and celebrate both the man and the long-awaited novel, it is all the more noteworthy, then, to find a Camusian expert like Conor Cruise O'Brien levelling against the book the charge of literary regression. Indeed, O'Brien entitles his extended review of the English edition, *The First Man*, 'The Fall'. The allusion to Camus's (arguably) most celebrated novel is not mere literary conceit; O'Brien makes the argument that his culminating text, notwithstanding its unfinished – and hence necessarily provisional – character, represents a step backward from the achievements of *The Fall*. In even stronger terms, O'Brien contends that if, as is generally accepted, most or all of *The First Man* was drafted after *The Fall*, then

> we must face an inescapable conclusion about Camus's development as a writer. On the basis of *The First Man*, and its return to the aestheticism and the self-righteousness of his earlier writings, we must conclude that as a writer Camus regressed, that he reneged upon his greatest literary and intellectual attainments.[9]

Even more central to O'Brien's critique than the novel's style or tone is the claim that Camus's alleged 'fall' from literary grace can be traced to extra-literary – indeed one might say to 'psycho-political' – sources: in O'Brien's words, 'to the situation of Camus's people, the *pieds-noirs*, the Europeans of Algeria, in the period between the completion of *The Fall* in 1956 and Camus's death in February [*sic*], 1960'.[10] O'Brien contends that Camus's over-identification with the worsening plight of the *pied-noir* as the Algerian war descended into its most murderous phase, and with no solution short of independence in sight, led him in his despair to indulge in a 'nostalgia' and 'melodrama of the self' that in *The Fall* had been the target of such effective derision.

I shall return to O'Brien's critique in due course; but first I want to make a detour in order to reflect upon how we might approach the use of the term 'nostalgia' in relation to Camus's last novel – a term that O'Brien is not alone in invoking, though most reviewers have done so without the negative connotations that clearly attach to O'Brien's ascription. And indeed in its conventional usage, 'nostalgia' usually refers to an evocation of the past that is imbued with warm, glowing feelings and pleasurable reminiscences. However, the very etymology of the word, from the Greek *nostos* meaning 'to return home' and *algos*, 'a painful condition', begins to suggest something of its more equivocal qualities.

Psychoanalysis has usefully elucidated the ambivalent psychical nature of nostalgia by identifying a pathological potential in this mode of remembering, where an idealization of the past is accompanied by a refusal to accept that this past can never return. In steadfastly clinging to a past cathected as a lost love object, nostalgia serves the function of denial and of a defence against, and substitute for, mourning. It activates what one psychoanalyst describes as 'a screen function in which the objects of nostalgic attachment are condensations of childhood values, derivatives of early fantasies that are used to idealize the past, preventing movement toward the future'.[11] Like other 'screen memories', these reminiscences are recalled with great clarity, though not because of their intrinsically memorable nature, but because they are the representational traces of more painful memories that have been subject to repression. The pleasant sensation that accompanies these memories is in turn described as a 'screen affect' whose function is to 'distort or camouflage painful feelings by pleasurable misrepresentations'.[12]

Many allegedly 'innocent' evocations of childhood memories could clearly be subjected to this kind of psychoanalytical scrutiny and the feelings of elation that accompany them could be unmasked to reveal the deeper workings of repression. My concern is not to subject Camus's childhood memories to this kind of critique in order to make the case for *Le Premier Homme* as psychobiography. In fact, it is not Camus's childhood memories as such that are my primary interest here, but other representations of the Franco-Algerian past that *Le Premier Homme* elicits. In order to explore these, I would like to retain a psychoanalytically-informed concept of nostalgia but extend it beyond the realm of the individual psyche and into the socio-historical domain. For if the 'psychopathology of nostalgia' that psychoanalysis identifies commands particular attention in the case of Camus and *Le Premier Homme*, it is because of the specific socio-historical context in which his childhood and early adulthood was lived and that provided the raw material for the novel's profusion of memories and representations of the past.

The anthropologist Renato Rosaldo has argued that a particular *kind* of nostalgia marks those memories deriving from a colonial era, since these are usually characterized by a mourning for the passing of what the colonialists themselves have transformed. 'Imperialist nostalgia', he claims, revolves around a paradox: '. . . someone deliberately alters a form of life and then regrets that things have not remained as they were prior to his or her intervention . . . In any of its versions, imperialist nostalgia uses a pose of "innocent yearning" both to capture people's imaginations and to conceal its complicity with often brutal domination.'[13] This notion of 'imperialist nostalgia' is particularly resonant with Edward Said's reading of Camus's fiction as a form of 'controlled nostalgia' in his book *Culture and Imperialism*.

Camus and his Critics

Published a year before *Le Premier Homme*, *Culture and Imperialism* subjects Camus's fiction to a searing – but measured – critique.[14] Said discerns behind the affective structure of Camus's novels 'an extraordinarily belated, in some ways, incapacitated colonial sensibility'. Said's discussion of Camus's *oeuvre* is detailed and nuanced and can only be adumbrated here. But it is first of all significant to note that Said praises an early book by Conor Cruise O'Brien on Camus as an 'agile demystification' of the relation between Camus's novels and the colonial context in which they were embedded. But because he ultimately believes that O'Brien too easily lets Camus 'off the hook', the main thrust of Said's critique is to extend and deepen O'Brien's attempt to locate Camus's narratives of existential isolation and confrontation in the geopolitical context with which they are intimately linked. This context, maintains Said, is at once France's brutal history of colonial domination of Algeria as well as the struggle for national independence that is making its presence powerfully felt even as Camus is writing fiction that chooses to ignore its existence.

Said's approach is not to treat Camus as representative of the French *colon* in any simple sense, and he acknowledges Camus's pre-war reports that documented Algeria's rural poverty and called for reforms of the colonial *status quo*. Instead, he poses three 'methodological' issues about the reception of Camus's fiction. Firstly, he asks how we are to construe Camus's use of an Algerian setting for stories (*L'Étranger, La Peste, L'Exil et le royaume*) that have been widely interpreted as parables for *another* context of domination: France under Nazi occupation. Secondly, when Camus does make reference to contemporary Algeria, according to Said he focuses exclusively on 'the actual state of Franco-Algerian affairs' and neglects any historical dimension that would otherwise expose the drama through which he is living as colonialism's last and final act. By relegating the colonial past and de-historicizing the colonial present, Said argues that Camus's novels must themselves be interpreted as 'interventions in the history of French efforts in Algeria, making and keeping it French . . . as affiliated historically both with the French colonial venture itself (since he assumes it to be immutable) and with outright opposition to Algerian independence' (p. 212).

Moreover, Camus's colonial sensibility is for Said not only a matter of what he symptomatically excludes from his fiction, but of what is manifestly present. And it is Camus's frequent invocation and usage of the Algerian landscape that furnishes the link for Said between Camus's novels and the unabated will-to-power of France's colonial adventure.

Said is not the first to attempt to establish this link. Many earlier studies have dwelt upon the Algerian subtext that traverses Camus's fiction, and especially the symbolic significance that he confers upon the country's geography and natural elements (the most well-known examples being the sensuous sea of *La Peste* and the murderous sun of *L'Étranger*).[15] While for some these references merely confirm Camus's visceral attachment to his homeland, for others they have provided the key to interpreting the political implications of such attachments. Albert Memmi, whose description of Camus as the left-liberal 'colonizer of good will' (*le colonisateur de bonne volonté*) has so often been cited, attempted in his early study *The Colonizer and the Colonized* to elaborate certain psychological features of what he called the 'colonialist's nationalism'. Memmi argued that this nationalism typically took the form of incorporating into the 'collective superego of the colonizers' an idealized image of the homeland such that 'its material features become quasi-ethical qualities'. In the colonial imagination, Algeria was 'the remote and never intimately known ideal . . . immutable and sheltered from time'. This idealized image must emphasize the inaccessible and the timeless, maintained Memmi, since 'the colonialist requires his homeland to be conservative'.[16]

Said's analysis follows in the footsteps of Memmi, and he is adamant that one can find in the narratives of Camus – whatever their ostensible moral or existential agenda – the same conservative representation of Algerian *territory*. When Camus evokes the French presence in Algeria, Said maintains, it is not the legacy of colonial violence that is called upon to explain this occupancy but a history of French settlement that is either assumed by the narrative or 'subject to neither time nor interpretation . . .' (p. 217). By thus excising from his narratives any reference to the protracted struggle to wrest the land from its indigenous inhabitants, Camus colludes in a vision of a country upon which the French-Algerian seems to have staked an irrefutable claim. Again, Said registers the important difference between the way the Algerian landscape is rendered in Camus and the tradition of settler literature that preceded him. Camus's fiction is not explicitly concerned with the task of historical legitimation of the colonial adventure, unlike much literature of the 'Algerianist' school, which made the settlers' lengthy struggle with the country's harsh physical elements the basis of their claim to colonial rule. Yet Said maintains that by uncritically accepting the claims embedded in the long tradition of colonial writing on Algeria, and by incorporating its 'idioms and discursive strategies' – not least the form of the realist novel itself – Camus's narratives 'lay severe and ontologically prior claims to Algeria's geography' (p. 217). Camus may sidestep colonial history in one sense, but in offering in its stead a chronicle of 'ceremonies of bonding with the territory', Camus's writing is profoundly implicated in that colonial history. The Algerian locale of Camus's fiction, insists Said, should not be seen as a mere backdrop for the *mise-en-scène* of essentially moral or existential dilemmas, but as a constitutive component of the 'political and interpretive contest to represent, inhabit, and possess the territory itself' (p. 213).[17]

With the publication of *Le Premier Homme*, Said's analysis gains an even more compelling dimension, since here we have a text that, amongst other narrative strands, explicitly thematizes the colonial past at the same time that it firmly locates the novel's present as the height of the Algerian war of independence.[18] A key question, then, arising from Said's critique, is how Camus treats this history and its relation to the novel's contemporary context. Does he indulge, like the settler literature of Louis Bertrand, Robert Randau and others, in what Said describes as mere 'commemorations of survival'? Or is there an awareness that successful settler implantation was predicated on a colonial violence that is the key to understanding the violence of the novel's present? The novel also makes frequent reference to the 'immense oblivion' of the Algerian landscape, to its 'interminable stretch of mountains' and 'barren and deserted space'. How do such territorial representations relate to the temporal and ethical sensibility of the *pieds-noirs* who are, undoubtedly, the main subjects of the novel? Finally, in so far as *Le Premier Homme* is structured primarily by modes of remembering, should these representations be seen as articulations of Camus's own 'colonial nostalgia' that betray the unconscious forces shaping his own colonial imagination?

This is in fact the substance of O'Brien's critique of the novel. Though he would probably disdain the appeal to a psychoanalytic perspective, O'Brien essentially argues that a 'screen affect' is at work in the novel wherein Camus's nostalgic mode of remembering functions to override a critical awareness of Algeria's colonial past, in favour of 'pleasurable misrepresentations' (to invoke psychoanalytic terminology) that sustain his unquestioned loyalty to the *pied-noir* community.

Said and O'Brien make unlikely political *confrères,* but I think O'Brien's critique of *The First Man* is one that Said might applaud to the extent that it seeks to relate the narrative and textual strategies of *The First Man* to the political and emotional sentiments that Camus harboured toward Algeria in the period of its composition. By contrast, most reviewers, while praising the author's evocation of his Algerian childhood (via his textual representative 'Jacques Cormery'), fail to situate this either with respect to the colonial past that the adult Cormery conjures, or to the novel's violent present (roughly between 1957 and 1959) that interrupts his child-hood reveries and reveals Algeria in the convulsive throes of decolonization.[19] However, I shall argue that O'Brien's approach contains its own misrepresentations – both with regard to the nature of Camus's political and emotional commitments in the Algerian arena, and to how these are articulated in the novel. In my view these lead O'Brien to impose a one-dimensional reading on the novel's multifarious exploration of French-Algerian identity during that moment of historical crisis. My defence of *Le Premier Homme/The First Man*'s multifaceted character will therefore follow closely the contours of O'Brien's own critique, since it seems to me that he raises the right questions about what is at stake in a contemporary appraisal of the novel, even though I disagree profoundly with his conclusions.

As Said reminds us, O'Brien is the author of a 1970 study, *Albert Camus of Europe and Africa*, whose title indicates the importance that O'Brien, too, attaches to the geopolitical context of Camus's writing.[20] Moreover, it is interesting to note that despite O'Brien's own political evolution (from a *tier-mondisme* that backed Sartre and Jeanson's support of Algerian independence, to a conservatism by no means sympathetic to such appeals elsewhere), he remains remarkably consistent in his judgement of why Camus resisted the nationalist solution. Camus, observed the early O'Brien, 'liked to express himself in universalist terms' but his 'actual positions were political and partisan'. Nowhere was this more evident than in

Camus's political writings on the Algerian war in *Actuelles III*, which O'Brien describes as 'categorical and resonant in tone, equivocal in substance'. Such equivocation arises, according to O'Brien, because Camus ultimately subordinated principles he had defended elsewhere – the right to rebel, condemnation of violence, openness to negotiation – to more primal loyalties he felt he owed to his 'tribe': the Europeans of Algeria. In his review of *The First Man*, O'Brien cites these same allegiances as the source of Camus's main political miscalculation – viz. his hope that an invasion of the Suez Canal Zone would clip the wings of Arab nationalism and weaken FLN determination – and as the cause of his eventual despair in the aftermath of the Franco-British withdrawal and intensification of FLN resolve. This is the moment – late 1956 – when, in O'Brien's view, Camus succumbs to a despair that finds expression in key episodes of *The First Man*.

Camus's suspicion that the bid for Algerian independence was partly a manifestation of Nasser's promotion of Arab nationalism (a 'new imperialism' that he in turn accused Russia of exploiting) certainly constituted one dimension of his analysis of the forces behind the Algerian uprising. However, O'Brien's characterization of the Suez invasion as 'Camus's panacea for the troubles of French Algeria' is simply a negation of his long-standing efforts on behalf of internal political reform, including his support, reiterated in his final statement of 1958, for a federal solution. Moreover, Camus also rejected the ideological grounds of the nationalist claim: that independence would restore to Algeria a nationhood confiscated by French colonization. He reacted to demands for Algerian sovereignty with the argument that:

> national independence is a formula driven by nothing other than passion. There has never yet been an Algerian nation. The Jews, Turks, Greeks, Italians, or Berbers would be as entitled to claim the leadership of this potential nation. As things stand, the Arabs alone do not comprise the whole of Algeria. The size and duration of the French settlement, in particular, are enough to create a problem that cannot be compared to anything else in history.[21]

There are two very different claims embedded in this citation, which Said describes as Camus's 'uncompromisingly severe political statement'. The first is the proposition that because Algerian nationhood was never a political reality before colonization, there is no historical basis to the nationalist demand for an Arab-dominated Algerian state; the second is that the size and longevity of the French community has produced a deep identification with the country and feelings of rootedness.

As a number of commentators have pointed out, the fact that pre-colonial Algeria displayed a weak or incipient national self-consciousness could hardly function as a decisive factor in a situation where the anti-colonial struggle itself was rapidly forging that very consciousness.[22] But behind such political rationalizations for and against independence loomed for Camus the second and more volatile issue of what kind of rights the non-Muslim population of Algeria could claim – and have recognized – when it came to adjudicating on their own and the country's future. O'Brien is right in considering *The First Man* as Camus's fictional response to this – for him, burning – question – a response that, whatever his rational appraisal of the situation, was equally 'driven by passion'.

Camus's complex identification with the *pied-noir* community cannot be treated at length here; but as Michael Walzer has eloquently argued, it was an identification that, far from contradicting his commitment to universal values, permitted him to clarify, deepen and actualize the meaning of that commitment. Camus's universalism, according to Walzer, was 'constructed out of repeated particularities; it worked by ... reiteration, not by abstraction'.[23] Rejecting O'Brien's dualism of universal values and local, affectively-based loyalties, Walzer maintains that Camus's constant affirmation of his profound attachment to his country and to his fellow *pieds-noirs* provided the essential ground for a 'social criticism from within'. This criticism was directed at a false universalism endemic to colonial Algeria that, in Camus's words, perpetuated the 'repeated lie of constantly proposed but never realized assimilation'.[24] And because such dissimulation reflected negatively on the country and people to which Camus felt bound, he felt equally obliged to take up the role of social critic and unpopular advocate of radical reform. When the option of reform was finally exhausted, owing to a combined lack of political will in the *metropole* and the intransigence of the *pied-noir* community, and the war pursued its violent course, Camus still did not sever those affective ties, but appealed to all sides for reconciliation, for a 'politics of reparation, not a politics of expiation'.[25] As Walzer demonstrates, Camus's own writings on the Algerian conflict provide ample evidence of the 'critical connection' – rather than immoderate and imprudent identification – that he sustained with his fellow *pieds-noirs*.

But even if O'Brien might concede this point in relation to Camus's journalism, it is clear he believes that we must turn to Camus's fictional output for true insight into his Algerian passions.

O'Brien's early study of Camus's novels directs its critical force to those commentators who either ignored, or (like Germaine Brée) idealized Camus's treatment of the relationship between the Arab and Berber population and the working-class Europeans amongst whom Camus grew up in the Belcourt quarter of Algiers. At a general level, O'Brien pointed out that during the war of independence 'working-class Europeans were among the most determined supporters of the French army and most bitter enemies of the Moslem *fellagha*'.[26] With respect to Camus in particular, O'Brien found little in his fictional writing that explored the dynamics of the Muslim–European relationship or elucidated the endemic racial barriers that made colonial Algeria a 'structurally segregated' society claiming adherence to republican universalism.[27] Indeed, O'Brien targets Camus's earlier writings, most notably a 1937 speech delivered at the Maison de la Culture on the theme of the unity of Mediterranean culture, for their complicity – if not with a proto-fascist discourse of the 'the Latin West' propounded by the likes of Mussolini – at least with a Eurocentric appropriation of Mediterranean culture to the exclusion of its indigenous languages and customs. Ignoring the fact that a majority of the inhabitants of Algeria spoke Arabic and extolling a unity based on the similarity of Romance languages, Camus, alleged O'Brien, was ultimately 'incapable of thinking in any categories other than those of a Frenchman'.[28] Here, O'Brien agreed with Memmi's prognosis that in having such contradictory sentiments, Camus was the prototype of Algeria's 'left-wing colonists' who unconsciously 'shared the assumptions of a colonialism which they consciously rejected'.[29] Moreover, living out this internal contradiction had psychological effects that manifested themselves, according to O'Brien, not as mere estrangement from social reality, but as an hallucinatory state of being in which one fantasized for oneself and one's cohabitants an identity that was wholly illusory in character. For O'Brien, Camus's own mode of affirming a common collective heritage and identity in the face of Algeria's deep schisms was not only indicative of the liberal's political naïveté, but symptomatic of the pathological self-delusion that Camus shared with his fellow French Algerians:

> ... when a brilliantly intelligent and well-educated man, who has lived all his life surrounded by an Arabic-speaking population, affirms the existence of a form of unity including the Arabs and based on the Romance languages, it is not excessive to speak of hallucination. It is important for the better understanding both of Camus's work and of his political development – and the two are intertwined – to try to grasp this situation from the outset. Camus is a stranger on the African shore, and surrounded by people who are strangers in that France of which they are legally supposed to be a part. The splendidly rationalist system of education which molded Camus was propagating, in relation to his own social context, a myth: that of French Algeria.[30]

I have quoted this passage at length because in its own condemnatory way, I think it provides a key to interpreting the crucial passages in *Le Premier Homme* where Camus the author, through Jacques Cormery, attempts to render the history and memory of the French colonial experience in a manner that at times indeed verges on the 'hallucinatory'. But I would argue that the function of this brief descent into madness is not to pander to an illusion of unproblematic national identity, as the early O'Brien asserts is the case with Camus's musings on Mediterranean culture, nor to indulge in a 'melodrama of the self', as the later O'Brien claims. Instead, I would argue that the novel's – at times delirious – ruminations on 'The First Man' – that is to say, the first-generation French settlers of Algeria – show Camus trying to come to terms with a legacy he well knows to be implicated in colonial oppression (and hence in the revolt through which he is living), yet one whose meaning he refuses to reduce to that fact alone. This last novel is, in my view, not a surrender to nostalgia but an attempt to mediate between the 'objective guilt' of the *pieds noirs* and the heroic myths they nurtured, and to come up with a historical memory that includes all the ambivalences but moderates the extremes.

It is worth noting here that Said remarked of the *colon* of Algeria that he embodied 'both the real human effort his community contributed and the obstacle of refusing to give up a systematically unjust political system' (p. 24). It is certainly true that Camus never proved able fully to embrace (or represent) what Said presents as 'the more difficult and challenging alternative of first judging, then refusing France's territorial seizure and political sovereignty' (ibid.). However, what we do find in *Le Premier Homme* is a testimony to that 'real human effort' *and* the anguished realization that the rights and historical entitlements that are assumed to derive from that effort are being pleaded by a community that Memmi famously designated as 'a minority which is historically in the wrong'. While Camus vehemently rejected the reduction of questions of agency and responsibility to the attribution of so-called objective guilt,[31] when this argument was wielded as a way of prescribing how French Algerians *should* respond to demands for independence, he felt obliged to confront the many and complex emotional investments that bound him and his community to the country they were being asked to renounce.[32] In so doing, in opting for an affectively charged rendition of the colonizers' experience, rather than its cold repudiation, the novel certainly runs the risk of legitimizing that history. But if Camus occasionally surrenders to the 'animating force' of nostalgia and pathos, as O'Brien alleges, I also believe that what Walzer argues is the case for Camus's political writings also holds true for this novel: that *only* by mobilizing this affective dimension is he able to grapple with the consequences for his own riven identity of what the novel describes as a history both 'dreadful and exalted'. It is this sense of division that, in my view, provides *Le Premier Homme* not only with its central narrative structure – the quest for origins – but with its main psychological drive.

Love, Death and War in Colonial Algeria

O'Brien bases his interpretation of *The First Man* on the assumption that Camus's protagonist is the mere mouthpiece of the author ('Cormery simply *is* Camus in every biographical respect . . .'). But if the heavily autobiographical element in the third-person narration of Jacques Cormery is undeniable, such an assertion excludes from consideration the other 'voices' the text contains that construct our perception of the character Cormery, including what in post-structural parlance would be identified as the 'split subjectivity' of Cormery/Camus himself. Yet surely such a reading is demanded by the novel's key motifs: an adult Jacques Cormery relates what he imagines to be the circumstances of his own birth, and then later conjures more primordial family origins in the period of colonization; interspersed with these imaginings, memories of a childhood and coming-of-age in Algiers are recalled by the same Cormery in the course of several journeys between France and Algeria. The element of fantasy, then, is not simply an embellishment of *Le Premier Homme* but an integral feature of it: it shapes the form and content of the childhood memories, which are undoubtedly based on the real-life experiences of Camus,[33] and it materializes a 'colonial family romance'[34] against the backdrop of an account of Algeria's settlement.

It is significant that O'Brien cites as the novel's 'most powerful passage' and prime example of Camus's descent into despair Jacques Cormery's conversation with a French-Algerian farmer, Veillard, who relates how his own father, a *colon*, responded to his expropriation from 'the forbidden zone' that had come under French army control during the course of this 'undeclared war'. The old man – 'a real settler. Of the old school' – decides after the grape harvest to empty all his wine vats, flood his fields, and uproot the vines all over his property. When an army officer demands an explanation, the old man tells him: 'Young man, since what we made here is a crime, it has to be wiped out.' He advises his Arab workers to join the guerrillas since '[t]hey're going to win. There're no men left in France.'[35] The passage ends with the son describing his father now living in Marseilles, in a modern apartment and pacing around his room in circles.

The passage is powerful, not only because it prophetically anticipates the 'scorched earth' policy that many hardline *pieds-noirs* executed before their departure in 1961–2, but because of the image it conjures of a hard-working man literally driven to distraction by the confiscation of everything to which he believes his labour and ownership had entitled him. Moreover, at this point in the novel, there is no counteracting voice that mitigates our sympathies and puts this sense of entitlement into perspective by reminding us of the prior expropriation upon which it was based. It would seem that by eliciting an empathetic response, Camus indeed comes perilously close to pleading the case of the *colon* as the dispossessed, the victim of a historical injustice. Veillard's own refusal to leave, explained in terms of the cyclical nature of European/Muslim conflict and the inevitable return to peaceful coexistence, may temper this bleak prediction, but it does so by appealing to the vagaries and constants of a debased human nature rather than to any acknowledgment of the need to change the colonial status quo: 'We were made to understand each other. Fools and brutes like us, but with the same blood of men. We'll kill each other for a little longer, cut off each other's balls and torture each other a bit. And then we'll go back to living as men together. The country wants it that way' (p. 181).

Such episodes seem to confirm Camus's descent into despair and resignation – a mood relieved only by a nostalgia (in the novel's lyrical evocation of childhood memories) that in O'Brien's words 'is the hope of those who feel condemned by history'. But, once again, rather than seeing *Le Premier Homme* as stranded between despair and nostalgia, I find the novel to be far more complex than O'Brien is prepared to allow. And I would locate the key site of this complexity in Camus's brief forays into Algerian colonial history, where he attempts to invent for himself and his community a *historical memory* that could be invoked as part of Algeria's collective heritage or *patrimoine*. In the course of their unfolding, however, these memories take on such an hallucinatory and ambivalent character that rather than confidently securing patrimonial claims, they seem to function as harbinger of the very ills over which the author anguishes.

In his fascinating psychological profile of Algeria's *pied-noir* community, written in 1960–1, Pierre Nora described this community's relation to its colonial past in the following terms: 'At the deepest level, their venture is so culpable that they dare not recognize nor write about it, except in the heroic-epic and braggartly virile mode. The French of Algeria have cut themselves off from their history; in the technical terms of psychological analysis, they have "scotomised" it.'[36] Nora's diagnosis of a community rendered psychically incapable of facing its own culpable history except by relating it as heroic epic renders all the more compelling Camus's almost coincidental attempt to render in the epic mode Jacques Cormery's quest for family origins and their place in *pied-noir* history.

The critical section here is one that in fictional chronology follows closely on the heels of Cormery's conversation with Veillard cited above. (It is recalled by Jacques in a state of semi-torpor on a plane journey back to Algiers.) Cormery, joined by Veillard, visits the old doctor who brought Jacques into the world. The doctor relates to him the story of his father's arrival at the settlement of Solférino and of his own birth, and comments on the Parisian-sounding names of the witnesses at his birth. Solférino, explains the doctor, was founded by 'forty-eighters'. Veillard confirms that his great-grandparents were among these original settlers, driven by unemployment and political unrest (they were veterans of the 1848 Revolution), and enticed by the land allocations voted by the Constituent Assembly. The men dreamed of 'the Promised Land', believed in 'Santa Claus' and in any case were resolved that '[t]hey hadn't made the revolution for nothing'. The doctor takes up the story, describing six barges that transported one group of Parisian settlers down the Seine amidst fanfares (a brass band playing the *Marseillaise*) and blessings from the clergy for undertaking their civilizing mission. But, he interjects, doubt crept in early, 'and even the strongest of spirits, the tough ones from the barricades, they fell silent, sick at heart' (p. 186). It is significant, then, that Camus evokes the image of the first pioneers not as zealous capitalist entrepreneurs or military adventurers, but as radical republicans, political exiles who embark on their journey with a strong sense of their own persecuted status and equally strong premonitions of the ordeals that lie ahead.

As the doctor continues the story of this particular journey, the ordeals are described in gruesome succession: the paddlewheeler, the *Labrador*, taking them across the Mediterranean, hits a storm that lasts five days and nights, leaving 'the conquerors at the bottom of the hold, deathly ill, vomiting on each other and wanting to die . . .' (p. 187). Arriving at the port of Bône, the travellers set out for their promised land 'under the hostile eyes of occasional groups of Arabs watching them from a distance'. At their destination – 'a wretched hostile place' – they endure eight days of rain, and these former comrades at the barricades find themselves reduced to 'brother-enemies in the filthy promiscuity of the great tents resonating under the interminable downpour' (p. 189). In the spring, their shacks finally built, 'they were entitled to cholera', which claimed 'ten a day'. That is when, related the doctor, 'they had an idea. You had to dance to stir up the blood'. Camus then offers what can only be described as 'hallucinatory' images of the 'conquerors', as they desperately attempt to stave off by any means their impending mortality:

> In the hot humid night – between the huts where the sick were sleeping, the violinist sitting on a crate, a lantern by him with mosquitoes and insects buzzing around it – the conquerors in long dresses and wearing sheets would dance, sedately sweating around a big fire of branches, while at the four corners of the encampment sentinels were on watch to defend the besieged people against black-maned lions, cattle thieves, Arab bands, and sometimes also raids by other French settlers who were in need of distraction or supplies (pp. 189/90).

By the time the illnesses abated and the village was built, 'two-thirds of the emigrants were dead, there as everywhere in Algeria, without having laid hands on a spade or a plow. The others remained Parisian in the fields, plowing in top hats, gun on the shoulder, a pipe between their teeth . . .' (p. 176).

As a *narrative* of colonization, this is more a tale of abject defeat than a celebration of the defiant virility evoked by Nora. But if this is a laudable corrective to the triumphalist stance of earlier settler literature, this does not mean that the novel escapes so easily its own transformation of history into myth.

In Jean Sarrocchi's largely sympathetic reading of the novel's attempt to contest the prevailing metropolitan stereotype of the *pied-noir*, there is nonetheless the allegation that:

> In thus representing Veillard and his wife, Solférino and its founding, Albert Camus, the son, appends his signature to an honourable account of colonization. He thereby inscribes the French of Algeria onto a list not so much of the favoured, but of the victims of destiny and offers them, at a time when they are being defamed, the right to enter into the golden legends of rogues.[37]

At the same time, it is clear from the annexes to *Le Premier Homme* that Camus had not merely relied on *pied-noir* cultural mythology but had researched historical sources for the novel's account of this early colonizing venture.[38] How are we therefore to weigh the charge of Camus's apologetic writing of the history of colonization against the author's evident aspiration to some measure of historical veracity?

The novel's account of the early settlement drive is based on actual historical circumstances: in September 1848, five million credits were voted to establish 42 agricultural settlements in Algeria. Settlers were to receive 2–12 hectares of land, a dwelling, livestock, tools, seeds, and food rations. Out of an astounding 100,000 applications, 14,000 were accepted for emigration by the end of that year.[39] As *Le Premier Homme* suggests, prominent amongst those selected were Parisian skilled workers, many made unemployed by the termination of the National Workshops in June. Indeed, it was admitted to the Legislative Assembly on 4 July 1850, in an oft-quoted phrase, that, concerning the Second Republic's motives for agricultural colonization: 'It was an attempt to sweep clean the streets of Paris but not to colonize Algeria. Africa was the means, but the aim was the tranquillity of the capital.'[40] These radical republicans, then, are Camus's prototypes for the *Labrador*'s passengers.

As the novel so poignantly relates, the settlers arrived to find no dwellings for them to inhabit and land that had never been tilled. The disastrous outcome of this settlement initiative – a high mortality rate and an equally high rate of inglorious return to the metropole[41] – led to the immediate suspension of the experiment and inspired a parliamentary investigation at which a number of returned *candidats colons* gave testimony. One of them, Gabriel Roger, was to explain to the inquiry: 'In February and June 1948 we fought for the right to work. Well! Here we found ourselves [at the settlement of Assi ben-Obka in Algeria] sentenced to hard labour. Those who in 1848 dreamed of becoming landowners became disillusioned, embittered.'[42]

If the novel's depiction of the misfortunes of the *Labrador*'s passengers seems to conform to a certain historical actuality, and Camus's settler profile to the likes of a Gabriel Roger, both the motives and the revolutionary sensibility attributed to this first wave of pioneers have been described in more recent historiographical literature as a 'tenacious myth'. Instead, it is alleged that 'these *candidats colons* were neither revolutionaries nor even followers of socialism but very much individualists'.[43] As Gabriel Roger's testimony suggests, these republican emigrants were driven abroad at least as much by the desire for land of their own as by persecution for their political convictions. Drawing any hard and fast distinctions between the economic and political motives influencing their decision to emigrate to Algeria may therefore be as difficult to accomplish as it is for many so-called 'economic migrants' today.

In any event, once installed, these individualists found themselves ill-suited temperamentally to the military administration that governed Algeria. The urban tradesmen amongst them were equally ill-suited to the physical demands of labouring the land – let alone the unfamiliar and intractable Algerian terrain. While some remained to take their chances in the Algerian outback, the majority headed straight for cities and towns. As one account notes, the republican *arriviste* 'rebelled against military discipline; attached to his prerogatives and rights, he planted on an unknown land his tree of liberty and his French flag in order to prove that he was still in France, unable to accept the separation'.[44]

And yet passionate attachment to the ideology of republican citizenship soon revealed its inherent limits and contradictions. Early settlers believed that the antagonisms that erupted with indigenous Algerians were being used by the military regime to justify its continued presence and authority, and that any animosities could be overcome by a concerted policy of assimilation. Implementing their civilizational mission with due haste and zeal would demonstrate the superiority of metropolitan culture at the same time that it would permit the extension of colonization to land still protected by tribal rights.[45] But these republican missionaries underestimated both the depth and strength of Muslim faith and the Muslim sense of primordial claims on the land. Faced with the *indigène*'s intransigent resistance to French colonizing imperatives, public opinion then held 'the perverse instincts of the Arab' responsible for the failures of republican assimilationism. As the esteemed historian of Algeria Charles-André Julien pointed out, despite their hostility to the capitalist practices of the *gros colon*, in the expansionist ambitions they harboured and the racial attitudes they displayed, these republican *petits colons* were indistinguishable from their class rivals:

> In fact in the Algerian context, the forty-eighter phraseology of transforming a social fraternity into a hypothetical fusion of races was only superficial and left untouched the irreducible hostility of the *colon* towards the indigenous population. The reactions of the large landowners and *petits blancs* were identical in this respect . . . A *colon* only considered himself a good republican by affirming his enmity towards the Muslims. The Parisian workers and artisans, who had stood the test of the June days, rapidly acquired the local mentality and revealed themselves as among the most hardened toward the Arabs.[46]

Following the 1848 settlement *débâcle*, the government of the Second Republic relinquished control over its planned colonization drive and 'wild colonization' (*la colonisation sauvage*) ensued. The policy of small-scale colonization (*la petite colonisation*), which had favoured owner-occupation of land allocations gave way to large-scale colonisation (*la grande colonisation*), in which absentee landlordism on large holdings prevailed. Those lured to Algeria by these sirens made no claim to rebel-republican status, but instead represented a wide social and political stratum, ranging, for example, from financiers interested only in the exploitation of the land for profit to peasants from the Massif Central, the Midi and Corsica, fleeing poverty or the phylloxera crisis in viticulture.[47]

The point of these historiographical corrections is not to condemn *Le Premier Homme* for historical naïveté – very few alternative accounts would have been available to Camus at the time of writing. Rather, they indicate why writing the history of Algeria's settlement as epic and elegiac narration, as the 'Algerian *Mayflower* myth',[48] emphasizing the ordeals of the early 'pioneers' yet not qualifying in important respects their rebel-republicanism, helped to underwrite the siege mentality of the *pied-noir* community.[49] And indeed, *Le Premier Homme* explicitly thematizes this link between a history of adversity and a defensive posture in the present when, after listening to the wretched account of the *Labrador*'s misfortunes, Jacques finally feels close to grasping how this experience is entangled with his own family history and personal identity.[50] He is able to project his father's arrival in Algeria back in time and to place him on the dock at Bône among the emigrants, 'resolute, somber, teeth clenched'. He imagines his father striking out forty years later on the road to Solférino with the same combination of trepidation and fortitude. And when Jacques takes a stroll around the village of his birth, where the army's loudspeakers are a reminder of the current hostilities that encircle it, he gazes at the faces of the French in the crowd and recognizes 'the same look, somber and turned to the future, like those who long ago had come here on the *Labrador*, or those who landed other places in the same circumstances, with the same suffering, fleeing poverty or persecution, finding sorrow and stone' (p. 192).

But I believe the novel is rescued from being a mere 'commemoration of survival' by the fact that it is not so much the anguish of hardship that Camus shows must be foreclosed in the memory of each 'first man', but the *ambivalences* indelibly inscribed in that memory, which constantly surface to destabilize confidence in the effort to 'reestablish the roots already established'.[51] Those now feeling besieged are the successors of those settlers who did persevere and prosper – not only by enduring hardship but, as Jacques fleetingly recalls, thanks to the special dispensations of racist colonial policies ('those Alsatians who in '71 had rejected German rule and chosen France [. . .] were given the land of the Arab rebels of '71').[52] These patriotic rebels became in their turn 'persecuted-persecutors', 'dissidents taking the places kept warm by insurgents'. And so to deal with this history of hard-won success built on a bedrock of misfortune *and* their complicity in the oppression of the indigenous population, each successive generation of 'first men' collectively endeavoured to turn its back on that past, adopting that 'sombre look' that arises from fixing thoughts only on the future,

[a]s if the history of men, that history that kept on plodding across one of its oldest territories while leaving so few traces on it, was evaporating under the constant sun

with the memory of those who made it, reduced to paroxysms of violence and murder, to blazes of hatred, to torrents of blood, quickly swollen and quickly dried up, like the seasonal streams of the country (p. 194).

The 'sombre look' that Jacques now sees replicated on the faces of his own besieged contemporaries is the only telling inscription of this history of perpetual violence and its enduring memorial legacy. As we have seen, he partly attributes this erasure of historical memory to an Algerian landscape 'where the wind and sand erases all trace of men on the open ranges' (p. 196). And in naturalizing this condition, in making the environment responsible for memory's evanescence, Camus perhaps comes closest to elevating material features to 'quasi-ethical qualities' in the manner critiqued by Memmi and Said. Moreover, as Sarrocchi points out, even where these 'crises of violence' are admitted as the consequence of colonialism, Camus proceeds to dissolve the specific culpability attached to them into a 'pluri-millennarian culpability'. Thus he has the old doctor remind Jacques that this memoryless landscape has played host to a succession of 'conquerors' who have each claimed their 'right of possession'. Nineteenth-century European colonizers may have asphyxiated anti-colonial insurgents in caves, admits the old doctor, but blood-letting between Arabs and Berbers preceded these colonial crimes 'and so on all the way back to the first criminal – you know, his name was Cain'.[53]

That Camus constructs a defensive historical memory dictated by an amnesic landscape and an originary fratricide is not disputed. However, *Le Premier Homme* also reveals an awareness that this mode of remembering has evolved as a function of human agency as well, and in particular of the *pied-noir*'s specific relation to historical time. It is shown – indeed celebrated – as a posture embraced by each generation as it resolutely constructs and consolidates an identity exclusively in relation to the present and future. In short, Camus shows the *pied-noir* community to be a community engaged in the *wilful foreclosure of historical memory*. For Jacques, deprived of a father who would tell him 'the family's secret, or a sorrow of long ago', and therefore also obliged to live without recourse to memory, this is a crucial moment of (almost Oedipal) self-recognition, of recognizing his own personal trajectory and fate in the figure of 'The First Man'. A descendant of those who had been coming to Algeria 'for more than a century', of those who had laboured the land and then disappeared 'without a trace', Jacques feels himself a native son *because* he is 'with no past, without ethics, without guidance, without religion, *but glad to be so . . .*' [my emphasis] (p. 193).

As this section draws to a close, Jacques is made aware once more of the violence of the present as he looks at 'the hard inscrutable faces of the Arabs' listening to the army loudspeakers, recalls 'the deathly look on his mother's face' at the time of an Algiers bombing, and realizes that this community of fate, to which he now feels inextricably bound, is threatened with 'eternal anonymity and the loss of the only consecrated traces of their passage on this earth, the illegible slabs in the cemetery that the night has now covered over' (pp. 195–6). This is surely the moment of greatest pathos in *Le Premier Homme*, and there is no doubt that Jacques's coming-to-consciousness should be interpreted as Camus's own declaration of solidarity with the fate of his 'tribe', the *pied-noir* community of the late 1950s, contemplating its own embattled existence. But rather than reducing his psychological pilgrimage to one of hopeless despair and unrestrained nostalgia, as O'Brien does, I would maintain that Camus has attempted a different affective itinerary. He has attempted to write himself into a *pied-noir* history that 'enveloped blood and courage and work and instinct . . . at once cruel and compassionate' (pp. 194–5), but one that was also deeply implicated in the 'culpable adventure' (Nora) of French colonialism. He has attempted, in other words, not merely to *claim* his place in Algeria's pioneer mythology, but to restore to the *pied-noir* community the ambivalences of a historical memory that, to its own eventual peril, it had chosen to repudiate.

Notes

Unless otherwise stated, translations from the French are my own.

1. '. . . [o]ù justice lui serait rendue par les siens et eux seuls.' See Jean Daniel, 'Retour à Camus', *Le Nouvel Observateur*, 27 November 1978.
2. See Albert Camus, *The Rebel* (London: Hamilton, 1953), pp. 291, 287.
3. Jean-Yves Guérin (ed.), *Camus et la politique* (Paris: L'Harmattan, 1986). See especially the contributions by Paul Thibaud, Annie Cohen-Solal, Hocine Aït Ahmed and Albert Memmi.
4. See especially Benjamin Stora, 'Deuxième guerre algérienne: Les habits anciens des combattants', originally published in *Les Temps modernes*, January 1995, and republished in his valuable collection of essays, *L'Algérie en 1995: La guerre, l'histoire, la politique* (Paris: Éditions Michalon, 1995).
5. This is a point forcefully made in Tony Judt, 'The Lost World of Albert Camus', *The New York Review of Books*, 6 October 1994. Olivier Todd's recent biography, *Albert Camus: une vie* (Paris: Gallimard, 1996), is perhaps the culminating expression of Camus's rehabilitation for the 1990s.
6. Herbert Lottman, *Albert Camus* (New York: Doubleday and Co., 1979), p. 6.
7. Albert Camus, *The First Man* (New York: Knopf, 1995), p. vi.
8. Bernard Fauconnier, 'Camus: une enfance en Algérie', *Magazine littéraire* 322, June 1994.

9. 'The Fall', by Conor Cruise O'Brien, *The New Republic*, 16 October 1995, p. 44.

10. Ibid., p. 44. Camus was killed on 8 January 1960.

11. The following remarks rely heavily on Harvey A. Kaplan's 'The Psycho-pathology of Nostalgia', *The Psychoanalytic Review*, vol. 74, no. 4, Winter 1987.

12. Lewin cited by Kaplan, ibid., p. 474.

13. Renalto Rosaldo, 'Imperialist Nostalgia', *Representations*, 26, Spring 1989, p. 108.

14. Edward Said, 'Camus and the French Imperial Experience', *Culture and Imperialism* (London: Chatto & Windus, 1993). Page references to this work appear in parentheses within the text.

15. See Roger Quilliot's classic study of this dimension in 'The Anguish of Algeria' in *The Sea and Prisons* (University, AL.: University of Alabama Press, 1970).

16. Albert Memmi, *The Colonizer and the Colonized* (New York: Orion Press, 1963), pp. 60–1.

17. Several stories from *L'Exil et le royaume* are particularly held open to this accusation. However, for an alternative reading of these, which argues that Algeria is presented in Camus's stories 'as a land in which no one can legitimately claim to be master and no one is destined to be slave', see David Carroll, 'Camus's Algeria: Birthrights, Colonial Injustice, and the Fiction of a French-Algerian People' in *Modern Language Notes*, September 1997.

18. As Jean Sarrocchi observes in his compelling study, *Le Dernier Camus ou Le Premier Homme* (Paris: Librarie A.-G. Nizet, 1995): '*Le Premier Homme* is a text which would be inconceivable in the period of colonial certainties . . . It germinates in the moment when French Algeria disaggregates, and receives its germinal force in an obscure will to conjure this moment through writing' (pp. 259–60). I return to Sarrocchi's book later in the text.

19. Notable exceptions include Judt, 'The Lost World of Albert Camus', Patrick McCarthy, 'The *pied-noir* story', *Times Literary Supplement*, 24 June 1994 and Jeanyves Guérin, 'Des *Chroniques algériennes* au *Premier Homme*', *Esprit*, May 1995.

20. Conor Cruise O'Brien, *Albert Camus of Europe and Africa* (New York: Viking, 1970).

21. I have used Said's translation of this statement, which seems to me closer in spirit to the French original. 'Camus and the French Imperial Experience', p. 217.

22. This view is firmly expressed by the esteemed historian of French colonization, Charles-André Julien, in his introduction to Pierre Nora's *Les Français d'Algérie* (Paris: René Julliard, 1961). After a brief survey of the historical existence of Algerian nationhood, he concludes: 'The Algerian nation forged

itself in the struggle which gave it the consciousness of its originality and its unity' (p. 34).

23. See Walzer's essay, 'Albert Camus's Algerian War' in *The Company of Critics: Social Criticism and Political Commitment in the Twentieth Century* (New York: Basic Books, 1988), p. 146.

24. 'Algérie 1958', *Actuelles III, Chroniques algériennes, 1939–1958* (Paris: Gallimard, 1994), p. 200.

25. The phrase is from the 'Avant Propos' to *Actuelles III*, p. 23. For a very detailed and incisive account of Camus's attempts at mediation during the early stages of the War of Independence, see Todd, *Albert Camus, une vie*, especially his gripping account of Camus's *Trêve Civile* meeting in Algiers in January 1956, pp. 621–9.

26. O'Brien, *Albert Camus of Europe and Africa*, p. 6.

27. The term is Pierre Bourdieu's in his classic sociological study of the Algerian economy and society, *The Algerians* (Boston: Beacon Press,1962). For lucid – but contrasting – interpretations of Camus's racial sensibility see Susan Tarrow, *Exile from the Kingdom: A Political Rereading of Albert Camus* (University, AL.: University of Alabama Press: 1985) and Philip Dine, *Images of the Algerian War: French Fiction and Film, 1954–62* (Oxford: Oxford University Press, 1994). An earlier discussion of Camus's attitude to the Muslim population can be found in Pierre Nora's *Les Français d'Algérie*. While generally sympathetic, Nora describes Camus as 'Français d'Algérie malgré tout' and cites *L'Etranger* as a symptomatic expression of the unconscious complexes that had led the *pied-noir* community to the brink of self-destruction.

28. O'Brien, *Albert Camus of Europe and Africa*, p. 19. Here O'Brien has chosen an easy target: Camus was 24 when he wrote this speech and a member of Algeria's Communist Party, which was pursuing a politics based on a 'melting-pot' vision of society. When the Party switched its emphasis to a resolute anti-fascism, Camus was expelled for continuing to promote dialogue with Algerian nationalists. Thanks are due to Susan Tarrow for emphasizing this point.

29. Ibid., p. 10.

30. Ibid., p. 11.

31. See Jeffrey C. Issac, *Arendt, Camus and Modern Rebellion* (New Haven: Yale University Press, 1992), p. 205, for an insightful discussion of this point. In the first entry to the 'Notes et plans' [Notes and Sketches] appended to *Le Premier homme*, Camus appears to respond to this charge of 'objective culpability' via an imaginary dialogue with an interlocutor whom we construe to be a former Muslim friend-turned-FLN militant:

'Conversation about terrorism:
Objectively she is responsible (answerable).

Change the adverb or I'll hit you.

What?

Don't take what's most asinine from the West. Don't say objectively or I'll hit you.

Why?

Did your mother lie down in front of the Algiers–Oran train? [the trolleybus] I don't understand.

The train blew up, four children died. Your mother didn't move. If object- ively she is nonetheless responsible,* then you approve of shooting hostages.

She didn't know.

Neither did *she*. Never say objectively again.

Concede that there are innocent people or I'll kill you too.

You know I could do it.

Yes, I've seen you' (pp. 290–1).

* answerable

32. See Sarrocchi's *Le Dernier Camus ou Le Premier Homme* for an analysis that explores Camus's *pied-noir* allegiances with considerable insight. Sarrocchi notes: '*Le Premier Homme* supports a defence. Its autobiographical tenor is not separable from the justificatory enterprise thanks to which a threatened ethnic minority must recognize above and beyond its rights or its official wrongs, the differential quality of the entitlements owed to it . . . [la qualité différentielle qui lui tient lieu d'hoirie]' (pp. 144–5).

33. A sign of this phantasmic dimension is provided by Camus's belief that his father was of Alsatian background and hence of exiled rebel stock, when in fact his family came from the Bordeaux region and arrived in Algeria a genera- tion earlier than Camus supposed. Lottman notes that it is curious Camus did not check the available public records, which would have corrected this misapprehension. See Lottman, *Albert Camus*, p. 9.

34. The term is borrowed from Stuart Hall in his analysis of Claire Denis's film *Chocolat*, an autobiographically-based story of Denis's childhood in colonial Cameroon. See D. Petrie (ed.), *Screening Europe* (London: BFI, 1992). But it is especially relevant to Cormery's account of his own birth, fantasized as the consequence of a loving union between his parents even though later in the novel he declares: '. . . at heart he did not even want to know what there had been between them, and so he had to give up on learning anything from [his mother]'.

35. *The First Man*, pp. 180–1. Page references to this English edition appear as parentheses in the text.

36. Pierre Nora, *Les Français d'Algérie*, p. 189.

37. *Le Dernier Camus ou Le Premier Homme*, p. 146.

38. See Camus's referencing of de Bandicorn, *Histoire de la colonisation de l'Algérie* in 'Interleaves', p. 287 and in the 'Notes and sketches', p. 291.

39. I have drawn on Jean Meyer, Jean Tarade, Annie Rey Golzeiguer and Jacques Thobie, *Histoire de la France coloniale, Tome 1. Des origines à 1914* (Paris: Armand Colin, 1991), especially 'La colonisation de peuplement' and Denise Bouche, *Histoire de la colonisation française, Tome 2. Flux et reflux 1815–1962* (Paris: Fayard, 1991), especially 'La colonisation algérienne et l'exportation de la crise'.

40. Quoted by Daniel Leconte in *Les pied-noirs: Histoire et portrait d'une communauté* (Paris: Seuil, 1980), p. 61. These emigrants should be distinguished from those republican political prisoners arrested following the June uprising who formed part of the first penal colony established in Algeria, and who were soon to be followed by those condemned following the *coup d'état* of 1852. These prisoners were amnestied in 1859 and for the most part returned to France. See *Histoire de la colonisation*, p. 151, and *Histoire de la France coloniale*, p. 417.

41. In *Histoire de la colonisation française* (p. 151), it is noted that one-sixth died soon after arrival and a third made a rapid return to France.

42. Quoted by Leconte, *Les Pieds-noirs*.

43. *Histoire de la France coloniale,* p. 416.

44. Ibid.

45. See Charles-André Julien, *Histoire de l'Algérie contemporaine, Vol. 1: La conquête et les débuts de la colonisation (1927–1871)* (Paris: PUF, 1964), p. 344.

46. Ibid.

47. Charles-Robert Ageron, 'Français, juifs et musulmans: l'union impossible' in *L'Algérie des Français* (Paris: Seuil, 1993).

48. The term is Ageron's, ibid.

49. Daniel Leconte points out that the difficult conditions of existence endured by Algeria's early settlers 'formed individuals constantly on the defensive, developing a siege mentality which the population of the colony would later exalt in the myth of the pioneers, upon which it in turn drew to legitimize its privileges.' Leconte, *Les Pieds-noirs*, p. 57.

50. Sarrocchi makes a similar case when he notes: 'In effect only paternal mediation opens to Camus the proper perspective on the history of the colony.' *Le Dernier Camus ou La Premier Homme*, p. 146.

51. David Carroll's phrase in 'Camus's Algeria . . .'. Carroll aptly describes this as a state of 'belated firstness' , 'the impossible, contradictory necessity of being first in a land already inhabited both by ancestors and by other peoples with whom one has no national, cultural, religious, or linguistic affinities. Being first does not make these new Adams "founding fathers" but rather belated

originators of a people who will never grow to maturity and old age, who will never have lasting traditions or a determined national-cultural identity, a people who will always remain virtual and never be "real".'

52. A total of 1,183 families from Alsace and Lorraine made up the 1871 settlement wave. See *Histoire de la colonisation française*, p. 152. As Camus notes, they were given land that had been expropriated from the indigenous inhabitants following the insurrection or 'Grand Revolt' in the Kabylia earlier that year – itself a protest against colonial policies of land expropriation.

53. Sarrocchi speaks of Camus's 'grandiose fashion of evading differences in shared iniquities, by instituting an eradication, an originary disinheritance which relegates colonial misdeeds to prehistory.' *Le Dernier Camus ou Le Premier Homme*, p. 254.

7

Remembering the Jews of Algeria

> J'ai quitté mon pays
> J'ai quitté ma maison
> Ma vie, ma triste vie
> se traîne sans raison
> J'ai quitté mon soleil
> J'ai quitté ma mer bleu
> Leurs souvenirs se réveillaient
> bien après mon adieu.
>
> Soleil, soleil de mon pays perdu!
> Des villes blanches que j'aimais
> Des filles que j'ai jadis connu.

These lyrics are sung by Enrico Macias, the enormously popular *chanteur*, described by *Le Monde* as the Charles Aznavour of France's *pied-noir* and Maghrebian community alike.[1] In his song 'Adieu mon pays', Macias recalls memories of the sun and of the blue sea of 'mon pays perdu', of last glimpses of his homeland as the ship puts distance between him and the quayside, and of the 'waves' of regret that overcome him. Macias, a Jew from Constantine, left Algeria in 1962, shortly after Raymond Leyris, spokesperson of the Constantine Jewish community and master singer of *malouf*, a version of arabo-andalusian music, was assassinated by two FLN militants during the final stages of the Algerian War. Leyris's death was the symbolic trigger for a rapid exodus of Jews from Algeria, including that of Macias, who, on the ship Le Ville-d'Alger, composed 'Adieu mon pays'.[2] However, if it is tempting to interpret the lyrics of Macias's song, and indeed his enormous popularity among France's *pied-noir* community, as symptomatic of the '*nostalgérie*' that is said to exercise such an enduring affective hold over former Français d'Algérie, in the case of Macias this interpretation would be both too simplistic and unjust. It would not account for the 8,000 Egyptian fans who turned up to his concert in 1979, the hundreds of Maghrebians who mingled with *pied-noirs* at his Paris concert in 1995, the women waving their headscarves as they danced to his music, nor for the insults – 'Sale juif', 'Ami des Arabes' – directed at him by the Front National.[3] Macias's Jewish-Algerianness is a more tangled identity to unravel, just as the memories evoked in his songs articulate an equally complex relationship to his 'pays perdu'.

Far from the venues of French popular culture, philosopher Jacques Derrida also confirms a 'disorder of identity' (*trouble d'identité*) that lies at the heart of his self-designation as a 'Jewish-Franco-Maghrebian'. The 'disorder' of which Derrida speaks, however, does not refer to the exodus of Algerian Jews during the War of Independence, but relates to a history when Algeria's colonial status quo was very much intact, and concerns the question of *citizenship*. Though Derrida admits that citizenship is not an identity in the way that cultural, linguistic or historical commonalities might confer on a community a sense of shared belonging, he nonetheless insists that citizenship is not either a 'superficial or superstructural predicate floating on the surface of experience'.[4] Moreover, its importance to a sense of selfhood is all the more revealed when it turns out that citizenship can be 'precarious, recent, threatened', as was the case for the Jews of Algeria. Granted French citizenship by the *décret Crémieux* in 1870, Algerian Jews were subsequently deprived of their citizenship by Vichy's *Statut des juifs* of 1940, without reclaiming any other citizenship in the process. '*No other*', Derrida emphatically reminds us.

In *Monolingualism of the Other*, Derrida evokes memories of having lost his French citizenship as a youth under Vichy, during an Occupation in which Algeria, as Derrida points out, was in fact never occupied – or at least not by the Germans. This was an entirely French affair – 'a Franco-French operation [. . .] an act of French Algeria in the absence of any German occupation'.[5] Thus, says Derrida, there is no alibi, no denial, no illusion possible. And while Derrida admits that his youthful self may not have fully grasped what citizenship and its loss fully signified, he has no doubt that this memory of exclusion is intimately related to the 'disorder of identity' that is part of his self-assignation as a Jewish-French-Maghrebian. And for the former Jewish community of Algeria as well, Derrida suggests, whether it remembers, or with great effort strives to forget this privation of citizenship, this precarious experience of national belonging is nonetheless inscribed within its collective memory. The question Derrida poses is whether this 'disorder of identity' could be said to 'heighten the desire of memory' or to 'drive the genealogical fantasy to despair'?[6]

Monolingualism of the Other is a multi-layed text into which Derrida weaves philosophical and personal reflections on questions of language, identity and memory. While Derrida is concerned not to reduce these reflections to his individual trajectory, he nonetheless insists that he could not have even broached them without engaging with his own 'Judeo-Franco-Maghrebian genealogy'. And when, in so doing, Derrida encounters a 'disorder of identity', it is soon clear that he is not seeking from this genealogy a solution that would allow him to vindicate and reclaim the fullness of a Jewish-Algerian identity. As his translator Geoff Bennington has pointed out, if Derrida experiences this memory of exclusion under the Vichy regime as a wound, and as the period which imprints upon him a certain 'belonging' to Judaism, it makes Derrida equally impatient with what Bennington calls 'gregarious identification' or the 'militancy of belonging'.[7] Nor is identity for Derrida in any event something that can be given, received or attained; what he argues is at stake, rather, is what he calls the 'interminable and indefinitely phantasmatic process of identification', the 'identificatory modality' that is secured by and within language.[8]

Within this context, however, his reflections on his Jewish-Algerian origins *do* have a specific place and function. They invoke a past – and above all a *status* – that, while not defining of all modalities of belonging to which Derrida lays claim, he nonetheless affirms as a distinct 'subset' (*sous-ensemble*). More acutely, reflections on this status pose for him the question of what modalities of identification *could* be available for Algeria's Jews given a collective inscription within a national culture that first defined them as 'indigenous Jews', subsequently confirmed them as French citizens and then negated that act of inclusion – all, as Derrida notes, within two generations. Algerian Jews 'could not properly *identify themselves*, in the double sense of "identifying oneself" and "identifying oneself with" the other'.[9] Even had the ignominy of Vichy not left its traumatic mark, identifying with the other had proved in any case a fraught exercise historically. Neither French, metropolitan, nor Catholic on the one hand, nor Arab nor Berber on the other, the place of Jews within colonial Algeria was inherently unstable, vulnerable to the forces of deracination and acculturation from which, as Derrida, poignantly remarks, 'I undoubtedly never completely emerged'.[10]

This instability is the subject of the remainder of my chapter, though I am concerned to locate its traces not primarily in personal testimonies but in what I perceive to be a new historiography of the Jews of Algeria. Indeed, Derrida and others have drawn upon this new historiography as they trace the historical coordinates of their personal and familial memories and attempt to give meaning to these.[11]

The history of the Jews of Algeria has been written over the past century and a half, so my claim is not that this is a repressed history now brought to light as France's culpability for colonial and collaborationist crimes has been progressively revealed. Instead, I want to suggest a link between history and memory, where this new historiography is serving as a vector of memory, not unlike the manner in which the new historiography of Vichy has been both cause and consequence of a renewed Franco-Jewish politics of memory and identity in the past two decades.[12] Admittedly, this vector potentially rallies a much smaller constituency, but the question nonetheless arises as to what might be the political stakes of any identity claims – however judiciously asserted – based on Jewish-Algerian memories.

To pursue my claim, I want to stake out the historiographical parameters of three crucial moments – the Crémieux Decree, Vichy and the Algerian War – and to signal some of the controversies and questions they elicit about the history and memory of Algerian Jews in particular.

The 'Gift' of Citizenship

In his contribution to *Les Lieux de mémoire*, Pierre Nora's project on national memory discussed in Chapter 1, Pierre Birnbaum describes Adolphe Crémieux, minister in several governments in the mid-nineteenth century, as a French Jew who so 'fully identified with the emancipatory goals of the Revolution', that he claimed to see embodied in the France of 1789, '"a divine flame" that had since become the expression of Judaism itself'.[13] Minister of Justice for the Government of National Defence, Crémieux was responsible for drafting the legislation that, on 24 October 1870, conferred French citizenship on Algeria's Jews. By this measure, France would gain thirty-four and a half thousand new citizens, and, as the historian Michel Abitbol has remarked, Algeria's Jews would 'leave Algerian history to enter that of France'.[14] This is not to say that Jews had not been recognized as *French* before this date: in order to deal with the status of Algeria's *indigènes*, that is to say Arabs, Berbers and Jews, the 1865 *Senatus Consulte* had created the category of French *subjects*, distinct from citizens, who could apply for citizenship if there were willing to give up their so-called *statut personnel* or personal status. This essentially entailed renouncing the authority of religious tribunals in matters such as marriage, divorce and inheritance, and agreeing to be subject to French civil law in these domains. Between 1865 and 1870, only 288 Algerian Jews out of 35,000 applied for citizenship under these conditions.[15] It should also be noted that an even smaller proportion of Muslims opted for this route to citizenship, and French insistence on the renunciation of Muslim personal status would scupper many reform measures until de Gaulle granted French citizenship to Muslims without this condition in 1946. The discrepancy between the minuscule number of demands for French citizenship by Jewish *indigènes* in these years, and their massive accession to full French citizenship, entailing the loss of personal status, in 1870, has recently led historians to pose a number of questions about the meaning to be ascribed to this momentous event. That the Crémieux Decree is a *lieu de mémoire* of Algerian Jewry is not in doubt; but the character of this memory is the subject of considerable contestation.

Derrida's appraisal, circumspect in many ways, is ultimately a negative one. He speaks of a process at the turn of the century whereby 'assimilation [. . .] and acculturation – the feverish bid for a "Frenchifying" which was also an embourgeoisification – were so frantic and so careless that the inspiration of Jewish culture seemed to succumb to an *asphyxia*: a state of apparent death, a ceasing of respiration, a fainting fit, a cessation of the pulse'.[16] Derrida's image of a thriving indigenous culture stifled by the very instrument of its political emancipation is one echoed by a strand of this new historiography that describes the Crémieux Decree as le *décret de sinistre mémoire*.[17] Algerian Jews, it is argued, anticipate their loss of personal status as too high a price to pay, given the religious freedom they had previously enjoyed and especially in light of the already considerable erosion of traditional life that had occurred in the prior decades.[18] In this interpretation, the well-meaning Crémieux is nonetheless cast as the Trojan horse of jacobin assimilationism, who recognizes that the decree *must* be imposed since citizenship for Algerian Jews will not be achieved by their own voluntary candidacy. For historians like Michel Abitbol, for example, Crémieux's victory is only the culmination of a longer process by which Algerian Jews became targets of the crusading spirit of French Jews, who projected their own historical trajectory of emancipation onto their co-religionists. At least from 1845, Abitbol points out, key positions in Algeria's Jewish *consistoires* had been occupied by metropolitan rabbis, and forms of social assimilation promoted by them. If by 1870, Algerian Jews accept reluctantly, or even in some cases with enthusiasm, an obligatory French citizenship, this is partly because they had internalized the 'civilizing' aspirations that had originated with ardent metropolitan advocates of a French-Jewish symbiosis.[19]

While the new historiography generally tends to accept Abitbol's thesis that the Crémieux Decree played a decisive role in the 'dejudaization' of the Jews of Algeria, other factors are entered into consideration that inflect this supposition in significantly different directions. Jacques Taïeb proposes that the Crémieux Decree be seen as the 'accelerator' or 'catalyst' for a *relative* 'decomposition' of Jewish identity in Algeria, rather than the primary cause of a profound dismantling. His argument is that the destabilizing forces of modernity had already impinged on the Jewish-Algerian community well before 1870, that 'westernization' and 'Frenchifying' (*francisation*) had been under way for several decades – whether by dint of scholarization, changing demographic patterns, or the rise of new non-traditional elites. Moreover, it was precisely these processes that had created a *demand* for naturalization on the part of a significant sector of Algeria's Jewish community, expressed through numerous petitions and the appeals of community and religious leaders. In this interpretation, the Crémieux Decree is the quintessential symbol of its time, and its disregard for cultural particularism the ideological essence of the 'republican pact' to which it owed its inspiration. In fact, Taïeb locates the detrimental consequences of the Crémieux Decree precisely here: in the fact that the assimilationist dogma of republican jacobinism in his words 'disarmed Algerian Jews into thinking that the decree was henceforth an inviolable and irrevocable principle within the French conception of citizenship' – a belief that would be shattered by the Vichy experience.[20]

Whatever the ambivalences of its reception by Algerian Jews, the Crémieux Decree claims a crucial place in the vicissitudes of turn-of-the-century French anti-Semitism. Edouard Drumont devotes a whole section of *La France Juive* to Crémieux and the allegedly corrosive effects of the decree on an organic national culture. 'Never', says Drumont, 'has the Jew shown himself more odiously indifferent to everything which concerns *la Patrie*, more implacably preoccupied with himself and his race, than in the case of the decrees submitted by Crémieux for the emancipation of the Algerian Israelites.'[21] Drumont, as Birnbaum has shown, used the Crémieux Decree as a spearhead for mobilizing the *political* anti-Semitism that would overlay traditional forms of French anti-Semitism and culminate in the Dreyfus affair, where the threat posed by Jews was seen to extend to the very heart of the French state.[22] In Algeria this political anti-Semitism focused in particular on the electoral power of the Jewish vote and the claim that this tended to be exercised *en bloc* and on behalf of the moderate republican party, the Opportunists. Not only did this arouse the predictable animosity of anti-republican parties, but, on the left of the political spectrum, Radicals reached for an anti-capitalist rhetoric infused with anti-Semitic stereotypes to express their own rancour. As Charles-Robert Ageron, amongst others, has pointed out, well before the turn of the century, '[a]nti-Jewishness had become the common denominator of the Algerian Left'.[23] By the end of the century, and fuelled by the Dreyfus affair, a hostility that had manifested itself primarily in anti-Semitic publications and anti-Semitic leagues had taken to the streets: Algiers, Oran and Constantine in particular, cities where the largest population of Jews lived, witnessed the sacking of Jewish shops, the pillaging of Jewish quarters, and physical attacks resulting in deaths and injuries. Drumont himself was given an ecstatic welcome on a visit to Algiers and in 1898 was elected a city deputy, while the well-known anti-Semite Max Régis was elected the city's major.

It is from this new historiography that an increasingly 'thick description' of the specific character of turn-of-the-century Algerian anti-Semitism emerges. In his fascinating study of Bône during this period, David Prochaska explains the especially virulent anti-Semitism of the so-called *petits blancs* – the Algerian settlers of Spanish, Italian and Maltese origin – as a 'classic case of status anxiety', and scapegoating by these more economically disadvantaged colonizers. He also argues that the anti-Semitic crisis of this period comprised more than a racial element, functioning also as a 'lightning rod which collected and deflected, as much as it focused, a whole range of collective resentments' – especially settler antipathy toward a metropole that was proving itself incapable of satisfying the settler's simultaneous demands for greater autonomy and protection of privileges.[24] Wherever the historiographical attention focuses, it is clear that, far from merely mimicking a metropolitan sensibility, Algeria's political anti-Semitism was a distinctive phenomenon – not something incidental to, but a constituent feature of, the colonial mentality, deeply embedded in the fear that granting citizenship rights to one group of *indigènes* had threatened the very foundations of the colonial status quo.[25]

Nowhere is this more evident than in recent historiographical interpretations of Muslim response to the Crémieux Decree. For some time, a historical orthodoxy has prevailed that asserts an angry Muslim response to the discriminatory implications of the Crémieux Decree, made manifest in the 1871 insurrection of Muslims in Kabylie, Aurès and the Constantine region. Anti-Semites like Drumont appeared to take up the Muslim defence, citing the latter's combat in the Franco-Prussian war as an additional justification for their anger faced with the collective natural-ization of Algeria's Jews.[26] Not surprisingly, the anti-Semites expended their campaigning energies on efforts to repeal the Crémieux Decree, not on agitating for the extension of citizenship to the Muslim population.[27] However, in the light of the still widely-held contemporary belief that the Crémieux Decree drove a wedge into Jewish–Muslim co-existence, I would only signal the thesis espoused recently by several historians that historical evidence does not corroborate this claim. Ageron, Richard Ayoun and others have instead trawled archival sources where testimonies from the period – including those by military personnel, dedicated anti-Semites and Muslim activists – deny this causal link between Jewish naturalization and the 1871 insurrection. In these accounts, for example, Muslims either state their unwillingness to follow the path of Jews and give up their personal status or see the Decree as paving the way for eventual Muslim enfranchisement. That this expectation would be thwarted for another 75 years by *pied-noir* intransigence does not diminish the significance of this 'revisionist' thesis. What this thesis maintains is that the myth of the insurrection's being provoked by the naturalization of the Jews was created *retrospectively*, and instrumentalized by anti-Semites like Drumont in a deliberate attempt to arouse Muslim resentment toward the Jews in a classic divide-and-rule strategy.[28] Not only was this attempt unsuccessful at the time, but it would also prove unsuccessful when later wielded for the same purposes – notably during the Vichy period.

Vichy's Algerian Syndrome

On 7 October 1940, as part of the series of infamous measures known as the *Statut des juifs*, the Crémieux Decree was abrogated. As Paxton and Maurrus note in their classic study, *Vichy France and the Jews*, one of the co-signatories to this measure was Marcel Peyrouton, a former governor-general of Algeria sympathetic to the European settlers, who became Vichy's Minister of the Interior in September 1940. In fact Paxton and Maurrus contend that rather than Vichy's putting pressure on Algeria with respect to racial laws, the situation was the reverse. Not only did Algeria apply with gusto the *Statut des juifs*, Algeria's Vichyists went beyond its provisions in order to exclude Jewish primary and secondary pupils from attending schools.[29] In remembering this period, Derrida recalls first of all the intense 'Pétainization' of his school in 1940–1, where though he was top pupil, he was prevented from raising the morning flag because of his Jewishness. By the first day of the school year in 1942, Derrida was expelled from school and sent home, joining 18,500 other children who fell above the 14 per cent quota of Jewish children allowed to attend school by Algeria's very own *numerus clausus*.[30]

While Derrida suggests that this memory of a 'degradation' constitutes the traumatic kernel of the Algerian-Jewish experience, it seems to me that what is surely the greater wound in this collective memory – and for this reason the more repressed – is the 'scandal' that this new historiography has increasingly emphasized: namely, the fact that it took eleven months for the Crémieux Decree to be reinstated *after* the Allied landing in North Africa in November 1942. Paxton and Maurrus, André Kaspi, Michel Abitbol and others reveal how Algeria's new rulers, under General Giraud's influence in particular, and now under the governor-generalship of Marcel Peyrouton (returned from duty as Vichy's former Interior Minister!) dragged their feet on the question of abrogating the *Statut des juifs* and especially of reinstating the Crémieux Decree.[31] Once again, the defence summoned is that such an expeditious action would provoke Muslim anger at a time when their support and military participation was needed for the liberation campaign. Indeed, when in March 1943, faced with British and American pressure, Giraud begins the process of abolishing the racial laws, he abrogates the Crémieux Decree for a second time, citing a desire to eliminate all racial discrimination between Muslims and Jews.[32] Only following de Gaulle's arrival and ongoing international protest was the decree finally reinstated in October 1943.

Was there any basis this time to this putative Muslim animus? All signs in recent historiography point to the contrary. Paxton, Maurrus and Kaspi document how Muslims generally abstained from the anti-Jewish campaign led by Algeria's Vichyists, or, in the case of the reformist Muslim elite, even declared their solidarity with the Jews. A letter of November 1942, signed by a group of Muslim leaders, made the observation that:

> [b]y putting down the Jew, one only brings him even closer together with the Moslem. It was thought that at the abrogation of the Crémieux decree, the Moslems would rejoice; but the latter can easily see the dubious worth of a citizenship that the granting authority can take away after seventy years' enjoyment.[33]

Ferhat Abbas, Muslim reformist, and later head of the FLN's Provisional Government, announced to the Vichyists: 'Your racism goes in every direction, today against the Jews, and always against the Arabs.'[34] At the same time, some Muslim nationalists pressed Algeria's Jewish leadership to follow the logic of their persecuted situation by refusing any eventual reinstatement of their citizenship and instead joining the nationalist camp in a common struggle on behalf of an independent *Algerian* citizenship.[35] This overture was politely but firmly refused.

From Jews to *Pied-Noirs*?

As we know, the decision on the part of Algeria's Jews to face their future as French citizens did indeed have profound consequences. By the time the Algerian War of

Independence breaks out, it is difficult to separate the reaction of Algeria's Jews from the rest of the *pied-noir* community. Writing in 1961, for example, in his lesser-known work *Les Français d'Algérie*, Pierre Nora observed:

> From the largest capitalist *colon* to the small Jewish tailor, from the descendants of old French families to Maltese workers, from the large merchant to the small *colon* of the interior, nationalist passion is at the same temperature. What unites psychologically all these categories is stronger than what separates them socially.[36]

This is echoed in a recent study of Algerian Jewry by Joëlle Allouche-Benayoun, who describes at length the social hierarchies to which this community was continually subject – even at the best of times. He then notes: 'The crossing of the Mediterranean, *la nostalgie du pays perdu*, achieved in France what had never occurred in Algeria: the proximity of Algeria's Jews and the "others", all having become *les pieds noirs*, bonding together in the myth of a fraternal Algeria.'[37]

This is where contemporary historiography concedes that much work remains to be done, though in the last few years, the specific nature of Algerian Jewish allegiance during the War of Independence has been further investigated.[38] In the main, recent historiography has shown that Jewish community organizations advocated and sustained a position of extreme moderation.[39] However, individuals adopted a diversity of positions across the political spectrum, and indeed changed their positions in radical ways as the conflict progressed, and as the *pied-noir* response evolved from confidence, to disquiet, to feelings of being duped and finally to despair. Research into an atypical Jewish support for the FLN on the one hand, and a more numerous – even if still minor – participation in the OAS on the other has met with considerable resistance on the part of the so-called repatriated community.[40] Jewish backing of the OAS is especially a 'taboo memory' within a community that prefers to remember itself only as a victim of the dereliction that characterized France's decolonization process.

On a number of occasions throughout the war, the Jewish community was specifically addressed by the FLN and urged once again to link its future with the independence cause. The decision not to do so has been widely accepted as evidence that, whatever iniquities members of this community had endured in the course of their gruelling apprenticeship as French citizens, this was nonetheless the fate they had chosen. Michel Abitbol asks whether this choice *could* have been otherwise, given a colonial situation that 'had erected unbridgeable barriers between diverse religious ethnies that had each adopted different strategies *vis-à-vis* the colonial state, its "codes" and policies.'[41]

In a sense an answer to this question must also be sought in conjunction with the new historiography of Algerian nationalism. Here I can only mention in passing the work of Mohamed Harbi, André Nouschi, Benjamin Stora (himself an Algerian

Jew) and others on the occlusion within Algerian memory of other strands of Algerian nationalism that played a crucial role in the formation of a national consciousness in the pre-independence period.[42] What were the constituents of this consciousness apart from the desire for an independent nation-state? Charles-Robert Ageron has argued that, while religion was not ostensibly foregrounded by the FLN, a contradictory discourse on the role Islam would play in the new Algerian state was embedded in a number of FLN statements.[43] For many Algerian nationalists, Muslim identity was indeed one of the stakes of the independence struggle, and had been so in the longer history of Algerian nationalism – associated with Messali Hadj – to which the FLN was a mere newcomer. This was a sentiment that the radical, secular-oriented FLN leadership simply could not afford to ignore. Thus it was not at all clear either within the FLN – or, as Ageron suggests, to Algerian Jews as well – what place would be accorded religious minorities if this aspiration for a nation defined in terms of religion prevailed. After 1960, as the war intensified, the targeting by the FLN of synagogues, rabbis, community venues and leading Jewish figures (like the philosopher Raymond Bénichou and the singer Raymond Leyris) clearly also sent messages to the Algerian Jewish community that appeals for their support of independence had now been superseded by more lethal means of persuasion. Algeria's Jews were among the first to leave the country, even before the mass exodus of summer 1962, and the question must be posed whether their precipitate departure was not in fact due to a collective premonition that their place in an independent Algeria was nowhere near as secure as the FLN statements had implied. This 'trou de mémoire' is one that can only be excavated by the combined efforts of Jewish *and* Algerian historiography.[44]

I raised earlier the question of what might be the political stakes of any identity claims based on the re-kindling of Jewish-Algerian memories and the new historiography that accompanies them. This is a question of considerable sensitivity in a situation where any reinterpretation of Algerian historiography has potentially far-reaching implications for an understanding of the sources of the country's present unspeakably violent conflict.[45]

A number of historians upon whom I've drawn deny that a nostalgia for roots lies behind the renewed affirmation of judeo-algerian specificity.[46] Yet, as I have indicated in Chapter 1, Pierre Nora is convinced that France is currently in the grip of a 'commemorative obsession' that has elevated 'patrimonial memory' to the status of a virtual obligation. As we've seen, Nora describes *la mémoire patrimoine* as memories rooted in specific loci of a particular region rather than in the narratives of the nation's past. This localized heritage, claimed as the cornerstone of one's singular identity, has allegedly reinforced the power of 'sectoral identities' in the French body politic to the detriment of the republican aspiration to represent an inclusive collective identity.[47] Yet Nora's assumption that this memorial militancy 'from below' also necessarily excludes those diasporic groups who cannot celebrate the kind of palpable attachments – material or symbolic 'sites' – valorized by patrimonial memory, does not, as we've seen, apply to the expatriated *pied-noir* community. On the contrary, precisely because Algeria is an absent site of patrimonial memory – a *non-lieu de mémoire* – remembrance is all the more psychically charged, and runs the risk of succumbing to *nostalgérie*, to an enduring melancholia over the traumatic loss of an idealized love object.[48] The tense and emotive circumstances of their departure may consign the former Jews of Algeria to this modality of memory; however, the specificity of their history and their location within the colonial context also differentiates their *mémoire patrimoine* from that of their *pied-noir* compatriots. I would suggest that the assertion of this distinction is one of the stakes of current identity claims.

This interpretation is borne out in a striking manner by a unique ethnography that anthropologist Joëlle Bahloul carried out in the 1980s amongst her own Jewish-Algerian relatives, formerly residents of Sétif and since their departure living in Marseilles and in the Paris metropolitan region. Bahloul's interest lay primarily in showing, in Bachelardian fashion, how a diasporic community is obliged to structure memory primarily in spatial terms. The 'uprooted memories' of a diasporic community, according to Bahloul, must compensate for lack of access to their own *lieux de mémoire* and the more 'intangible relation to the past' that such physical distance may impose, by summoning memories whose key locus is the very spatial parameters from which the community is physically estranged. Surcharged memories of places – especially domestic spaces – are, according to Bahloul, 'part of the syndrome of exile'. They are an 'embodiment of the life cycle' and therefore an 'embodiment of genealogy' – highly-cathected substitutes for the physical traces of lineage their bearers have been forced to abandon. Their function is to 'erase deracination by re-creating genealogical loci'.[49] Bahloul's relatives, the Senoussi family, had preserved the affective intensity of their symbolic connection to their Algerian homeland by summoning a wealth of memories that crystallized around the Sétif residence occupied by this extended family and their Muslim neighbours. Individual and family narratives – the temporal dimension of memory – were reconstructed around the experiences, rituals and interactions that occurred within this domestic space and its immediate environs.

Within this 'architecture of memory' (to use Bahloul's elegant term), a subtle picture emerges of the character of Jewish–Muslim interaction over a period of several decades that resonates in largely reinforcing ways with the historiographical discourses I have earlier sketched. Most notably, recollections by both the Senoussi family and their Muslim neighbours invariably place emphasis on a legacy of co-residence 'without animosity', and any discord that is recalled is attributed to the provocations of French anti-Semites rather than internally-induced racial tensions. As Bahloul notes: 'Jewish and Muslim voices concur on the theme that the Christians created discord between the two dominated communities.'[50] Even when

Bahloul's interlocutors recall conflicts between the two communities whose tensions directly infiltrate the space of the Senoussi household – the Sétif pogrom of 1935, the latter stages of the War of Independence – the theme of 'mutual protection' prevails over any discussion of their discordant effects. At the same time, Bahloul observes that if such memories paint a rather idyllic portrait of harmonious co-existence on the part of two 'outsider' communities, there is also an insistence on a 'distinction without hostility' that marked everyday rituals and interactions. And while many of these were religiously-determined and concerned boundaries marked by dietary, social and linguistic codes, Bahloul remarks on the eagerness displayed especially in Jewish memories to emphasize such distinctions, 'using a wealth of details that reflects the narrators' drive to put behind them some of their indigenous Maghrebian traits and embrace Western modernity'.[51] Perhaps in this (very human) desire to have it both ways – the desire for 'harmony without anarchic mingling', in Bahloul's apt expression – such memories serve to articulate both the historical reality of Jewish-Muslim existence *and* promote the 'genealogical fantasy' of which Derrida speaks.[52]

A question remains: why are claims of Jewish-Algerian specificity surfacing now – whether in historiography or popular memory – more than three decades after an exodus to the metropole during which such distinctions were neither recognized nor sought? The fact that an assertion of judeo-algerian identity is making its presence felt at this particular conjuncture cannot be without significance. Undoubtedly, this relates to the wider reconfiguration of French Judaism faced with the so-called crisis of republican identity. But there are other contingencies to consider as well, though these must be elucidated with some care. As Algeria's civil war – recently described by one oppositionist as 'une guerre *contre* les civils'[53] or war *against* civilians – intensifies, former Algerian Jews have been prominent amongst those expressing solidarity with Algeria's beleaguered democratic forces (Derrida, Cixous, Jean Daniel to name but a few).[54] In these gestures, however much they are geared to Algeria's contemporary crisis, there is in my view a surplus of signification that harks back to the long and complex vicissitudes of Jewish–Muslim coexistence in Algeria – some features of which I have tried schematically to outline.[55]

Which is perhaps only to re-state the basic Halbwachsian premiss: that historical memory is once again in the service of present political needs; but one can only hope that at the very least its current usage will help to advance the democratic outcome upon which Algeria's future so desperately depends.

Notes

Unless otherwise stated, translations from the French are my own.

1. See José-Alain Fralon, 'Enrico, paroles de paix', *Le Monde*, 15 November1995. The verse form is not conducive to translation, but the gist is the following: 'I left my country/I left my house/My life, my sad life/purposelessly drags on/I left my sun/I left my blue sea/Their memories are reawakened/long after my good-bye/Sun, sun of my lost country!/White villages that I loved/Girls that I once knew.'
2. Fralon, 'Enrico, paroles de paix'.
3. Ibid.
4. Jacques Derrida, *Monolingualism of the Other; or, The Prosthesis of Origin*, trans. Patrick Mensah (Stanford, CA: Stanford University Press, 1998), p. 15; originally published as *Le Monolinguisme de l'autre* (Paris: Galilée, 1996).
5. *Monolingualism of the Other*, p. 17.
6. Ibid., p. 18.
7. See Geoff Bennington, 'Curriculum Vitae', *Jacques Derrida* (Chicago: University of Chicago Press, 1993), pp. 326–7.
8. *Monolingualism of the Other*, p. 28.
9. Ibid., p. 52.
10. Ibid., p. 53.
11. See, for example, Hélène Cixous's ruminations on her Jewish-Algerian past in 'My Algeriance, in other words To Depart not to Arrive from Algeria', paper delivered at the conference 'French and/in Algeria', Cornell University, October 1996, organized by Anne Berger. In this paper, Cixous argues that the war *was* 'time's pivot', ordering all thought into the modes of before, during and after. Cixous's father, a French army lieutenant on the Tunisian front in 1939, a doctor forbidden from practising medicine by Vichy's racial laws, became a podiatrist to provide for his family. In Cixous's wry observation: 'Vichy, which had forbidden him the treatment of bodies, had nonetheless abandoned to him the corns of the feet' (p. 12). Vichy, alleges Cixous, signified to the Jewish community of Algeria that it had 'sold its soul to France and for nothing . . .' (p. 6), the Crémieux Decree proving to be, in Cixous's words, the 'true *Gift*, an example of the gift-poison . . .' (p. 9).
12. See Henry Rousso, *The Vichy Syndrome: History and Memory in France since 1944* (London: Harvard University Press, 1991) and Chapter 5 for a longer discussion of Rousso's evolving views on the vicissitudes of this 'syndrome' in France and the ambivalent position of Vichy historiography as a vector of memory.

13. For the English version of Birnbaum's original contribution to *Les Lieux de mémoire*, see 'Grégoire, Dreyfus, Drancy, and the Rue Copernic: Jews at the Heart of French History', in Pierre Nora (ed.), *Realms of Memory: The Construction of the French Past, Vol. 1: Conflicts and Divisions*, trans. Arthur Goldhammer (New York: Columbia University Press,1996), p. 389.

14. '. . . quitter l'histoire de l'Algérie pour entrer dans celle de la France'. Michel Abitbol, 'La citoyenneté imposée, du décret Crémieux à la guerre d'Algérie', in Pierre Birnbaum (ed.), *Histoire politique des Juifs de France entre universalisme et particularisme* (Paris: Presses de la Fondation nationale des sciences politiques, 1990).

15. This figure is given by Richard Ayoun in 'Le décret Crémieux et l'insurrection de 1871 en Algérie', *Revue d'histoire moderne et contemporaine*, vol. 35, Jan.–March 1988, p. 61. In 'My Algeriance', Cixous notes that her family was one of the few to apply for citizenship under the *Senatus Consulte*.

16. Derrida, *The Monolingualism of the Other*, p. 53.

17. The term 'decree of sinister memory' is drawn from an unattributed source in the journal *L'Arche* and cited by Joëlle Allouche-Benayoun in 'Une histoire d'intégration: Les Juifs d'Algérie et la France', *Les nouveaux cahiers*, no. 116, Spring 1994, p. 32.

18. A number of historians emphasize that before French colonization, Jews had the status of *dhimmi* – a status that applied to all non-Muslims under Muslim rule. This implied both protection and subordination, religious freedom and forms of cultural discrimination and humiliation. See Richard Ayoun's description of *dhimmi* in 'Une Presence Plurimillenaire', *Les Juifs d'Algérie. Images et Textes* (Paris: Éditions du Scribe,1987).

19. See Abitbol, 'La Citoyenneté imposée'; Shmuel Trigano, 'L'Avenir d'un déracinement', *Les Juifs d'Algérie: Images et Textes.*

20. Jacques Taïeb, 'Tumulte autour d'un décret: Le décret Crémieux ou la première logique coloniale', *Les nouveaux cahiers*, no. 123, Winter 1995/6. I borrow the term 'dejudaization' from Taïeb, whose article also explicitly highlights the negative interpretation of the effects of the decree as a 'revisionist' turn within this new historiography.

21. See Edouard Drumont, *La France Juive: Essai d'Histoire Contemporaine*, tome II (Vingtième Edition) (Paris: C. Marpon and E. Flammerion, no date), p. 11. Drumont also expresses the hope that Algeria will be the launching pad for the anti-Semitic campaign of the metropole.

22. Pierre Birnbaum, 'The Empire Abandoned: From the Crémieux Decree to the Blum–Violette Plan', *Anti-Semitism in France* (Oxford: Blackwell, 1992).

23. Charles-Robert Ageron, cited by David Prochaska, *Making Algeria French: Colonialism in Bône, 1870–1920* (Cambridge: Cambridge University Press, 1990).

24. See Prochaska, *Making Algeria French* and Pierre Hebey, *Alger 1898: La grande vague antijuive* (Paris: NiL éditions, 1996).

25. Pierre Nora describes the Dreyfus affair in France as only one aspect of a more general nationalist crisis, whereas in Algeria, '. . . anti-Semitism typified the crisis, and represented a crucial – perhaps decisive – moment in the formation of the reprobate sensibility of French Algerians and in their contradictory self-perception.' See Nora, *Les Français d'Algérie* (Paris: Julliard, 1961), pp. 100–1.

26. Drumont, *La France Juive*. Drumont (p. 12) speaks of the Prussian admiration for the Arab contingent of France's forces, evoking the 'fantasy-like effect' that 'their savage cries, their joy at hearing gunpowder, and their manner of pouncing like tigers' had on the enemy.

27. Drumont does hint that the Government of National Defence might have rewarded these 'heroic Arabs' with citizenship; but nowhere does this become a battlecry of his anti-Semitic platform.

28. This argument is elaborated in great detail by Richard Ayoun in 'Le décret Crémieux'. Ayoun's article includes documentation of official investigations into the insurrection by the Constantine and Algiers judicial authorities, as well as extended testimony about the uprising given in 1872 by a Muslim peasant. In light of the fact that this was the period of transfer of power over Algeria from the French military to a civilian government, Ayoun's conclusion is that the uprising was primarily caused by the anticipated loss of influence of the Muslim aristocracy once the *colons* gained political power. He argues that 'before, during and after the 1871 insurrection, Muslim opinion concerning naturalization remained the same, regarding Jewish accession to full political rights with perfect indifference' (p. 74).

29. See Michael Maurrus and Robert O. Paxton, 'A Special Case: Algeria' in *Vichy France and the Jews* (Stanford, CA: Stanford University Press, 1995), pp. 191–7.

30. See Bennington, 'Curriculum Vitae' and Derrida, *The Postcard: From Socrates to Freud and Beyond* (Chicago: Chicago University Press,1987). In *The Postcard*, Derrida writes: 'The only school official whose name I remember today: he has me come into his office: "You are going to go home, my little friend, your parents will get a note." At the moment I understood nothing, but since?' p. 86. Cixous, 'My Algeriance', also recalls herself and her brother being sent home under the *numerus clausus*. Alternative schools were set up by many Jewish communities – Camus was recruited by his friend André Bénichou to teach excluded secondary pupils for a limited time.

31. See Maurrus and Paxton, 'A Special Case: Algeria'; Michel Ansky, *Les Juifs d'Algérie, du décret Crémieux à la Libération* (Paris: Éditions du Centre,1950); Michel Abitbol, *Les juifs d'Afrique du Nord sous Vichy* (Paris: Maisonneuve

& Larose, 1988); André Kaspi, *Les Juifs pendant l'Occupation* (Paris: Seuil, 1991); Joëlle Alouche-Benayoun and Doris Bensimon, *Les Juifs d'Algérie* (Paris: BHP,1989). Concluding his detailed study of this period, Abitbol remarks: 'In invading France and preparing the path for the installation of the Vichy regime, the Germans were at the origin of the application of the racial laws in the metropole and in North Africa. But three years later, it was Frenchmen – and Frenchmen free of any external constraint – who were singularly responsible for delaying the annulment of these laws' (p. 174).

32. See Ansky, *Les Juifs d'Algérie*, who quotes from the *Oran Républicain* of 15 March 1943 Giraud's justification that 'relations between Muslims and Israelites must be those of men required to complement each other economically, whether working in workshops or in the interior, without either having the edge on the other' (p. 285).

33. Cited by Paxton and Maurrus, 'A Special Case: Algeria', p. 195.

34. Cited by Jean-Louis Planche, 'Violence et Nationalismes en Algérie (1942–1945)', *Les Temps Modernes* 590, Oct.–Nov. 1996, p. 125.

35. Ibid. Planche offers an important account of the radicalization of Algerian nationalist sentiment between 1942 and 1945. Planche shows that both the Vichyist government of Algeria and the authorities installed after the Allied landing were well aware of the intensification of nationalist activity during this period, highlighted in 1943 by the issuing of the *Manifeste du People algérienne,* which demanded an independent Algerian state. This desire not to fuel nationalist resentment was embraced by both camps as another reason for the delay in reinstating the Crémieux Decree.

36. Pierre Nora, *Les Français d'Algérie*, p. 47. Nora's observations on the relations between Jews and Muslims are sharp and critical of prejudices on both sides. He notes a Jewish attitude that invokes an endemic anti-Semitism amongst Algeria's Arab population, at the same time that it appeals to the long-standing capacity for peaceful coexistence between the two groups. This 'apparent contradiction', maintains Nora, 'defines perfectly the ambiguity of their situation' (p. 137). He also offers a scathing description of Algeria as a country founded on 'le colonialisme foncier et la présence militaire, d'opinion conservatrice, catholique, pétainiste, giraudiste, franquiste, mussolinienne et collaboratrice . . .' (p. 140).

37. Joëlle Allouche-Benayoun, "Une histoire d'intégration', p. 72.

38. See in particular, the journals *Les nouveaux cahiers* (especially no. 116) and *Archives Juives* (especially no. 29/1, 1996), that also confirm the difficulty of researching this topic because of the military sensitivity of some archival material, and the reticence on the part of the community to speak about the war.

39. See in particular Jacques Lazarus, 'Rapport sur la situation des Juifs en Algérie au début de l'année 1958', *Archives Juives*, vol. 29, no. 1, 1996. Lazarus was

director of the *Comité juif algérien d'études sociales*, one of the main social organizations of Algeria's Jews. In this report, written during the War of Independence, Lazarus shows an acute awareness of Algeria's vulnerability to political anti-Semitism. And while he emphasizes that 'il n'y a de politique juive', at the same time he insists: 'to be Jewish is also a political – and not only religious or social – phenomenon' (p. 52). The report cites the warm relations of Jews and Arabs' during the Vichy period, yet at the same time affirms the attachment of Algerian Jews to their French citizenship. Lazarus urges moderation and an attitude consistent with their identity as 'Français, Juifs, républicains et libéraux'.

40. See Jean Laloum, 'Portrait d'un Juif du FLN', *Archives Juives*, vol. 29, no.1, 1996; Doris Bensimon, 'La Guerre et l'évolution de la communauté juive', in Jean-Pierre Roux (ed.), *La guerre d'Algérie et les Français* (Paris: Fayard, 1990), and Richard Ayoun, 'Les Juifs d'Algérie pendant la guerre d'indépendence (1954–62)', *Archives Juives*, vol. 29, no.1, 1996.

41. Abitbol, 'La Citoyenneté imposée', p. 215.

42. There is an abundant literature on this topic, but see in particular Mohamed Harbi, *Le FLN: Mirage et réalité* (Paris: Jeune Afrique,1980); André Nouschi, *L'Algérie amère* (Paris: Éditions de la Maison des Sciences de l'Homme, 1996); Benjamin Stora, *La gangrène et l'oubli* (Paris: La Découverte, 1991); *Histoire de l'Algérie coloniale, 1830–1954* (Paris: La Découverte, 1994).

43. Charles-Robert Ageron, 'Une guerre religieuse?', *Archives Juives*, vol. 29, no. 1, 1996. See also Richard Ayoun, 'Le décret Crémieux'.

44. For example, the attitude of Ferhat Abbas was highly ambivalent on this question. Richard Ayoun in 'Le décret Crémieux' quotes several statements where Abbas explicitly links the fate of Algerian Jews with the French, and refutes their future right of emigration in an independent Algerian state.

45. See, for example, Benjamin Stora, *L'Algérie en 1995: La guerre, l'histoire, la politique* (Paris: Éditions Michalon, 1995), a book of essays that attempts to demonstrate the link between nationalist violence during the War of Independence and the violence of the contemporary conflict.

46. See, for example, Joëlle Allouche-Benayoun, 'Une histoire d'intégration', who suggests that the main pole of this identity is a liberal and anti-racist attitude, not a *pied-noir* nostalgia.

47. This diagnosis of France's politics of memory is elaborated further in Chapter 1 and in Pierre Nora, 'L'Ère de la commémoration', in *Les Lieux de mémoire, Vol. 3, Les France* (Paris: Gallimard, 1992), pp. 977–1012.

48. For a careful consideration of these issues, see Joëlle Hureau, 'La mémoire rapatriée', in *La France en Guerre d'Algérie* (Paris: BDIC, 1992), and *La mémoire des Pieds-Noirs* (Paris: Olivier Orban, 1987).

49. See Joëlle Bahloul, *The Architecture of Memory: A Jewish-Muslim Household*

in Colonial Algeria 1937–1962 (Cambridge: Cambridge University Press, 1996), p. 115.

50. Ibid., p. 119.

51. Ibid., p. 83.

52. The theme of Jewish–Muslim coexistence is reiterated in the fascinating film *Le Grand Pardon* (Alexandre Arcady, France, 1981). A police thriller, the film traces the fortunes and misfortunes of the wealthy (and shady) Bettoun clan, Jewish-Algerians who were part of the 1962 exodus and now run a gambling empire in France. The clan's chief rival is a *pied-noir* of Spanish origin, though for some time the clan believe they are being undermined by an Algerian boss (linked to the FLN) who is out to settle old scores. The resolution of the plot turns on recognizing the ultimately trustworthy relations between Jews and Muslims and the duplicity of *pieds-noirs*. Thanks are due to Ginette Vincendeau for alerting me to this film.

53. The term was used by Saïd Sadi, leader of the Rassemblement culturel et démocratique (RCD), at a meeting at the Mutualité, Paris, February 1997.

54. See Derrida's address to a 1994 meeting organized by CISIA (Comité International de Soutien aux Intellectuels Algériens) entitled 'Parti Pris Pour l'Algérie', published in *Les Temps Modernes*, January 1995, and translated into English by Boris Belay in 'Translating 'algeria'', *parallax* 7, 1998. Derrida speaks of 'an Algeria to which I have often come back and which in the end I know to have never really ceased inhabiting or bearing in my innermost, a love for Algeria to which, if not the love of a citizen, and thus the patriotic tie to a Nation-state, is none the less what makes it impossible to dissociate here the heart, the thinking, and the political position-taking . . .' (p. 19). I don't mean to imply that the political allegiances of former Jewish Algerians are self-evident, nor that the evolving political situation in Algeria and fractious divisions within the Algerian opposition and amongst French intellectuals have not complicated solidarity to a point where it is difficult to make any confident generalizations. However, I do want to maintain that a certain 'will to solidarity' amongst former Jews of Algeria has been a modest but visible dimension of support activity.

55. This is the reading invited by a recent collection edited by Leïla Sebbar, *Une Enfance Algérienne* (Paris: Gallimard, 1997). Amongst contributions by Algerians and former Français d'Algérie, one finds essays by Albert Bensoussan, Hélène Cixous, Annie Cohen and Jean Daniel. A Jewish sub-text is more or less evident in these essays, but their primary function seems to be to recall childhood memories that are both highly personal and revelatory of a particular historical and social milieu. There is no introductory essay, but the bookjacket speaks of bringing together writers 'comme ils ne l'ont jamais été sur la terre natale [as they never were on their native soil]'.

8

Memory by Analogy: *Hiroshima, mon amour*

In an influential article on understanding history *as* trauma, the literary critic Cathy Caruth mobilizes the following definition of trauma's particular structure of pathology: 'The event is not assimilated or experienced fully at the time, but only belatedly, in its repeated *possession* of the one who experiences it. To be traumatized is precisely to be possessed by an image or event.'[1] In Alain Resnais' *Hiroshima, mon amour* (scripted by the novelist Marguerite Duras),[2] both protagonists are indeed 'possessed' by memories of the traumatic events they have respectively endured, and it is only thanks to a passionate love affair that their captivation by images from the past is converted into speech. It is as if the eroticized body triggers the release of traumatic memories and the experiencing *for the first time* of the affect that has hitherto been denied discursive expression.

But the relationship that the film establishes between traumatic memories and eroticized bodies is itself routed through another level of signification, which has proved to be the film's most ambiguous and vexing dimension. For most spectators, it is the film's recourse to analogy that generates the greatest unease. It is not simply that the film juxtaposes memories of historical events that potentially destabilize the edifying narratives of the end of the Second World War – the 'excesses' associated with France's Liberation on the one hand, and the atomic annihilation of Hiroshima and Nagasaki on the other. The discomfort that the film is still capable of provoking arises from the kinds of analogy it constructs between the personal memories of *une femme tondue* – women whose heads were shaven for (literally) 'sleeping with the enemy' – and the collective commemoration of an atomic conflagration.[3]

In an earlier chapter, I invoked an analogy between the resentments of Holocaust survivors and those generated by recent genocidal conflicts, and I signalled that it was not the events that were strictly comparable, but memories of abandonment by the larger polity that their victims had in common. In a similar spirit, I wish to use *Hiroshima, mon amour*, a film that explictly thematizes the link between two traumatic – but otherwise incomparable – events, to reflect on how analogy illuminates and limits our encounter with history-as-trauma.

Of course, a certain discomfort about the film's manner of linking the trauma of an individual with that of an entire nation was registered by critics at the time of the film's release; and in a number of interviews that Resnais gave in 1959–60, he was quick to refute the charge that any simple equation or comparison had been proposed between the individual drama of 'Elle', a former *femme tondue*, and the enormous tragedy of Hiroshima. Resnais argued that 'any pain is incommensurable' with another, and that the film had merely attempted to draw these two dramas – two kinds of grief – closer ('nous avons rapproché ces deux drames') in order better to apprehend each of them.[4] But the distinctive feature of the film's *mise en rapport* of two kinds of pain lies precisely in the compelling force of an analogy that the film elicits.[5]

The problem of interpreting the film's analogical strategy is immediately evident in two contrasting interpretations of *Hiroshima, mon amour* of recent years, both of which are critically attuned to the issues involved in representing memories of a traumatic past. The French film critic Marie Claire Ropars-Wuilleumier offers a reading of the film in which the story of Elle's traumatic past serves as the narrative scaffolding bearing the weight of the otherwise 'unrepresentable' nature of Hiroshima's atomic holocaust.[6] By contrast, the philosopher Alain Brossat emphasizes that Hiroshima provides the wider ethico-political context for understanding the collective chastisement that was inflicted on French women who fell in love with German soldiers.[7] To draw the contrast more starkly, in one reading the stakes of the film's analogy are the 'limits of representation' of this – and perhaps any other – mass annihilation; in another, they are History's cruel indifference to the claims of a love exempt from political judgement. I want to consider each of these interpretations in turn – though not with a view to reconciling their opposing emphases. Instead, I hope to show that in both readings of *Hiroshima, mon amour*, analogy is deemed to be a crucial – indeed indispensable – mnemonic mechanism because it initiates the 'working-through' of traumatic events via an encounter with the memory of the other.

The Limits of Representation

The famous fifteen-minute opening sequence is for Ropars-Wuilleumier the clearest expression of the film's deliberate engagement with the 'limits of representation' of the atomic firestorm that engulfed Hiroshima. The film begins with several images in which a glittering dust rains down gently on two bodies locked in a perpetual embrace. A luminous dust coats the bodies' surfaces, suggesting a haunting resemblance to landscapes in the aftermath of a volcanic eruption (see Figure 3). Thus is the horror of Hiroshima's atomic destruction initially evoked, via the abstractions of an erotic encounter. The bodies themselves – fragmented by extreme close-ups – remain unidentifiable throughout the sequence; only the male and female voice-overs give any indication of character. But this abstraction soon gives way to the 'referential illusion' as these close-ups are intercut with newsreel and reconstructed images of Hiroshima's destructive aftermath. Through this juxtaposition, the fragmented corporeality that has opened the sequence is brutally de-meta-phorized by images that now show destroyed flesh, disfigured and dismembered limbs. Against a musical backdrop, a woman's voice recounts what she has seen in the museums and hospitals of Hiroshima; a male voice insistently negates her affirmations. Ropars-Wuilleumier argues that with this opening *écriture* or cinematic 'writing', *Hiroshima, mon amour* proclaims its intention to resist the impulse of only recreating a simulacrum of Hiroshima's destruction, and instead employs sounds and images that designate by their very 'syntax' the impossibility of their referential task.[8] Juxtaposition is not in the service of comparison, Ropars-Wuilleumier insists; on the contrary, the effect of this calculated *figural* analogy is to introduce a profound 'disorder [. . .] into our scale of values' and thereby to suggest the 'impotence of sight and knowledge' faced with an event that, by its very nature, exposes the limits of familiar representational and moral categories.[9]

If, by deploying cinematic *écriture*, *Hiroshima, mon amour* foregrounds the quandary of representing a catastrophe like Hiroshima, this figural strategy is by no means offered as a privileged solution. Indeed, to avoid remaining trapped in the hermetic world of the couple's lovemaking, the film then harnesses *écriture* to the mechanisms of narration, thus, according to Ropars-Wuilleumier, making the 'event readable by inserting it into a logical continuity'. And this is where the function of the Nevers story assumes its full representational significance. Ropars-Wuilleumier maintains that the 'unrepresentable' of Hiroshima's catastrophe is transferred onto the 'narratable' of Elle's story of a doomed love affair in Nevers.[10]

This notion of 'transference' introduces another level of analogy into the film – between a narration that harnesses the force generated by cinematic *écriture*, and the position of the analyst in the psychoanalytic encounter onto whom is transferred the affective charge of the analysand's discourse. Indeed, for psychoanalysis, the very condition of 'working-through' in the therapeutic situation depends on the analysand's memories activating the 'affect' that was originally attached to them.[11] By reviving the affect and then adopting a role in the accompanying recollections of the analysand, the analyst helps to give form and expression to an emotive force that has until then exercised virtual blind rule over the analysand's psychic landscape. As Ropars-Wuilleumier points out, 'Lui', the Japanese lover, assumes exactly this identificatory position of the analyst in relation to Elle's narration of her Nevers past at the moment when he accepts being addressed as her dead German lover, when he demands of Elle: 'Quand tu es dans la cave, je suis mort?' ['When you are in the cellar, am I dead?'].[12] But, consistently with Ropars-Wuilleumier reading of *Hiroshima, mon amour*'s analogical strategy, she insists that we should not see this 'psychoanalytic simulacrum' as operating primarily on behalf of the 'working-through' of the traumatic memory of *une femme tondue*. Rather, the elaboration of the Nevers story in this transferential mode implicitly poses the question of what it means to 'work through' the legacy of an atomic catastrophe

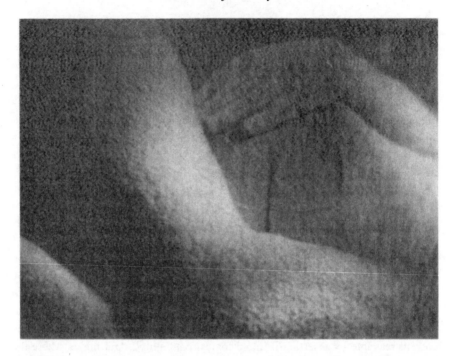

Figure 3

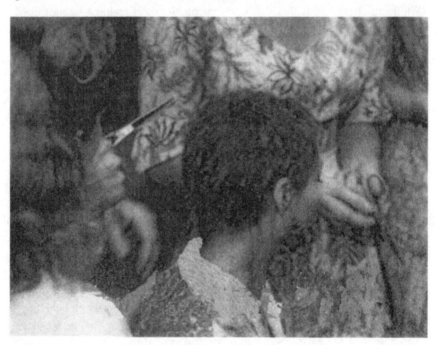

Figure 4

(or indeed any mass catastrophe), what comparable labour of mourning can release survivors – and societies – from the 'psychic numbing' that the devastation induced as the very condition of survival?[13] The 'simple story' of Nevers is thus designated to assume the enormous affective weight of 'the opaque memory of an event whose importance cannot be formulated'.[14]

In early sequences, when Elle relates the evidence of destruction she has seen on her visits to hospitals and museums, Lui tells her: 'Tu n'a rien vu à Hiroshima [. . .] Tu ne sais rien' ['You saw nothing in Hiroshima. You know nothing']. Elle in turn insists that she has seen 'everything', knows 'everything' and has thus become convinced that she will never forget Hiroshima. But it is only after the transmission of her story of Nevers in three flashback sequences[15] that Lui – and by extension the film's spectators – realize that Elle has been seeking to inscribe in her memory images of Hiroshima's destruction and its aftermath in order to do battle with the forces of forgetting that overwhelm even the strongest compulsion to remember. Early in the film, Elle tells Lui that they both share the desire to resist any attenuation of the memories that bind them to their respective traumatic pasts: 'Comme toi, je connais l'oubli [. . .] comme toi, je suis douée de mémoire [. . .] comme toi, moi aussi, j'ai essayé de lutter de toutes mes forces contre l'oubli. Comme toi, j'ai oublié. Comme toi, j'ai désiré avoir une inconsolable mémoire, une mémoire d'ombres et de pierres.' ['Like you, I know what it is to forget [. . .] like you, I'm over-endowed with memory [. . .] like you, I too have tried with all my might not to forget. Like you, I forgot. Like you, I wanted to have an inconsolable memory, a memory of shadows and stones.'] The first intrusion of another memory that also once seemed unforgettable – a flashing image of the hand of her dead German soldier – makes her realize that her conviction that she will preserve an indelible memory of what she has seen in Hiroshima must also be an illusion.[16]

Through telling to Lui the story of Nevers – of love with a German soldier, his assassination by the Resistance and her punishment as a *femme tondue* – Elle undertakes her long-belated labour of mourning. Only as her narration nears completion does this traumatic – but nonetheless precious – memory of her German lover lying dead on the Quai de la Loire, which has made Elle captive to her past, achieve full representation. And only once it achieves representation does the memory in turn risk being subjected to the forces of forgetting. This, the film suggests, is the ambiguous fate awaiting memories of Hiroshima. In the final scene, when Elle cries out in anguish 'Je t'oublierai! Je t'oublie déjà!', ['I'll forget you! I'm forgetting you already!'], we know that she is not only experiencing the pain of progressively forgetting the death of her 'first love', but that she suffers by anticipation the pain of forgetting 'Lui' and Hiroshima. From this perspective, then, 'working-through' the memory that has possessed her is shown to be generative of a therapeutic process of forgetting, wherein forgetting is not simply the consequence of repression or social neglect, but of a cathartic and necessary 'letting go' of the traumatic memory itself. Thus, through the film's recourse to the analogy of an individual's compulsion to remember and need to forget, Ropars-Wuilleumier maintains that 'the horror of Hiroshima is not eclipsed, but it becomes the object of a secret reflection upon the terms of both enunciation and expulsion of the historical event.'[17]

The Judgement of History

However this argument deliberately sidesteps the specific representation of *une femme tondue*, and I want to return to this question, because however compelling we find the film's analogical engagement with the 'limits of representation' of mass catastrophe, the personal tragedy of Elle cannot be so easily subsumed into this larger problematic. Let us recall the words with which Elle describes her youthful self towards the end of the film: 'Petite fille de Nevers. Petite coureuse de Nevers [. . .] Petite fille de rien [. . .] Morte d'amour à Nevers. Petite tondue de Nevers je te donne à l'oubli ce soir. Histoire de quatre sous.' ['Little girl from Nevers. Little slut from Nevers [. . .] Who died of love in Nevers. Little shaven head from Nevers, I deliver you up to oblivion this evening. Another penny dreadful.'] According to the analysis of Alain Brossat, the voice that disparages Elle's own loss and subsequent humiliation is the voice of 'History', which condemns a love that remained indifferent to the demands of public morality. What Elle realizes by these words, observes Brossat, is that she was 'a "collabo" by virtue of being in love'.[18]

Brossat's discussion of *Hiroshima, mon amour* forms part of his larger study of *les femmes tondues*. Brossat's own interest in these women derives in part from what he sees as the failure of historians of the Liberation to account for the intense 'memorial agitation' that still surrounds all reference to these women in French popular culture. Yet it is precisely the belated 'affect' aroused by memories and images of *les femmes tondues* in the present that, in Brossat's view, testifies to their traumatic nature in French collective memory. The similarly 'belated' historiographical interest in *les tondues* is not because these women have been 'absent from history' – indeed, they have been manifestly present in nomadic and 'capillary' cultural channels: songs, novels, local rumours, and *fait divers*. Their absence from the main fields of historiographical enquiry into the events of the Liberation instead suggests to Brossat that here, too, they have functioned as a 'painful spasm' (*une douloureuse contracture*), reminding historians of French memory of 'a past that will not pass'.[19]

There is not space here to discuss Brossat's provocative and fascinating study, nor the heated criticism that his work on the Liberation has generated.[20] But it is nonetheless worth noting that while historiographical accounts have stressed the 'scapegoating' function that these women served in the context of the various humiliations suffered by an occupied France, Brossat has argued that the full symbolic significance of this ritualized sexual violence has still not been adequately explained. He asks the pointed question: 'What is this woman's *real* 'crime' which justifies such a bizarre form of torture?'[21] To be sure, French men who collaborated with the Germans were also subject to violent recriminations during the so-called purges or *épuration* of 1944. But the kind of punishments they received, although more physically severe and often extending to summary execution, did not explicitly target their sexual difference. Why, then, was the punishment of women accused of 'horizontal collaboration' targeted at a part of their bodies that marked sexual difference, and why did it also require their sexual humiliation (after being shorn, the women were often stripped naked and paraded through the streets or put on public display)?[22] Brossat agrees that this 'carnivalesque behaviour' probably served to enact for many communities the cathartic trial of a betrayed and sullied nation. But he insists that the corporeal dimensions of this expiating ritual must be situated within the wider claims that nations make on the bodies of women – and of women alone: 'These women', Brossat contends, 'were symbolically accused of having 'deceived' the nation and of having sullied it across their very body, as if this body belonged to the collectivity.'[23]

Hiroshima, mon amour offers a vivid *mise-en-scène* of the corporeal punishments inflicted on Elle by the good citizens of Nevers, who judged her love for a German soldier as a betrayal of the town and of the entire nation (see Figure 4). But the film's extraordinary provocation, in 1959, is to show Elle's 'crime' to be that of youthful love alone, of an *amour fou* that ignored the strictures that 'History' had imposed on intimate life.[24] Elle's only 'crime', the film suggests, was not to bow to History's *diktat*, to regard her love as immune from the demand that in a war, desire, too, must take sides. And for this naïveté, she pays the price of madness in the cellar, remorse that she did not 'die of love' on the Quai de la Loire and subsequent psychic imprisonment by the repetitive, hallucinatory image of her lover's death. Certainly this is one of the film's most flagrant violations of French national memory: it solicits our empathetic identification with the loss suffered by *une femme tondue*: the death of her *German* soldier-lover on the Quai de la Loire.

Like Ropars-Wuilleumier, Brossat also highlights the indispensability of Lui to Elle's re-externalization of her traumatic memory; but he stresses that this role is overdetermined by an analogy that the film mobilizes between the historical definitions ascribed to each of Elle's lovers. It is Lui's *alterity* – his designation 'in the time of History, as the absolute Other' – that permits him to occupy the phantasmic place of the dead German soldier in the transference. Like her German lover whom History defined solely as 'the enemy', Lui occupies a place in a system of binary oppositions that opposes the French woman to the Japanese man, the victor to the vanquished, the European to the Asian, the democrat to the ex-fascist.[25]

This leads us to an issue that it seems to me Brossat overlooks. If we accept the view that it is the alterity of her German lover that defines her original transgression, and the alterity of Lui that enables the transference, is it not also the case that Elle is shown to desire these men precisely for this quality? Elle knew her German lover was objectively 'un ennemi de la France', as she tells Lui, and yet this knowledge, far from impeding her actions, gives her memories of her *amour fou* for the young soldier their particular *élan*.[26] In other words, the transgressive nature of Elle's love for a man objectively defined as 'the enemy' provided her desire with the force it needed to act out the rebellion of her youth, to express her emergent sexuality, and her sense of social confinement. When she suffers the punishment of being shaven, her spirit of transgression continues in her refusal to feel any remorse for her lethal desire. She tells Lui: 'Je suis d'une moralité douteuse, tu sais' ['I have doubtful morals, you know']; and when he asks her what this means, she replies that it is 'douter de la morale des autres' ['being doubtful about the morals of other people']. The 'innocence' of which Brossat speaks is thus shown in the film to be not so much the consequence of *l'amour fou*, but of the belief that such transgression would *not* incur the vengeance of History's moral arbiters.[27]

By the same token, Elle's desire for Lui is conditioned by the very fact that it, too, cannot endure. Once its force is expended in the re-enactment of an earlier *amour fou*, she *must* leave Hiroshima, despite his pleas that she stay. The price of her cure, of mastery over the 'tyranny' of her traumatic memory, is the dissipation of her desire, and hence her decision to depart.

This leaves us with the question of the function that Hiroshima serves in this intimate scenario. Brossat argues that by refracting the tale of this '*petite tonte* [. . .] without a name' from the 'small town of Nevers' through the mirror of the 'universal event *par excellence* which Hiroshima represents', the film attempts to highlight not a comparison between the traumatic events each protagonist has endured, but the common, debilitating relation to a memory of catastrophe that they have both borne until their erotic encounter: 'It is in this disastrous relation to the past that the symbolic homology between Nevers and Hiroshima resides.'[28] And while Lui's own memories are relegated to the film's margins, it is evident that in telling her story, Elle also becomes the 'midwife' of his traumatic memories. Her story of taking flight to Paris after her hair has grown, and hearing *en route* of the bombings of Hiroshima and Nagasaki, elicits from him a bitterly ironic recollection of world reaction to his city's mass destruction: 'Le monde entière était joyeux [. . .] C'était un beau jour d'été à Paris [. . .] j'ai entendu dire . . .' ['The whole world rejoiced [. . .] I heard it was a beautiful summer's day in Paris . . .'].

From their struggles, then, to extricate themselves from the 'tyranny' of their respective traumatic memories, the combatants of the film finally emerge as 'survivors' of their violent legacy: '*Hiroshima* articulates a modest ambition: to live, despite everything, with this memory of the deadly bullet and of the scissors for one, of the lethal flash of light for the other.'[29] Elle and Lui's common status as 'survivors' of History's memorial ruins thus emerges as the final level of analogy that Brossat identifies. Elle and Lui come to experience and ultimately to affirm their own 'survivorship' of a catastrophe through an intimate encounter with the spectre of death that has compulsively haunted the other.[30] In her commentary, which is appended to the film's script, Marguerite Duras affirms that it is this 'gift' of her story, and of her own death encounter, that Elle offers as a memorial homage to the pain of Lui and Hiroshima: 'She gives this Japanese man – *at Hiroshima* – her most precious possession: herself as she now is, her *survival* after the death of her love *at Nevers*.'[31] The film ends with the reciprocal gesture by which Lui accepts the name of 'Hiroshima' as his survivor-appellation and confers on Elle an analogous title of 'Nevers-en-France'.

* * *

Cathy Caruth has argued that '[i]n a catastrophic age [. . .] trauma itself may provide the very link between cultures'.[32] In other words, it is the *latency* inherent in the traumatic event – the belated, assimilation of its affective legacy – that confers on all of us the status of emotional survivors of this catastrophic era. From this perspective, *Hiroshima, mon amour* affirms not only the shared survivorship of Elle and Lui, but elicits an empathetic identification between them and the psycho-historical position of the film's spectators.

This inclusive notion of 'survivorship' is certainly appealing, especially to those who feel engaged by the memorial legacy of past traumas. But it is here that we also run up against the 'limits' of the analogical enterprise itself. If we are all nominated as History's 'survivors', merely by virtue of living vicariously through and after traumatic events, we risk diminishing the 'incommensurable pain' that real survivors of this century's catastrophes have suffered, and that a film like *Hiroshima, mon amour* sets out to represent and commemorate.

Notes

Unless otherwise stated, translations from the French are my own.

1. Cathy Caruth, 'Introduction', *American Imago*, vol. 48, no.1, 1991, p. 3. Reprinted in Caruth (ed.), *Unclaimed Experience: Trauma, Narrative and History* (Baltimore: Johns Hopkins University Press, 1996).
2. See Marguerite Duras, *Hiroshima, Mon Amour: scénario et dialogues* (Paris: nrf/Gallimard, 1960).

3. *Hiroshima, mon amour* was withdrawn from competition at the Cannes Film Festival in 1959 following pressure exerted by the French political and cultural authorities. But, contrary to assumptions we might have today about this action, it was not the images of *une femme tondue* that prompted this measure, but French officialdom's anticipation of *American* displeasure with the scenes of Hiroshima. See 'Alain Resnais: *Hiroshima, mon amour*, film scandaleux?', *Les Lettres françaises*, 14–20 May 1959.

4. 'Réponse à *Clarté*', in Alain Resnais, *Premier Plan*, no.18, October 1961, p. 47.

5. In his 1963 film *Muriel*, Resnais was to mobilize another analogy – this time between the Second World War and the Algerian war. For an incisive discussion of the strengths and weaknesses of this strategy, see Philip Dine, 'The inescapable allusion: the Occupation and the Resistance in French fiction and film of the Algerian war', in H. R. Kedward and Nancy Wood (eds), *The Liberation of France: Image and Event* (Oxford: Berg, 1995).

6. Marie-Claire Ropars-Wuilleumier, 'How history begets meaning: Alain Resnais's *Hiroshima, mon amour*', in Susan Hayward and Ginette Vincendeau (eds), *French Film: Texts and Contexts* (London: Routledge, 1990).

7. Alain Brossat, *Les Tondues: Un carnaval moche* (Paris: Editions Manya, 1992).

8. For the notion of *écriture*, see Roland Barthes, 'From Work to Text' in *Image-Music-Text* (London: Fontana/Collins, 1977).

9. Ropars-Wuilleumier, 'How history begets meaning', pp. 179–80. The influence of debates concerning the representation of the Holocaust is evident here, and the reader is once again referred to the seminal text, Saul Friedländer (ed.), *Probing the Limits of Representation: Nazism and the "Final Solution"'* (London: Harvard University Press, 1992).

10. Ibid.

11. See J. Laplanche and J.-B. Pontalis, 'Transference', in *The Language of Psycho-Analysis* (London: The Hogarth Press and the Institute of Psycho-Analysis, 1980), pp. 455–62.

12. Precisely because the film dialogue aspires to a form of *écriture*, I have left the original French in the text. The English translations are drawn (with minor modifications) from Marguerite Duras, *Hiroshima Mon Amour*, trans. Richard Seaver (London: Calder and Boyars, 1966).

13. I borrow the notion of 'psychic numbing' from Robert Jay Lifton, whose study, *Death in Life: The Survivors of Hiroshima* (London: Weidenfeld, 1967), is a moving and indispensable exploration of the psychological effects of the bomb on Hiroshima's survivors, or '*Hibakusha*'. See especially pp. 500–10 for an elaboration of the concept. The following testimony of one *Hibakusha*, a physicist, renders the concept vividly: 'As I walked along, the horrible things I saw became more and more extreme and more and more intolerable. At a

certain point I must have become more or less saturated, so that I became no longer sensitive, in fact insensitive, to what I saw around me. I think human emotions reach a point beyond which they cannot extend – something like a photographic process. If under certain conditions you expose a photographic plate to light, it becomes black; but if you continue to expose it, then it reaches a point where it turns white [. . .] Only later can one recognize having reached this maximum state' (p. 33).

14. Ropars-Wuilleumier, 'How history begets meaning', p. 181.

15. An excellent analysis of these flashback sequeces is offered by Maureen Turim, 'Disjunction in the Modernist Flashback', in *Flashbacks in Film: Memory and History* (London: Routledge, 1989).

16. The memory flashback occurs as she stands staring transfixed at the hand of her sleeping Japanese lover, as if trying to register a mental imprint of this erotic moment. On this 'involuntary memory', see Turim, 'Disjunction in the Modernist Flashback', pp. 211–12.

17. Ropars-Wuilleumier, 'How history begets meaning', p. 182. In her remarks on *Hiroshima, mon amour* in *Black Sun*, Julia Kristeva suggests that the tenacity of Elle's memory of the death of her lover is a function of a melancholia in which '[t]o love, from her point of view, is to love a dead person'. Hence her attachment to Hiroshima might be formulated as: '*I love Hiroshima for its suffering is my Eros . . .*'. See Julia Kristeva, 'The Malady of Grief: Duras', in *Black Sun: Depression and Melancholia* (New York: Columbia University Press, 1989), pp. 231–6.

18. Brossat, *Les Tondues*, p. 55.

19. Ibid., p. 10. Since the publication of *Les Tondues*, these women, far from being neglected by historians, have become a focus of intense research interest. However, there is still a resistance to theorizing these rituals of sexual humiliation as practices that have more than a functional dimension.

20. Brossat is criticized by historians for many sins, but mostly for not making sufficient use of archival sources. See Henry Rousso's remarks in *Vichy, un passé qui ne passe pas* (Paris: Fayard, 1994), p. 104, n.1. See also my discussion of Brossat's provocations in 'Memorial Militancy in France: A "Working-Through" of the Politics of Anachronism' in *Patterns of Prejudice*, vol. 29, nos. 2/3, summer 1995.

21. Brossat, *Les Tondues*. See also Corran Laurens, '"*La Femme au Turban*": *Les Femmes Tondues*', in H. R. Kedward and Nancy Wood (eds), *The Liberation of France: Image and Event*, pp. 155–79.

22. See Laurens, '"La Femme au turban"', for a series of astounding photographs that document these rituals.

23. Brossat, *Les Tondues*, p. 18.

24. Ibid., p. 54.

25. Ibid., p. 60.
26. Maureen Turim perceptively identifies the transgressive desire embedded in this lyrical flashback: 'Within the second set of flashback images, the full weight of the ideological taboo crossed by this love affair is unspoken, and the lyricism of the images, the racing across fields for clandestine encounters, counteracts the charged context of the War.' See 'Disjunction in the Modernist Flashback', p. 213.
27. For a similar reading of youthful sexual transgression during the Occupation, see H. R. Kedward, '*Lacombe Lucien*: The Carnival of Liberation' in Ginette Vincendeau and Susan Hayward (eds), *French Film: Texts and Contexts* (London: Routledge, 1999).
28. Brossat, *Les Tondues*, p. 63.
29. Ibid., p. 62.
30. In this regard, it is relevant to note that Robert Jay Lifton has described every death encounter as a 'reactivation of earlier survivals'. Cited by Eric L. Santner, 'History Beyond the Pleasure Principle: Some Thoughts on the Representation of Trauma', in Saul Friedlander (ed.), *Probing the Limits of Representation* (London: Harvard University Press, 1992), p. 364.
31. Duras, *Hiroshima Mon Amour*, p. 140.
32. Cathy Caruth, 'Introduction', *American Imago*, vol. 48, no. 1, 1991.

Conclusion

As this book was going to press, two historical events were the focus of public remembrance throughout Europe: the end of the First World War eighty years ago, and the 1973 putsch in Chile that brought down the democratically-elected government of Salvador Allende and led to massive repression and the disappearance and death of thousands of Chilean citizens as well as non-nationals. It might be instructive, by way of a brief conclusion, to raise some questions concerning what the memory of these events might reveal – or conceal – about a contemporary public's relationship to the recent and more distant past.

In the first case, intense public interest in the eightieth commemoration of the end of the Great War – an annual symbolic ritual, after all – seemed to be explained by the fact that this was likely to be the last notable commemoration at which veterans would be present. It had also been preceded by a flurry of publications and extensive media coverage that concentrated on two themes in particular: (1) the needless death of untold thousands of soldiers as a result of an incompetent and ruthless politico-military Establishment; and (2) the injustice meted out to those soldiers executed by dawn firing squads for desertion or dereliction of duty. As details emerged in print, film and television, testifying to the sheer visceral horrors of the conflict and the heartlessness of officers who sent traumatized soldiers into futile combat situations, there was clearly a public desire to recast ordinary soldiers as victims of their Establishment superiors and to rehabilitate and pardon those unjustly accused of cowardice.

But like most instances of public memory that I've discussed in this book, beneath the ostensible meanings of this commemoration lurk a set of questions that complicate any over-confident interpretations of its memorial salience in the present. Why, for example, does memory of the suffering endured by First World War veterans in the trenches elicit such an empathetic response on the part of a younger generation whose experience of war is largely limited to sanitized images of 'collateral damage' beamed onto our television screens from the nose cones of cruise missiles? And if images from the war in Bosnia of hand-to-hand combat, trench warfare, antiquated weaponry and bodily dismemberment were precisely reminiscent of the terms of engagement of the First World War, why was it only several years after the end of this genocidal conflict that commemorations of the Great War focused so centrally on this visceral element? Is the fact that 'shell-shock' has now been recognized as a variant of Post-Traumatic Stress Disorder

(PTSD), itself a fairly recent but increasingly widespread diagnostic category, behind a public desire to make retrospective amends to all soldiers whose reaction to conditions of combat was judged according to the military's uncompromising moral vocabulary? Finally, is it perhaps easier as we approach the end of the millennium to identify with combatants of a war whose ideological stakes are only recalled faintly – if at all? To identify with the reluctant patriot or pacifist of the First World War does not raise the same ideological quandaries or suspicions in a public increasingly cynical of wars waged in the name of fighting fascism, communism and evil dictatorships.[1] These are a cluster of questions and speculations that would require extended consideration, but they do suggest that the public desire to commemorate the First World War is by no means self-evident, but is 'overdetermined' by a set of circumstances relating to the specific nature of wars and their legacy in the late twentieth century.

In the second case, public memory was aroused unexpectedly by an entirely fortuitous sequence of events: in October 1998, while seeking medical treatment in the UK, Chile's General Augusto Pinochet was arrested in response to a Spanish extradition request that accused him of genocide and torture. For a whole generation of former student, trade union and human rights activists, and for left-leaning opinion more generally, the media coverage devoted to the ensuing legal battle revived memories of grisly crimes committed against (mostly young) Chilean civilians. Meanwhile, Chileans were being confronted with the very traumatic memories whose relegation to social oblivion had been the bargain struck for a peaceful transition to democracy. For well over a decade, it had been left to the relatives of the dead and 'disappeared' alone to keep a permanent memorial vigil, while those responsible for crimes against humanity, including the former Head of State and life-long Senator, seemed assured of immunity from prosecution. Now legal action initiated by another state threatened belatedly to confront Chileans with the price they had paid for acceding to the 'will to forget' and for the social truce that had kept bitter political divisions at bay.

Later that month, a British High Court decided that the British arrest was illegal because, as a former Head of State, Pinochet enjoyed 'sovereign immunity' from prosecution even in foreign courts. In late November, with public opinion and the media alike pressing the case for prosecution, this decision was dramatically overturned by the British Law Lords, who held that in crimes of this nature, international law prevailed over claims to immunity. In December, the British Home Secretary upheld this ruling. The mood of public jubilation throughout Europe was palpable. Not only did British juridical recognition of Pinochet's responsibility for the fate of victims of his dictatorship achieve what the The Hague Tribunal for the former Yugoslavia had thus far failed to do – bring to legal account a high-level perpetrator of crimes against humanity[2] – but the decision signalled that no head of state could henceforth claim immunity from prosecution for similar crimes.

The verdict also had a deeper symbolic significance. As Chilean writer Ariel Dorfman commented following the Law Lords' decision: if the internal controversy over Pinochet's detention might test the stability of Chilean democracy in the short run, only by finally confronting in the public domain the traumatic legacy of his dictatorship could Chile's 'moral well-being' be restored.[3] This appraisal resonates with one central premiss of this book: that traumatic experiences in the life of a collectivity that are not dealt with in the public domain are all too likely to turn into the proverbial 'festering wound' evoked by Nietzsche.[4]

And yet . . . if we accept that 'working-through' a traumatic past is a precondition of the moral health of democratic states, at what point does such a process also demand some form of provisional closure so that it does not become an end in its own right, preventing future-oriented perspectives that are also vital to social dynamism? Another central concern of this book has been to highlight instances when memory's performativity has served primarily as grist to the mill of identity-politics, encouraging a retreat from, rather than participation in, 'transformative politics'.[5] This is the gist of Pierre Nora's critique of 'patrimonial memory', and the ensuing 'commemorative obsession' that he believes has hijacked the French political imaginary, as well as that of other European nation-states. I have identified an 'entropic' dimension to the contemporary politics of memory that cannot 'convert' the energy devoted to redressing past wrongs into action directed at halting present crimes – as I believe has been demonstrated by Europe's failure to halt genocide in the former Yugoslavia. Jürgen Habermas has lamented the 'neutralizing effect' that perpetual discussions about Holocaust commemoration are having in Germany as its participants shy away from meaningful action in the public sphere and resort to a 'reflexive level of discussions about discussions'.[6] Henry Rousso has targeted his criticism at the 'memorial militancy' of recent years, which, in its haste to claim the media spotlight, has obscured the true nature of France's implication in the Final Solution and the lessons for the present that should be drawn from such culpable complicity.

In more general terms, Rousso has recently pointed out that there is an 'insoluble dilemma' that *le devoir de mémoire* or obligation to remember engages: on the one hand, there is the recognition that certain crimes, like crimes against humanity, are 'irreparable'; on the other hand, there is the ongoing demand for an eventual reparation – a reparation, moreover, that is often proclaimed less on behalf of victims, than on behalf of whole societies or constituencies who feel betrayed by crimes belatedly acknowledged or revealed. Thus, argues Rousso, memorial militancy has tended to subsume its pedagogical function beneath a moral posture that contemporary societies are urged to adopt *writ large* in relation to the past. This is a posture that invokes the notion of 'an inexhaustible debt' (*une dette inépuisable*) owed to past victims of crimes against humanity – a debt that, because it can never be repaid, demands a permanent upping of the memorial ante as the guarantee of our own moral rectitude. Moreover, in the guise of transmitting such an obligation to younger generations, we are in danger of encouraging a 'fascination with the victims' rather than an understanding of how such crimes came to be committed within modern (and postmodern) societies in the first place.[7] For these reasons, Rousso believes that the task facing us is much harder than demonstrating an ongoing memorial vigilance. It is one that requires us to think about 'the modalities, rituals and forms of transmission of the past that permit us to live *with* the memory of tragedy, rather than trying to live *without* it, as happened after the war, or *against* it, as is the case today'.[8]

Such critiques point to the need for a new realignment of forces between the obligation to remember and the capacity to forget – a capacity that must also be 'performed' if a society is to extricate itself from the potentially incapacitating grip that a politics of memory can exert. For many, South Africa's 'Truth and Reconciliation Commission' was an exemplary 'vector of memory' that attempted such a realignment, allowing the details of past crimes committed under apartheid to emerge without imposing the kinds of punitive measures that might ultimately have destabilized a still-fragile democracy. The Commission's defenders argued that even if what emerged in this performativity of memory were only partial truths, because these exposed the systemic lies that for so long had gone unchallenged, the *process* in which the nation was engaged had a symbolic significance and healing power that far outstripped any likely juridical outcomes. They also insisted that the amnesty granted to perpetrators in return for full disclosure of offences committed with a political objective was not an invitation to social amnesia, but a calculated decision to forgo prosecution – a juridical forgetting that, they argued, was a necessary price to pay for the non-violent dismantling of the apartheid regime.

For the Commission's critics, however, the verdict is still out on the moral efficacy of a process that may have extracted the truth of crimes committed, but let their perpetrators off the ethico-juridical hook. Victims or their families now have knowledge of who did what, and such knowledge is essential if families are to at last 'bury the dead' (hence the importance of juridical investigation into Chile's 'disappeared'). However, if the most victims and their families could expect from perpetrators were 'confessions' of heinous crimes, can we really be surprised if victims refused in their turn to exercise 'forgiveness', so that a sullied page in the nation's history could be turned once and for all? This was poignantly illustrated during the Commission's hearings when a woman whose husband had been abducted and killed by a former member of South Africa's security services, was asked whether, after hearing the killer's 'confession', she was prepared to forgive him. Her halting reply was the following: 'No government can forgive . . . No commission can forgive . . . Only I can forgive . . . And I am not ready to forgive.'[9] The 'victim's resentment' expressed here (and defended so trenchantly by Jean Améry), refuses to concede a social temporality of forgiveness that does not coincide with her own sense of injury. Moreover, forgiveness presupposes the perpetrator's request for pardon, and it is clear that South Africa's Truth and Reconciliation Commission heard all too few and genuine expressions of remorse or repentence.[10] Not only were such requests for pardon rarely forthcoming; as this woman insists, only victims have the right to grant pardon, and some crimes are of such a nature that they cannot be pardoned whatever contrition is displayed.[11] To the extent that the Commission's conception of reconciliation was couched in terms of a 'Christian morality of forgiveness',[12] the aims may not only have been unachievable, but ethically indefensible.

However, far from undermining the foundations of newly-democratized societies, such enduring 'resentments' do have a valuable function: they serve to awaken their citizens to the inevitable contradictions between justice and memory, between a victim's right not to forgive and a society's need for civil peace, and thus to the challenge and necessity of 'living with unresolvable conflicts'.[13] As one former Commissioner put it, at the end of the truth and reconciliation process it cannot be imagined that victims and perpetrators will have been transformed into 'friends', but it is to be hoped that the process will have paved the way for the antagonists to live a 'non-lethal coexistence' as South African citizens.[14] This sombre conclusion contains important lessons for all of us engaged in a politics of memory – whatever memories these may be.

Notes

1. I would argue that *Saving Private Ryan* (Steven Spielberg, US, 1998) though a film about the Second World War, fits this hypothesis equally well, in so far as its popular appeal derives precisely from the film's ultra-realist depiction of gruesome battle scenes combined with its evacuation of any deeper meanings to the soldier's valorous behaviour than their desire to return to home and family.

2. At the time of writing, General Radislav Krstic, a Bosnian Serb general who commanded the troops that took Srebrenica in 1995, appeared before the Hague Tribunal, sparking (false) hopes that General Ratko Mladic, Radovan Karadzic and Slobodan Milosevic might soon follow in his footsteps.

3. Ariel Dorfman, 'No Safe Haven', *The Guardian*, 26 November 1998, p. 24. There is to my mind one still-unexplained feature of public reaction to the Law Lords' decision: the widespread rejoicing by younger generations who would only have known of these historic events had assiduous parents or teachers transmitted such knowledge to them. It is curious that young people, who, after

all, were undoubtedly more familiar with the faces of Slobodan Milosevic, Radovan Karadzic and Saddam Hussain than that of Augusto Pinochet, claimed victory on behalf of *their* cultural memories.

4. Of course the fact that the public domain for this *mise-en-scène* of the recent Chilean past will be neither the Chilean courts nor an international legal forum has already been cited as a major setback to the process of working-through its traumatic legacy – and not just by Pinochet supporters, but by a number of Chilean human rights activists. Moreover, as this book goes to press an appeal by Pinochet's lawyers has been upheld by another Law Lords' decision, on the grounds that one of the Lords in the earlier ruling was a close associate of Amnesty International.

5. See Charles Maier, 'A Surfeit of Memory', *History and Memory*, vol. 5, no. 2, Fall/Winter, 1993, pp. 136–51.

6. See Habermas, 'On How Postwar Germany Has Faced Its Recent Past', *Common Knowledge*, vol. 5, no. 2, 1996, p. 3.

7. The term comes from a critique of *le devoir de mémoire* by Emma Schnur that interrogates how we transmit memory of the Shoah to younger generations. See 'Pédagogiser la Shoah?', *Le Débat*, no. 96, Sept.–Oct. 1997 and her interview 'Ne prenons pas les jeunes en otage pour nous libérer', *Le Monde*, 5 December 1997.

8. Henry Rousso, *La Hantise du Passé: entretien avec Philippe Petit* (Paris: Les éditions Textuels, 1998), p. 47.

9. Cited by Timothy Garton Ash, 'True Confessions', *New York Review of Books*, 17 July 1997, p. 37.

10. For a very insightful reflection on why the Commission could not 'dispense forgiveness', see Anthony Holiday, 'Forgiving and Forgetting: the Truth and Reconciliation Commission', in Sarah Nuttall and Carli Coetzee, *Negotiating the Past: The Making of Memory in South Africa* (Cape Town: Oxford, 1998). See also Paul Ricoeur, 'Le Pardon peut-il guérir?, *Esprit*, Mar.–Apr. 1995, for a philosophical enquiry into the question of memory and pardon.

11. This is a point stressed by Ricoeur: 'To enter the arena of the pardon, is to be prepared to be confronted with the ever-present possibility of the unpardonable. The pardon demanded is not the pardon owed' (ibid., p. 81; my translation).

12. This was the criticism directed at Archbishop Desmond Tutu in particular.

13. Garton Ash, 'True Confessions'.

14. This point was made by Dumisa Ntsebeza, former Head of Investigations of the Truth and Reconciliation Commission, at a conference held at the University of Sussex, 18–19 September 1998.

Index

Abbas, Ferhat, 174, 183n44
Abitbol, Michel, 170, 171, 175
Adorno, Theodor, 40, 41–2
Ageron, Charles-Robert, 172, 173, 176
Algeria, 10, 143–66 *passim*, 167–184 *passim*
Allende, Salvador, 197
Allouche-Benayoun, Joëlle, 175
Améry, Jean, 8, 61–77 *passim*, 132, 200
Arendt, Hannah, 71, 74, 79, 113
Ayoun, Richard, 173, 181n28

Bahloul, Joëlle, 177
Barbie, Klaus, 7, 117–18, 130
Bartov, Omer, 79, 82, 91, 92–3
Baruch, Marc-Olivier, 126–7
Bédarida, François, 82, 128
Bénichou, Raymond, 176
Bennington, Geoff, 168
Birnbaum, Pierre, 170, 172
Bitburg, 45–6
Bousquet, René, 115, 119–20, 126
Brossat, Alain, 186, 190–3
Browning, Christopher, 83–111 *passim*
    Ordinary Men, 83–111 *passim*

Camus, Albert, 10
    Le Premier Homme (*The First Man*), 10,
    144–66
    The Fall, 145
Camus, Catherine, 144
Carroll, David, 61, 165n51
Caruth, Cathy, 185, 193
Castagnède, Jean-Louis, 134
Cixous, Hélène, 178, 179n11
Conan, Éric, 115, 119, 120, 123, 128, 130–1,
    132, 133
Crémieux Decree, 169, 170–3, 174

Daniel, Jean, 143
de Gaulle, Charles, 120, 129, 170, 174
de Pellepoix, Darquier, 119

Derrida, Jacques, 168–9, 170, 173, 178,
    184n54
Diner, Dan, 6, 55, 101–2
Dorfman, Ariel, 199
Drumont, Edouard, 171–1
Duras, Marguerite, 185, 193

Esprit, 15, 32

FLN (*Front de Libération Nationale*), 143, 150,
    175–6
Friedländer, Saul, 79, 100, 110n63, 138n32

Giraud, General, 174
Goldhagen, Daniel J., 8, 9, 55, 79–111 *passim*
    Hitler's Willing Executioners, 9, 55, 79–111
    passim
Goodheart, Eugene, 65, 67–9
Greilsamer, Laurent, 114

Habermas, Jürgen, 2, 7, 39–60 *passim*, 58n47,
    59n54, 199
Hadj, Messali, 176
Halbwachs, Maurice, 1–4, 17, 178
Harbi, Mohamed, 175
Hilberg, Raul, 84, 103n8, 103n10, 104n13,
Hillgruber, Andreas, 48–9
Hiroshima, mon amour, 10, 185–96 *passim*
Historikerstreit, 7, 9, 46–9, 131
Huyssen, Andreas, 5, 9, 10

Jaspers, Karl, 44, 50, 113
Jeanson, Francis, 143, 149
Julien, Charles-André, 158
July, Serge, 114, 115, 128

Kandel, Liliane, 91
Kaspi, André, 174
Kierkegaard, Soren, 51
Kohl, Chancellor Helmut, 45, 46
Klarsfeld, Serge, 119

Klarsfeld, Arno, 128, 142n74

LaCapra, Dominick, 40, 56n3, 57n29, 58n46,
    95, 107n44, 108n52, 110n63
Lang, Jack, 28
Lanzmann, Claude, 81, 104n10, 124
Laub, Dori, 132–4
Laval, Pierre, 127, 128
Leguay, Jean, 115, 117
Levy, Primo, 8, 61–77 *passim*, 132
Leyris, Raymond, 167, 176
Librach, Léon, 135–6
Lottmann, Herbert, 144

Macias, Enrico, 167
Marrus, Michael, 79, 129, 173, 174
Memmi, Albert, 147–8, 152
Mérignac, 122, 134, 135
Mitscherlich, Alexander and Margarete, 42–4
Mitterrand, François, 29, 116, 119, 129
Mongin, Olivier, 32
Moulin, Jean, 117

Nietzsche, Friedrich, 8, 63–4, 72, 74, 76n6
Nolte, Ernst, 46–8
Nora, Pierre, 3–5, 6, 11, 15–37 *passim*, 34n3,
    37n55, 155, 170, 176, 199
    Les Lieux de mémoire, 15–37 *passim*
    Les Français d'Algérie, 163n27, 175,
    182n36
Nouschi, André, 175

O'Brien, Conor Cruise, 145, 147, 149–53, 154,
    155, 161
Ozick, Cynthia, 66–7, 69

Papon, Maurice, 7, 9, 113–142 *passim*
Paxton, Robert, 79, 126, 173, 174
Peyrouton, Marcel, 173, 174
Pinochet, General Augusto, 198
Pisar, Samuel, 133

Prochaska, David, 172

Reagan, Ronald, 45
Resnais, Alain, 10, 185–6
Roger, Gabriel, 157
Ropars-Wuilleumier, Marie Claire, 186–90
Rosaldo, Renato, 146
Rose, Gillian, 91
Rosenfeld, Sidney, 62
Rousso, Henry, 1, 5–6, 114–15, 119, 123, 124,
    131, 133, 199–200
Rushdie, Salman, 75

Said, Edward, 146–8, 150, 153
Sarajevo, 75
Sarrocchi, Jean, 156, 160
Sartre, Jean-Paul, 143, 149
Schinazi, Sabatino, 134–5
Schindler's List, 82, 91–2
Slitinsky, Michel, 134, 136
Statut des juifs, 142n70, 168, 173, 174
Stille, Alexander, 66, 74
Stora, Benjamin, 161n4, 175

Taïeb, Jacques, 171
Thibaud, Paul, 122, 143
Todorov, Tzvetan, 119
Touvier, Paul, 7, 117, 118–19, 123, 125
Truth and Reconciliation Commission, 200–1

Varaut, Maître Jean-Marc, 121
Vél d'Hiv, 29, 116, 130
Vergès, Maître Jacques, 117–8
Vichy, 6, 7, 23, 33, 113–42 *passim*, 168–9

Walzer, Michael, 151, 153
Wehrmacht, 48, 98
Weill, Nicolas, 129, 131
White, Hayden, 87, 93, 106n27

Young, James, 74
Yugoslavia (former), 6, 74, 198, 199

Lightning Source UK Ltd.
Milton Keynes UK
UKOW01f0341291215

265467UK00004B/31/P